Edmondo de Amicis

Holland and its People

Edmondo de Amicis

Holland and its People

ISBN/EAN: 9783743321786

Manufactured in Europe, USA, Canada, Australia, Japa

Cover: Foto ©ninafisch / pixelio.de

Manufactured and distributed by brebook publishing software (www.brebook.com)

Edmondo de Amicis

Holland and its People

HOLLAND

AND ITS PEOPLE

BY

EDMONDO DE AMICIS

Author of 'Constantinople,' 'Studies of Paris,' &c., &c.

TRANSLATED FROM THE ITALIAN

BY

CAROLINE TILTON

NEW YORK
G. P. PUTNAM'S SONS
27 & 29 W. 23D ST.
1881

CONTENTS.

	PAGE
HOLLAND	1
ZEALAND	17
ROTTERDAM	37
DELFT	94
THE HAGUE	125
LEYDEN	205
HAARLEM	224
AMSTERDAM	244
UTRECHT	272
BROEK	284
ZAANDAM	301
ALKMAAR	311
HELDER	326
THE ZUYDER ZEE	342
FRIESLAND	355
GRONINGEN	382
FROM GRONINGEN TO ARNHEM	401

HOLLAND.

Whoever looks for the first time at a large map of Holland, wonders that a country so constituted can continue to exist. At the first glance, it is difficult to say whether land or water predominates, or whether Holland belongs most to the continent or to the sea. Those broken and compressed coasts, those deep bays, those great rivers that, losing the aspect of rivers, seem bringing new seas to the sea; and that sea, which, changing itself into rivers, penetrates the land and breaks it into archipelagoes; the lakes, the vast morasses, the canals crossing and recrossing each other, all combine to give the idea of a country that may at any moment disintegrate and disappear. Seals and beavers would seem to be its rightful inhabitants; but since there are men bold enough to live in it, they surely cannot ever sleep in peace.

These were my thoughts as I looked for the first time at a map of Holland, and experienced a desire to know something about the formation of so strange a country; and as that which I learned induced me to write this book, I put it down here, with the hope that it may induce others to read it.

What sort of a country Holland is, has been told by many in few words.

Napoleon said that it was an alluvion of French rivers, —the Rhine, the Scheldt, and the Meuse,—and with this pretext he added it to the empire. One writer has defined it as a sort of transition between land and sea. Another, as an immense crust of earth floating on the water. Others, an annex of the old continent, the China of Europe, the end of the earth and the beginning of the ocean, a measureless raft of mud and sand; and Phillip II. called it the country nearest to hell.

But they all agreed upon one point, and all expressed it in the same words:—Holland is a conquest made by man over the sea—it is an artificial country—the Hollanders made it—it exists because the Hollanders preserve it—it will vanish whenever the Hollanders shall abandon it.

To comprehend this truth, we must imagine Holland as it was when first inhabited by the first German tribes that wandered away in search of a country.

It was almost uninhabitable. There were vast tempestuous lakes, like seas, touching one another; morass beside morass; one tract covered with brushwood after another; immense forests of pines, oaks, and alders, traversed by herds of wild horses; and so thick were these forests that tradition says one could travel leagues passing from tree to tree without ever putting foot to the ground. The deep bays and gulfs carried into the heart of the country the fury of the northern tempests. Some provinces disappeared once every year under the waters of the sea, and were nothing but muddy tracts, neither land nor water, where it was impossible either to walk or to sail. The large rivers, without sufficient inclination to descend to the sea, wandered here and there uncertain of their way, and slept in monstrous pools and ponds among the sands of the coasts. It was a sinister place, swept by furious winds, beaten by obstinate rains, veiled in a perpetual fog, where nothing was heard but the roar of the sea, and the voices of wild beasts and birds of the ocean. The first people who had the courage to plant their tents there, had to raise with their own hands dykes of earth to keep out the rivers and the sea, and lived within them like shipwrecked men upon desolate islands, venturing forth at the subsidence of the waters in quest of food in the shape of fish and game, and gathering the eggs of marine birds upon the sand.

Cæsar, passing by, was the first to name this people. The other Latin historians speak with compassion and respect of those intrepid barbarians who lived upon a "floating land," exposed to the intemperance of a cruel sky, and the fury of the mysterious northern sea; and the imagination pictures the Roman soldiers, who, from the heights of the uttermost citadels of the empire, beaten by the waves, contemplated with wonder and pity those wandering tribes upon their desolate land, like a race accursed of heaven.

Now, if we remember that such a region has become one of the most fertile, wealthiest, and best regulated of the countries of the world, we shall understand the justice of the saying that Holland is a conquest made by man. But, it must be added, the conquest goes on for ever.

To explain this fact, to show how the existence of Holland, in spite of the great defensive works constructed by the inhabitants, demands an incessant and most perilous struggle, it will be enough to touch here and there upon a few of the principal vicissitudes of her physical history, from the time when her inhabitants had already reduced her to a habitable country.

Tradition speaks of a great inundation in Friesland in the sixth century. From that time every gulf, every island, and, it may be said, every city in Holland has its catastrophe to record. In thirteen centuries, it is recorded that one great inundation, besides smaller ones, has occurred every seven years; and the country being all plain, these inundations were veritable floods. Towards the end of the thirteenth century, the sea destroyed a part of a fertile peninsula near the mouth of the Ems, and swallowed up more than thirty villages. In the course of the same century, a series of inundations opened an immense chasm in northern Holland, and formed the Zuyder Zee, causing the death of more than eighty thousand persons. In 1421 a tempest swelled the Meuse, so that in one night the waters overwhelmed seventy-two villages and one hundred thousand inhabitants. In 1532 the sea burst the dykes of Zealand, destroying hundreds of villages, and covering for ever a large tract of country. In 1570 a storm caused another inundation in Zealand, in the province of Utrecht, Amsterdam was invaded by the waters, and in Friesland twenty thousand people were drowned. Other great inundations took place in the seventeenth century; two terrible ones at the beginning and the end of the eighteenth; one in 1825 that desolated North Holland, Friesland, Over-Yssel, and Gueldres; and another great one of the Rhine, in 1855, which invaded Gueldres and the province of Utrecht, and covered a great part of North Brabant. Besides these great catastrophes, there happened in different centuries innumerable smaller ones, which would have been famous in any other country, and which in Holland are scarcely remembered; like the rising of the lake of Harlem, itself the result of an inundation of the sea; flourishing cities of the gulf of Zuyder Zee vanished under the waters; the islands of Zealand covered again and again by the sea, and again emerging; villages of the coast, from Helder to the mouths of the Meuse, from time to time inundated and destroyed; and in all these inundations immense loss of life of men and animals. It is plain that miracles of courage, constancy and industry, must have been accomplished by the Hollanders, first in creating and afterwards in preserving such a country. The enemy from which they had to wrest it, was triple: the sea, the lakes, the rivers. They drained the lakes, drove back the sea, and imprisoned the rivers.

To drain the lakes the Hollanders pressed the air into

their service. The lakes, the marshes, were surrounded by dykes, the dykes by canals; and an army of windmills, putting in motion force-pumps, turned the water into the canals, which carried it off to the rivers and the sea. Thus vast tracts of land buried under the water, saw the sun, and were transformed, as if by magic, into fertile fields, covered with villages, and intersected by canals and roads. In the seventeenth century, in less than forty years, twenty-six lakes were drained. At the beginning of the present century, in North Holland alone, more than six thousand *hectares* (or fifteen thousand acres) were thus redeemed from the waters; in South Holland, before 1844, twenty-nine thousand *hectares;* in the whole of Holland, from 1500 to 1858, three hundred and fifty-five thousand *hectares.* Substituting steam-mills for windmills, in thirty-nine months was completed the great undertaking of the draining of the lake of Harlem, which measured forty-four kilometres in circumference, and for ever threatened with its tempests the cities of Harlem, Amsterdam, and Leyden. And they are now meditating the prodigious work of drying up the Zuyder Zee, which embraces an area of more than seven hundred square kilometres.

The rivers, another internal enemy, cost no less of labour and sacrifice. Some, like the Rhine, which lost itself in the sands before reaching the sea, had to be channelled and defended at their mouths, against the tides, by formidable cataracts; others, like the Meuse, bordered by dykes as powerful as those that were raised against the ocean; others, turned from their course; the wandering waters gathered together; the course of the affluents regulated; the waters divided with rigorous measure in order to maintain that enormous mass of liquid in equilibrium, where the slightest inequality might cost a province; and in this way all the rivers that formerly spread their devastating floods about the country, were disciplined into streams and constrained to do service.

But the most tremendous struggle was the battle with the ocean. Holland is in great part lower than the level of the sea; consequently, everywhere that the coast is not defended by sand-banks, it has to be protected by dykes. If these interminable bulwarks of earth, granite, and wood were not there to attest the indomitable courage and perseverance of the Hollanders, it would not be believed that the hand of man could, even in many centuries, have accomplished such a work. In Zealand alone the dykes extend to a distance of more than four hundred kilometres. The western coast of the island of Walcheren is defended by a dyke, in which it is computed that the expense of construction added to that of preservation, if it were put out at interest, would amount to a sum equal in value to that which the dyke itself would be worth were it made of massive copper. Around the city of Helder, at the northern extremity of North Holland, extends a dyke ten kilometres long, constructed of masses of Norwegian granite, which descends more than sixty metres into the sea. The whole province of Friesland, for the length of eighty-eight kilometres, is defended by three rows of piles sustained by masses of Norwegian and German granite. Amsterdam, all the cities of the Zuyder Zee, and all the islands—fragments of vanished lands—which are strung like beads between Friesland and North Holland, are protected by dykes. From the mouths of the Ems to those of the Scheldt Holland is an impenetrable fortress, of whose immense bastions the mills are the towers, the cataracts are the gates, the islands the advanced forts; and like a true fortress, it shows to its enemy, the sea, only the tops of its bell-towers and the roofs of its houses, as if in defiance and derision.

Holland is a fortress, and her people live as in a fortress, on a war-footing with the sea. An army of engineers, directed by the Minister of the Interior, spread over the country, and ordered like an army, continually spy the enemy, watch over the internal waters, foresee the bursting of the dykes, order and direct the defensive works. The expenses of the war are divided; one part to the State, one part to the provinces; every proprietor pays, besides the general imposts, a special impost for the dykes, in proportion to the extent of his lands and their proximity to the water. An accidental rupture, an inadvertence, may cause a flood; the peril is unceasing; the sentinels are at their posts upon the bulwarks; at the first assault of the sea, they shout the war-cry, and Holland sends men, material, and money. And even when there is no great battle, a quiet, silent struggle is for ever going on. The innumerable mills, even in the drained districts, continue to work unresting, to absorb and turn into the canals the water that falls in rain and that which filters in from the sea. Every day the cataracts of the bays and rivers close their gigantic gates against the high tide trying to rush into the heart of the land. The work of strengthening dykes, fortifying sand-banks with plantations, throwing out new dykes where the banks are low, straight as great lances, vibrating in the bosom of the sea, and breaking the first impetus of the wave, is for ever going on. And the sea externally knocks at the river-gates, beats upon the ramparts, growls on every side her ceaseless menace, lifting her curious waves as if to see the land she counts as hers, piling up banks of sand before the gates to kill the commerce of the cities, for ever gnawing, scratching, digging at the coast; and failing to overthrow the ramparts upon which she foams and fumes in angry effort, she casts at their feet ships full of the dead, that they may announce to the rebellious country her fury and her strength.

In the midst of this great and terrible struggle Holland is transformed: Holland is the land of transformations. A geographical map of that country as it existed eight centuries ago is not recognisable. Transforming the sea, men also are transformed. The sea, at some points, drives back the land: it takes portions from the continent, leaves them, and takes them again; joins islands to the mainland with ropes of sand, as in the case of Zealand; breaks off bits from the mainland and makes new islands, as in Wieringen; retires from certain coasts and makes land cities out of what were cities of the sea, as Leuvarde; converts vast tracts of plain into archipelagoes of a hundred islets, as Biisbosch; separates a city from the land, as Dordrecht; forms new gulfs two leagues broad, like the gulf of Dollart; divides two provinces with a new sea, like North Holland and Friesland. The effect of the inundations is to cause the level of the sea to rise in some places and to sink in others; sterile lands are fertilised by the slime of the rivers, fertile lands are changed into deserts of sand. With the transformations of the waters alternate the transformations of labour. Islands are united to continents, like the island of Ameland; entire provinces are reduced to island, as North Holland will be by the new canal of Amsterdam, which is to separate it from South Holland; lakes as large as provinces disappear altogether, like the lake of Beemster; by the extraction of peat, land is converted into lakes, and these lakes are again transformed into meadows. And thus the country changes its aspect according to the violence of nature or the needs of men. And while one goes over it with the latest map in hand, one may be sure that the map will be useless in a few years, because even now there are new gulfs in process of formation, tracts of land just ready to be detached from the mainland, and great canals being cut that will carry life to uninhabited districts.

But Holland has done more than defend herself against the waters; she has made herself mistress of them, and has used them for her own defence. Should a foreign army invade her territory, she has but to open her dykes and unchain the sea and the rivers, as she did against the Romans, against the Spaniards, against the army of Louis XIV., and defend the land cities with her fleet. Water was the source of her poverty, she has made it the source of wealth. Over the whole country extends an immense net-work of canals which serve both for the irrigation of the land and as a means of communication. The cities, by means of canals, communicate with the sea; canals run from town to town, and from them to villages, which are themselves bound together by these watery ways, and are connected even to the houses scattered over the country; smaller canals surround the fields and orchards, pastures and kitchen-gardens, serving at once as boundary-wall, hedge, and road-way; every house is a little port. Ships, boats, rafts move about in all directions, as in other places carts and carriages. The canals are the arteries of Holland, and the water her life-blood.

But even setting aside the canals, the draining of the lakes, and the defensive works, on every side are seen the traces of marvellous undertakings. The soil, which in other countries is a gift of nature, is in Holland a work of men's hands. Holland draws the greater part of her wealth from commerce; but before commerce comes the cultivation of the soil; and the soil had to be created. There were sand-banks, interspersed with layers of peat, broad downs swept by the winds, great tracts of barren land apparently condemned to an eternal sterility. The first elements of manufacture, iron and coal, were wanting; there was no wood, because the forests had already been destroyed by tempests when agriculture began; there was no stone, there were no metals. Nature, says a Dutch poet, had refused all her gifts to Holland; the Hollanders had to do everything in spite of nature. They began by fertilising the sand.

In some places they formed a productive soil with earth brought from a distance, as a garden is made; they spread the siliceous dust of the downs over the too watery meadows; they mixed with the sandy earth the remains of peat taken from the bottoms; they extracted clay to lend fertility to the surface of their lands; they laboured to break up the downs with the plough; and thus in a thousand ways, and continually fighting off the menacing waters, they succeeded in bringing Holland to a state of cultivation not inferior to that of more favoured regions. That Holland, the sandy, marshy country that the ancients considered all but uninhabitable, now sends out yearly from her confines agricultural products to the value of a hundred millions of francs, possesses about one million three hundred thousand head of cattle, and, in proportion to the extent of her territory, may be accounted one of the most populous of European states.

It may be easily understood how the physical peculiarities of their country must influence the Dutch people; and their genius is in perfect harmony with the character of Holland. It is sufficient to contemplate the monuments of their great struggle with the sea in order to understand that their distinctive characteristics must be firmness and patience, accompanied by a calm and constant courage. That glorious battle, and the consciousness of owing everything to their own strength, must have infused and fortified in them a high sense of dignity and an indomitable spirit of liberty and independence. The necessity of a constant struggle, of a continuous labour, and perpetual sacrifices in defence of their existence, for ever taking them back to a sense of reality, must have made them a highly practical and economical people; good sense should be their most salient quality, economy one of their chief virtues; they must be excellent in all useful arts, sparing of diversion, simple even in their greatness; succeeding in what they undertake, by dint of tenacity and a thoughtful and orderly activity; more wise than heroic; more conservative than creative; giving no great architects to the edifice of modern thought, but the ablest of workmen, a legion of patient and laborious artisans. And by virtue of these qualities of prudence, phlegmatic activity, and the spirit of conservatism, they are ever advancing, though by slow degrees; they acquire gradually, but never lose what they have gained; holding stubbornly to their ancient customs; preserving almost intact, and despite the neighbourhood of three great nations, their own originality; preserving it through every form of government, through foreign invasions, through political and religious wars, and in spite of the immense concourse of strangers from every country that are always coming among them; and remaining, in short, of all the northern races, that one which, though ever advancing in the path of civilisation, has kept its antique stamp most clearly.

It is enough also to remember its form in order to comprehend that this country of three millions and a half of inhabitants, although bound in so compact a political union, although recognisable among all the other northern peoples by certain traits peculiar to the population of all its provinces, must present a great variety. And so it is in fact. Between Zealand and Holland proper, between Holland and Friesland, between Friesland and Gueldres, between Groningen and Brabant, in spite of vicinity and so many common ties, there is no less difference than between the more distant provinces of Italy and France: difference of language, costume, and character; difference of race and of religion. The communal *regimé* has impressed an indelible mark upon this people, because in no other country does it so conform to the nature of things. The country is divided into various groups of interests organised in the same manner as the hydraulic system. Whence, association and mutual help against the common enemy, the sea; but liberty for local institutions and forces. Monarchy has not extinguished the ancient municipal spirit, and this it is that renders impossible a complete fusion of the State, in all the great States that have made the attempt. The great rivers and gulfs are at the same time commercial roads serving as national bonds between the different provinces, and barriers, which defend old traditions and old customs in each.

But however wonderful may be the physical history of Holland, her political history is still more so. This small territory, invaded from the beginning by different tribes of the Germanic races, subjugated by the Romans and the Franks, devastated by the Normans and by the Danes, desolated by centuries of civil war with all its horrors, this small people of fishermen and traders, saves its civil liberty and its freedom of conscience by a war of eighty years against the formidable monarchy of Philip II., and founds a republic which becomes the ark of salvation to the liberties of all the world, the adopted country of science, the Exchange of Europe, the station for the commerce of the world; a republic which extends its domination to Java, Sumatra, Hindostan, Ceylon, New Holland, Japan, Brazil, Guiana, the Cape of Good Hope, the West Indies, and New York; a republic which vanquishes England on the sea, which resists the united arms of Charles II. and Louis XIV., and which treats an equal terms with the greatest nations, and is, for a time, one of the three Powers that decide the fate of Europe.

She is not now the great Holland of the seventeenth century; but she is still, after England, the first colonizing State in the world; instead of her ancient greatness, she has tranquil prosperity; she restricts herself to commerce acquired by agriculture; she retains the substance of the republican *regimé* although she has lost the form; a family of patriot princes, dear to the people, governs tranquilly in the midst of her liberties, ancient and modern. There is wealth without ostentation, freedom without insolence, and there are taxes without poverty. She is, perhaps, of all European states the one where there is most popular education and least corruption of manners. Alone, at the extremity of the continent, occupied with her dykes and her colonies, she enjoys in peace the fruits of her labours, with the comforting conviction that no people in the world have conquered at the price of greater sacrifices liberty of conscience and the independence of the State.

All these things I revolved in my mind to the stimulation of my curiosity, as at Antwerp one fine summer morning I went on board the ship which was to take me by the way of the Scheldt to Zealand, the most mysterious of the provinces of the low countries

ZEALAND.

If before I had made up my mind to go to Holland some professor of geography had stopped me in the street and demanded suddenly—Where is Zealand? I should have remained speechless; and I think I am not mistaken in supposing that numbers of my fellow-citizens to whom the question might be put would not easily find an answer. Zealand is a mystery even for the Hollanders themselves; very few of them have been there, and of these the greater part have only passed through it in a boat; consequently it is seldom spoken of, and always as a very distant country. The first words that reached my ears among the travellers who came on board the vessel with me, and who were almost all Belgians and Dutch, informed me that they also were about to visit that province for the first time; we were all, therefore, full of curiosity, and the ship had not left her moorings when we entered into conversation, and questions which no one could answer passed from one to another.

The ship sailed at sunrise, and for a time we enjoyed the spectacle of the steeple of Antwerp Cathedral, made out of Mechlin lace, as Napoleon, who was in love with it, used to say; and after having touched at the fortress of Lille and the village of Doel, we came out of Belgium and entered Zealand.

At the moment of passing for the first time the frontier of a state, although it is evident that the prospect will not change all at once, everyone seems to imagine that it must do so. We all, therefore, stood at the side of the vessel to behold the apparition of Zealand.

But for a good while our expectations were deluded: nothing was to be seen but the green flat shores of the Scheldt, wide as an arm of the sea, and sprinkled with sand-banks, upon which alighted flocks of screaming sea-gulls; and the pure, clear sky did not seem the sky of Holland. The ship sailed in between the island of Zuid-Beveland and that strip of land which forms the left bank of the Scheldt, called Flanders of the States, or Flemish Zealand.

The story of this strip of land is very curious. For the stranger entering Holland it is, as it were, the first page of that great epic which is entitled—the battle with the sea. In the middle ages there was nothing here but a vast gulf with a few scattered islets. In the beginning of the sixteenth century this gulf no longer existed; four hundred years of slow and patient labour had changed it into a fertile plain defended by dykes, intersected by canals, and populated with villages, under the name of Flemish Zealand. When the war of independence broke out, the inhabitants of Flemish Zealand, rather than give it up to the Spaniards, cut their dykes, let in the sea, and destroying in one day the labour of four centuries, it became once more the gulf of the middle ages. The war of independence over, the work of reformation was again commenced, and in three hundred years Flemish Zealand again emerged from the waters, and was restored to the continent, like a daughter that had been dead and was alive again. Flemish Zealand, divided from Belgian Flanders by a double political and religious barrier, and separated from Holland by the Scheldt, preserves its customs and its faith as they were in the sixteenth century. The traditions of the war with Spain are as speaking and vivid as any event of the day. The soil is fertile, the inhabitants enjoy a more than ordinary prosperity, they have schools and printing-presses, their manners are severe and simple, and they live peaceably on their fragment of country, risen from the sea but yesterday, until the day when the sea shall once more claim it for its third burial. A Belgian fellow-passenger, who gave me this information, called my attention to the fact that the inhabitants of Flemish Zealand, when they inundated their country and rose against the Spanish domination, were still Catholics; consequently the strange circumstance occurred that while they went down into the waters good Catholics, they rose to the surface Protestants.

To my great amazement, the ship, instead of continuing to descend the Scheldt and skirting the island of Zuid-Beveland, when it reached a certain point, entered a narrow canal which cuts that island into two parts and joins the two branches of the river which are made by the island itself.

It was the first Dutch canal that I had seen, and the impression was a new one. It is bordered by two lofty dykes which hide the country; the ship glided along as if it were in ambush and meant to rush out at the other end to somebody's confusion; and as there was not a boat on the canal nor a living being on the banks, the silence and solitude gave a still more piratical air to the proceeding.

Issuing out into the eastern branch of the Scheldt we were in the heart of Zealand. To our right lay the island of Tholen; to the left, that of North Beveland; behind, that of South Beveland; before, that of Schonwen. Except the island of Walcheren, all the principal islands of the mysterious archipelago were around us.

The mystery lay in the fact that the islands were only to be divined, not seen. To the right and left of the wide river, before and behind our vessel, the straight lines of the dykes lay like green strips upon the waters; and beyond these strips, here and there, the tops of trees and steeples and the red roofs of houses seemed rising up to peep at us.

Not a hill, not a bit of rising ground, not a house could be descried on any side; everything seemed hidden, immersed in the water; the islands might have been on the point of sinking into the depths of the waves; we appeared to be traversing a country on the day of a great flood, and were sensible of some consolation at the thought that we were in a ship. Now and then the vessel stopped to let out a passenger who got into a small boat and was rowed to shore. I was myself very curious to see Zealand, and yet I looked at these people with a feeling of compassion, as if those objects which seemed islands were really only monstrous whales that would vanish under the waters at the boat's approach.

The captain of our ship, a Hollander, stopping to look at a small map of Zealand which I was studying, I seized the occasion to bombard him with questions. Fortunately I had fallen upon one of those few Dutchmen who, in common with us Latins, have the weakness of loving the sound of their own voices.

"Here in Zealand," said he, with the gravity of a schoolmaster giving a lesson, "the dykes are, even more than in the other provinces, a question of life and death. At high tide all Zealand is under water. At every broken dyke an island would vanish. And the worst of it is that the dykes have to resist not only the direct attack of the waves, but still another even more dangerous force. The rivers throw themselves into the sea, the sea rushes against the rivers, and in this continual struggle undercurrents are formed which gnaw at the base of the dykes, so that they crumble in all at once like a wall that has been undermined. The Zealanders have to stand ever on the alert. When a dyke is in peril, they build another one within it, and await the assault of the waters behind that, and so gain time, until they can either rebuild the first dyke or continue to strengthen those within, and the current diverges and they are saved."

"And may it not be," said I, always hungry for poetic possibilities, "that some day Zealand may no longer exist?"

"Quite the contrary," he answered, to my great regret; "the day may come in which Zealand will be no longer an archipelago, but *terra firma*. The Scheldt and the Meuse constantly bring down deposits of mud which remain at the bottom of the arms of the sea, and which, gradually rising, enlarge the islands and enclose within the land cities and villages which were once upon the shore and had their ports. Azel, Goes, Veere, Arneminden, Middelburg, were once maritime towns, and are such no longer. A day will come when Zealand shall be divided by no waters but those of her rivers, and when a network of railways shall extend over the whole country, which will be joined to the mainland as Zuid-Beveland is joined. Zealand grows greater in her battle with the sea. The sea may succeed in doing something in other parts of Holland, but here it will get the worst of it. You know the arms of Zealand, do you not? A lion swimming, and the motto, *Luctor et emergo*."

Here he was silent for a moment, and a gleam of pride sparkled for a moment in his eye, and was quenched; then he began again with all his former gravity:

"*Emergo*; but not always immersed. Everyone of the islands of Zealand, one after the other, slept for more or less time under the waters. Three centuries ago Schonwen was inundated by the sea, drowning inhabitants and cattle from one end to the other, and leaving it a desert. North Beveland was entirely submerged a short time after, and for several years only the tops of her steeples could be seen above the water. South Beveland had the same fate in the middle of the fourteenth century. Tholen the same in 1825. Walcheren the same in 1808; and in Middelburg, her capital city, several miles distant from the coast, the water was up to the roofs of the houses."

What with hearing for ever of water and floods, of countries submerged and people drowned, I began to think it strange that I was not drowned myself. I asked the captain what sort of people these were who inhabited the invisible islands with water under their feet and over their heads.

"Agricultural people and shepherds," he answered. "In point of agriculture Zealand is the richest province in the low countries. The soil is one of wonderful fertility. Grain, flax, colza, madder, grow as in few other places. There are fine large cattle and colossal horses; bigger than the Flemish horses. The people are strong and well made, preserving their ancient customs and living contented in their prosperity and peace. Zealand is a hidden paradise."

Whilst the captain talked, the ship entered the canal of Keete, which divides the islands of Schonwen and Tholen, famous as having been forded by the Spaniards in 1575, as the eastern arm of the Scheldt is famous for the ford of 1572. All Zealand is full of memorials of that war. This little sandy archipelago, half buried in the sea, was the very hotbed of war and heresy, both because of its connection with William of Orange, hereditary lord of many of the islands, and because of the impediments of every kind which it opposed to the invader, and the

Duke of Alva burned to get possession of it Consequently the most obstinate struggles went on upon its shores with all the mingled horrors of land fights and sea fights. The soldiers forded the canals at night, holding on to each other, with water up to their necks, in peril from the tides, beaten by the rain, fired at from the shores; horses and artillery sank into the mud; the wounded were caught by the currents and buried alive in the quagmires; the air resounded with the voices of Germans, Italians, Flemings, Walloons; torches illuminated here and there the great arquebuses, pompous plumes, strange visages, and the battle seemed a fantastic funeral; and it was indeed the funeral of the great Spanish monarchy, which was being slowly drowned in the waters of Holland and covered with mud and maledictions. He who is guilty of any overwhelming tenderness for Spain has only to go to Holland. There never, perhaps, existed two nations who had better cause to hate each other with all the strength of their souls, or who have proved it with more furious wrath.

The ship now passed between the island of Schonwen and the smaller one of San Philipsland, and in a few moments came out into the large arm of the Meuse called Krammer, which divides the island of Overflakkee from the mainland. We appeared to be sailing through a chain of large lakes. The shores were distant and presented the same aspect as those of the Scheldt: long perspectives of dykes, tops of trees, steeples and roofs behind them. Only upon some projection of the shore, forming a sort of breach in the immense bastion of the islands, could be seen a sort of sketch of a Dutch landscape, a colored house, a windmill, a boat, looking like the revelation of a hidden thing, made to sharpen the curiosity of travellers, and to delude it.

Going towards the prow of the vessel I made a pleasant discovery. There was a group of peasants, men and women, wearing the costume of Zealand, I do not remember of which island, for the costume differs, as does the dialect, which is a mixture of Dutch and Flemish, if that may be said of two languages which differ but slightly from each other. The men wore round felt hats with an embroidered band; jackets of dark cloth, short and tight, and opening in front to display a sort of vest bordered with red, yellow and green, buttoned with a row of silver buttons, so close together as to resemble a chain; short breeches of the same colour as the jacket, bound round the waist by a belt, furnished with a large stud or buckle of chased silver; a scarlet cravat, and fine woollen stockings coming to the knee. One of them had coins for buttons, a not uncommon custom. The women wore a straw hat in the shape of a truncated cone, very tall, something like a bucket turned upside down, with a quantity of blue ribbons fluttering about it; a dark-coloured gown open on the bosom over an embroidered chemise; their arms bare to the elbow; and enormous gold or gilded ear-rings that projected nearly over the cheeks.

Although I did my best to copy Victor Hugo, and "admire everything like a brute," I could not succeed in persuading myself that that fashion of dress was beautiful. But I was prepared for this sort of contrariety. I knew that in Holland one seeks the new rather than the beautiful, and the good rather than the new; and therefore I was more disposed for observation than enthusiasm. I comforted myself for the disappointment of my taste for the picturesque with the thought that all those peasants certainly knew how to read and write; that they had, perhaps, that very evening committed to memory some of the verses of their great poet, Jacob Catz; and that probably they were then going, with their excellent programme in their pockets, to some rural meeting, where some of them were to confute with the arguments of their modest experience the propositions of a learned agronome of Goes or Middelburg.

Ludovico Guicciardini, a Florentine gentleman, and author of a fine work on the Low Countries, printed in Antwerp in the sixteenth century, says that in Zealand there is scarcely a person of either sex who speaks French or Spanish, but that many speak Italian. This, which was perhaps an exaggeration even in his time, is now an absolute fable; but it is certain, however, that there is an extraordinary amount of intellectual culture among them, superior to that of the French, Belgian, or German peasant, and superior also to that of the other parts of Holland.

The ship skirted the island of San Philipsland, and we were out of Zealand.

So this province, mysterious before we entered it, appeared still more mysterious when we got out of it. We had been through it, but we had not seen it. We went in and came out with our curiosity ungratified. The only thing we

had seen was the fact that Zealand was invisible. But it would be a mistake to suppose that it is a country of mystery merely because it is hidden. Everything in Zealand is mysterious. In the first place, how was it formed? Was it a group of very small islands, separated by canals and uninhabited, which, as some believe, joined themselves together and became large islands? or was it, as others believe, *terra firma* when the Scheldt emptied itself into the Meuse? But leaving the question of its origin, in what other country in the world do the things happen which happen in Zealand? In what other country do the fishermen catch a Siren in their nets, and the husband, having in vain entreated with tears that she should be restored to him, catches up a handful of sand and throws it at them, prophesying at the same time that that sand shall choke up the city ports, and the prophecy is accomplished? In what country, as on the shores of the island of Walcheren, do the souls of the dead, lost at sea, come and wake up the fishermen, and oblige them to carry them in their boats to the English coast? In what country do the tempests bring, as on the shores of the island of Schonwen, corpses from the Polar seas, of monsters, half man, half boat, mummies dressed in trunks of trees that float? and is there not one to be seen now in the Municipal Hall of Zeirikzee? In what country, except near Wemeldinge, does it happen to a man to fall head first into a canal and remain under one hour, during which time he sees his dead wife and children, who converse with him from Paradise, and he is then taken out alive, and relates the prodigy to Victor Hugo, who believes it true and writes a commentary upon it, concluding that the soul may leave the body for a time and return to it again? In what country, save Domburg, do they fish up at low water antique temples and statues of unknown divinities? In what country, except at Wemeldinge, does the sword of a Spanish captain, Mondragone, serve as a lightning-rod to a tower? In what country but the island of Schonwen, do they make unfaithful wives walk naked through the streets, with two stones tied to their necks, and an iron cylinder upon their heads? But come, this last wonder is no more to be seen; but the stones exist still, and anyone may see them in the Town Hall of Brauwershaven.

The ship now entered that portion of the southern branch of the Meuse, which is called Vokerak; the scene was still the same: dykes, and again dykes, tops of steeples, roofs of houses, here and there a vessel. One thing only was changed—the sky.

I saw there for the first time the sky of Holland under its usual aspect, and looked on at one of those battles of light, proper to the Low Countries, which the great Dutch landscape painters rendered with such unrivalled excellence. Until then the sky had been serene, a lovely summer's day, the waters blue, the shores bright green, the air warm, and not a puff of wind. Suddenly a dense cloud hid the sun, and in less time than it takes to write it, everything changed its aspect, as if in one instant season, latitude, and time had changed. The water became dark, the green of the shores grew dull, the horizon hid itself behind a grey veil, every object appeared surrounded by a dim light that softened and confused the outlines, and a malignant breeze arose that froze one's very bones. It seemed December, and we felt the damp chill of winter, and that uneasiness which is brought by any sudden, unexpected change in nature. Then, from the whole circle of the horizon, leaden clouds began to rise, moving with great rapidity, seeming to seek with a sort of painful impatience a direction and a form, and the water became agitated, streaked with luminous reflections, broad, greenish, violet, whitish, clay-colored, and black strips; and at length the irritation of nature resolved itself into a thick, heavy rain, confusing sea and land and sky into one grey mass, hardly interrupted by a slightly darker shade where lay the distant shore, or where the sails of some vessel stood up here and there like a dim phantom on the waters of the rivers.

"We are now really in Holland," said the captain to a group of passengers who stood contemplating the scene. "These sudden changes are seen nowhere but here."

Then, in answer to a question from one of us, he added:

"Holland has a meteorology of her own. The winter is long, the summer short, the spring nothing but the end of winter, and now and then, as we see, winter looks back at us even in summer. There is a saying among us that we may see the four seasons in one day. We have the most inconstant sky in the world, and we are for ever talking about the weather. The atmosphere is the most variable spectacle that we can boast. But it is a dreary climate. The sea sends rain from three quarters, and the winds sweep over us without resistance; even on the finest days the earth exhales vapors that obscure the horizon; for many months the air has no transparency. See the winter; there are days when it seems as if we should never see the sky again; the darkness comes from above, like the light; the north-west wind brings the icy air from the poles and lashes the sea into a fury that seems capable of destroying the coast." Here he turned to me with a smile, and said: "You are better off in Italy." Then he became grave again, and added: "But every country has its good and its evil."

The ship now coming out of the Volkerak, passed before the fortress of Willemstadt, built in 1583 by the Prince of Orange, and entered the Hollandsdiep, a large branch of the Meuse with separates South Holland from North Brabant. A great stretch of water, two dark lines to right and left, and an ash-colored sky, were all that could be seen from the vessel. A French lady, amid the general silence, exclaimed with a yawn: "How lovely Holland is!" and everybody, but the Hollanders, laughed.

"Ah, Captain," said a little old gentleman, a Belgian, one of those pillars of the café who are for ever airing their political opinions, "every country has its good and its evil side, and we Belgians and Hollanders must at least be persuaded of this truth, and sympathise with each other in order to live in peace and harmony. When we think that we are a State of nine millions, we with our manufactures, and you with your commerce, with two capitals like Amsterdam and Brussels, and two commercial cities like Antwerp and Rotterdam! we should count for something in the world, eh, Captain?"

The captain made no reply. Another Dutchman said: "To be sure; with religious wars going on twelve months in the year."

The little old Belgian, rather disconcerted, continued in a low voice to me:

"It is a fact, *Signor mio*. It is a trifle, especially on our side. You will see in Holland: Amsterdam is not Brussels; no, indeed, and the country is as flat and as tiresome as it can be; but as for prosperity, you will see. They spend a florin, which is more than two francs, where we spend a franc. You will find that out in the hotel bills. They are twice as rich as we are. The blow was given by William I., who wanted to make a Dutch Belgium, and pushed us to extremities. You know how things went on," &c.

In the Hollandsdiep we began to see large boats, fishing vessels, and some large ships from Hellevoetsluis, a great maritime port on the right bank of the Meuse, near the mouth, where all the vessels that make the voyage to India stop. The rain ceased, the sky gradually, almost unwillingly, cleared in part, the water and the shores again took on their fresh and vivid colors, and we were in summer once more.

In a short time the ship was off the village of Moerdigk. There is to be seen one of the largest bridges in the world. It is an iron bridge, one mile and a half in length, over which passes the railway to Dordrecht and Rotterdam. From a distance it presents the aspect as of fourteen enormous buildings of equal size placed across the river, these edifices being the piers of the arches which sustain the rails. Passing over it, as I did some months afterwards, one sees nothing but sky and water. It is not a pleasant sensation. The ship turned to the left in front of the bridge and entered a narrow arm of the Meuse, called Dordshe kil, bordered by dykes, and having more the look of a canal than a river. It was the seventh turn she had made since we crossed the frontier. We now began to see around us something like the appearance of a great city. Long piles of trees upon the banks, bushes, small houses, canals on either side, and a coming and going of boats large and small. The name of Dordrecht was in everybody's mouth, and all seemed making ready for some spectacle. The ship turned for the eighth time and entered the Oude-Maas, or old Meuse, and in a few minutes we saw the first houses of the environs of Dordrecht.

It was like the sudden apparition of Holland, the instantaneous satisfaction of all our curiosity, the revelation of all the mysteries that tormented our imaginations; we awakened in a new world.

On every side we saw very high windmills with their long arms; houses were sprinkled along the river, of a thousand strange forms, villas, pavilions, kiosks, with red roofs, black walls, and walls of rose, blue, and ash color, the windows and doors surrounded by broad snow-white bands. Canals great and small divided these houses, and were bordered by rows of trees; ships lay all along; boats before every door; sails gleamed at the bottoms of the streets; pennons, ships' flags, and arms of windmills rose confusedly above the trees and roofs; bridges, small stair-

TURF-PIT NEAR DORDRECHT. (*Page* 32.)

ways, gardens hanging over the water, and a coming and going of men, women, and children on the banks of the canals and over the bridges, making a lively and varied spectacle. There was something of theatrical and childish, a little Chinese, a little European, a little of no country, mingled with an air of blessed peace and innocence.

So appeared to me Dordrecht for the first time, one of the oldest as well as one of the freshest and gayest of Dutch cities; queen of commerce in the middle ages; fertile mother of painters and learned men; honoured by first assembly of deputies from the United Provinces in 1572; the seat at different times of memorable synods; and especially famous for that assembly of Protestant theologians in 1618, which was a sort of Œcumenical Council of Reform, which fixed the form of the national religion, and caused the beginning of that series of agitat'ons and persecutions which ended with the fatal execution of Barnevelt and the bloody triumph of Maurice of Orange.

Dordrecht is still one of the most flourishing of the cities of the United Provinces, thanks to its easy communication with the sea, with Belgium, and the interior of Holland. At Dordrecht arrive the immense provisions of wood which come down the Rhine from the Black Forest and Switzerland, the wines of the Rhine, lime, cement, and stone; in her small port there is a continual coming and going of sails, clouds of smoke, and flags, bringing greetings from Arnhem, from Bois-le-Duc, from Nimeguen, Rotterdam, Antwerp, and all her mysterious sisters of Zealand.

Our ship stopped a few minutes at Dordrecht, and I

was strongly tempted to land and look about me, but reflecting that I should have better opportunities and more to see at Rotterdam, I refrained; and we presently turned (our ninth turning) into a narrow branch of the Meuse called *De Noord*, one of the thousand threads of the inextricable watery network that covers South Holland.

The position of Dordrecht is most singular. It is placed upon the extremity of a tract of land, separated from the continent, forming an island in the midst of land, surrounded by rivers, partly natural, partly artificial, of which one, the large stream called the New Merwede, was entirely formed by the hand of man. The imprisonment of this piece of land upon which Dordrecht stands is an episode of one of Holland's great battles with the sea. The archipelago of Biesbosch did not exist before the fifteenth century, and in its place extended a beautiful plain, dotted with populous villages. On the night of the 18th of November 1421, the waters of the Waal and the Meuse burst the dykes, destroyed more than seventy villages, drowned a hundred thousand people, and broke up the plain into a hundred or so of small islands, leaving only one tower erect amid the ruin, some remains of which, called *Casa Merwede*, are still to be seen.

Thus was Dordrecht separated from the mainland, and the archipelago of Biesbosch made its appearance upon the earth, which, as if to show that it has some reason to exist, offers hay, canes, and reeds to a small village that is stuck like a swallow's nest upon one of the surrounding dykes. But this is not all the singularity of Dordrecht.

Tradition relates that the entire city, with its houses, its mills, its canals, was, in the time of that memorable inundation, transported all in one piece from one place to another; and that when the inhabitants of the neighbouring towns came to it after the catastrophe they could not find it. And this prodigy is explained by the fact that Dordrecht is founded upon a stratum of clay, and that this stratum of clay slid bodily down with the city upon it. I write it as I heard it, or read it.

Before the ship left the canal of Noord my hope of seeing my first sunset in Holland was deluded by another sudden change of weather. The sky grew dark, the water became livid, and the horizon vanished behind a dense vapory veil.

At that point where the Meuse takes prisoner and carries with her the waters of the main branch of the Rhine, the Vaal, and receives those of the Leck and the Yssel, the width is very great, and the banks are crowned by long rows of trees, interspersed with houses, manufactories, workshops, and arsenals, that extend all the way to Rotterdam. The first time that one sees the Meuse, and thinks of the disasters, the transformations, the thousand calamities, and innumerable victims of that capricious and terrible river, one examines it with a sort of anxious curiosity, as if it were some famous brigand, and one's eyes run along the dykes with a sentiment of grateful satisfaction, as when one beholds the famous bandit manacled and in the hands of the *carabinieri*. Whilst we stood expecting the first view of Rotterdam, a passenger told us that, when the Meuse is frozen, the current which comes from warmer regions bursts from beneath the ice that covers the stream, and with a terrible noise, piles it against the dykes in immense masses, thus arrestting the course of the water and making it overflow. Then begins a strange battle. To the threats of the Meuse the Hollanders reply with cannon, and charges of grapeshot break the towers and barricades of ice which choke the current into a tempest of briny and icy rain. "I think," concluded the passenger, "that we Hollanders are the only people who are forced to fight their rivers with cannon."

When we arrived in sight of Rotterdam it rained and was foggy; we could see, as through a veil, only an immense confusion of ships, houses, windmills, towers, trees, and people in motion on the dykes and bridges; there were lights everywhere; a great city with such an aspect as I had never seen before, and which fog and darkness soon hid from me altogether. When I had taken leave of my travelling companions, and had put my luggage in order, it was night. "So much the better," I thought, as I entered a carriage; "I shall see the first Dutch city by night, which must be a strange spectacle." And, indeed, when M. Bismarck was at Rotterdam, he wrote to his wife that at night he saw spectres on the roofs.

ROTTERDAM.

It is difficult to make much of the city of Rotterdam, entering it at night. The carriage passed almost immediately over a bridge that resounded hollowly beneath it, and whilst I thought myself, and was in fact, within the city, I saw with amazement, on my right and left, two rows of ships vanishing in the gloom.

Leaving the bridge, we passed through a street, lighted, and full of people, and found ourselves upon another bridge, and between two rows of vessels, as before. And so on from bridge to street, from street to bridge, and to increase the confusion, an illumination of lamps at the corners of houses, lanterns on masts of ships, lighthouses on the bridges, small lights under the houses, and all these lights reflected in the water. All at once the carriage stopped, people crowded about; I looked out, and saw a bridge in the air. In answer to my question, someone said that a vessel was passing. We went on again, seeing a perspective of canals and bridges, crossing and recrossing each other, until we came to a great square, sparkling with lights, and bristling with masts of ships, and finally we reached our inn in an adjacent street.

My first care on entering my room, was to see whether Dutch cleanliness deserved its fame. It did, indeed, and may be called the religion of cleanliness. The linen was snow white, the window-panes transparent as the air, the furniture shining like crystal, the floors so clean that a microscope could not discover a black speck. There was a basket for waste-paper, a tablet for scratching matches, a dish for cigar ashes, a box for cigar stumps, a spittoon, and a bootjack; in short, there was no possible pretext for soiling anything.

My room examined, I spread a map of Rotterdam upon the table, and made some preparatory studies for the morrow.

It is a singular thing that the great cities of Holland, although built upon a shifting soil, and amid difficulties of every kind, have all great regularity of form. Amsterdam is a semicircle, the Hague square, Rotterdam an equilateral triangle. The base of the triangle is an immense dyke, which defends the city from the Meuse, and is called the Boompjes, signifying, in Dutch, small trees, from a row of little elms, now very tall, that were planted when it was first constructed.

Another great dyke forms a second bulwark against the river, which divides the city into two almost equal parts, from the middle of the left side to the opposite angle. That part of Rotterdam which is comprised between the two dykes, is all canals, islands, and bridges, and is the new city; that which extends beyond the second dyke is the old city. Two great canals extend along the other two sides of the town to the apex, where they meet, and receive the waters of the river Rotte, which with the affix of *dam*, or dyke, gives its name to the city.

Having thus fulfilled my conscientious duty as a traveller, and with many precautions not to soil, even by a breath, the purity of that jewel of a chamber, I abandoned myself with humility to my first Dutch bed.

Dutch beds, I speak of those in the hotels, are generally short and wide, and occupied, in a great part, by an immense feather pillow in which a giant's head would be overwhelmed; I may add that the ordinary light is a copper candlestick, of the size of a dinner-plate, which might sustain a torch, but holds, instead, a tiny candle about the size of a Spanish lady's finger.

In the morning I made haste to rise and issue forth into the strange streets, unlike anything in Europe. The first I saw was the Hoog Straat, a long straight thoroughfare running along the interior dyke.

The unplastered houses, of every shade of brick, from the darkest red to light rose color, chiefly two windows wide and two stories high, have the front wall rising above and concealing the roof, and in the shape of a blunt triangle surmounted by a parapet. Some of these pointed façades rise into two curves, like a long neck without a head; some are cut into steps like the houses that children build with blocks; some present the aspect of a conical pavilion, some of a village church, some of theatrical cabins. The parapets are, in general, surrounded by white stripes, coarse arabesques in plaster, and other ornaments in very bad taste; the doors and windows are bordered by broad white stripes; other white lines divide the different stories; the spaces between the doors in front are marked by white wooden panels; so that two colors, white and red, prevail everywhere, and as in the distance the darker red looks black, the prospect is half festive, half funereal, all the houses looking as if they were hung with white linen. At first I had an inclination to laugh, for it seemed impossible that it could have been done seriously, and that quiet sober people lived in those houses. They looked as if they had been run up for a festival, and would presently disappear, like the paper framework of a grand display of fireworks.

Whilst I stood looking vaguely at the street, I noticed one house that puzzled me somewhat; and thinking that my eyes had been deceived, I looked more carefully at it, and compared it with its neighbours. Turning into the next street, the same thing met my astonished gaze. There is no doubt about it; the whole city of Rotterdam presents the appearance of a town that has been shaken smartly by an earthquake, and is on the point of falling into ruin.

All the houses—in any street one may count the exceptions on their fingers—lean more or less, but the greater part of them so much that at the roof they lean forward at least a foot beyond their neighbours, which may be straight, or not so visibly inclined; one leans forward as if it would fall into the street; another backwards, another to the left, another to the right, at some points six or seven contiguous houses all lean forward together, those in the middle most, those at the ends less, looking like a paling with the crowd pressing against it. At another point, two houses lean together as if supporting one another. In certain streets the houses for a long distance lean all one way, like trees beaten by a prevailing wind; and then another long row will lean in the opposite direction, as if the wind had changed. Sometimes there is a certain regularity of inclination that is scarcely noticeable; and again, at crossings and in the smaller streets, there is an indescribable confusion of lines, a real architectural frolic, a dance of houses, a disorder that seems animated. There are houses that nod forwards as if asleep, others that start backwards as if frightened, some bending towards each other, their roofs almost touching, as if in secret conference; some falling upon one another as if they were drunk, some leaning backwards between others that lean forwards like malefactors dragged onwards by their guards; rows of houses that curtsey to a steeple, groups of small houses all inclined towards one in the middle, like conspirators in conclave.

Observe them attentively one by one, from top to bottom, and they are as interesting as pictures.

In some, upon the summit of the façade, there projects from the middle of the parapet a beam, with cord and pulley to pull up baskets and buckets. In others, jutting from a round window, is the carved head of a deer, a sheep, or a goat. Under the head, a line of whitewashed stone or wood cuts the whole façade in half. Under this line there are two broad windows with projecting awnings of striped linen. Under these again, over the upper panes, a little green curtain. Below this green curtain, two white ones, divided in the middle to show a suspended birdcage or a basket of flowers. And below the basket or the cage, the lower panes are covered by a network of fine wire that prevents the passer-by from seeing into the room. Within, behind the netting, there stands a table covered with objects in porcelain, crystal, flowers, and toys of various kinds. Outside, on the stone sill, is a row of small flower-pots. From the stone sill, or from one side, projects an iron stem curving upwards, which sustains two small mirrors joined in the form of a book, movable, and surmounted by another, also movable, so that those inside the house can see, without being seen, everything that passes in the street. On some of the houses there is a lamp projecting between the two windows, and below is the door of the house, or a shop-door. If it is a shop, over the door there is the carved head of a Moor with his mouth wide open, or that of a Turk with a hideous grimace; sometimes there is an elephant, or a goose; sometimes a horse's or a bull's head, a serpent, a half-moon, a windmill, or an arm extended, the hand holding some object of the kind sold in the shop. If it is the house-door—always kept closed—there is a brass plate with the name of the occupant, another with a slit for letters, another with the handle of a bell, the whole, including the locks and bolts, shining like gold. Before the door there is a small bridge of wood, because in many of the houses the ground-floor or basement is much lower than the street; and before the bridge two little stone columns surmounted by two balls; two more columns in front of these are united by iron chains, the large links of which are in the form of crosses, stars, and polygons; in the space between the street and the house, are pots of flowers; and at the windows of the ground-floor, more flower-pots and curtains. In the more retired streets there are birdcages on both sides of the windows, boxes full of green growing things, clothes hung out to air or dry, a thousand objects and colors, like a universal fair.

But without going out of the older town one need only go away from the centre to see something new at every step.

In some narrow straight streets one may see the end suddenly closed as if by a curtain concealing the view; but it disappears as it came, and is recognised as the sail of a vessel moving in a canal. In other streets a network of cordage seems to stop the way; the rigging of vessels lying in some basin. In one direction there is a draw-bridge raised, and looking like a gigantic swing provided for the diversion of the people who live in those preposterous houses; and in another there is a windmill, tall as a steeple and black as an antique tower, moving its arms like a monstrous firework. On every side, finally, among the houses, above the roofs, between the distant trees, are seen masts of vessels, flags, and sails and rigging, reminding us that we are surrounded by water and that the city is a seaport.

Meantime the shops were opened and the streets became full of people. There was great animation, but no hurry, the absence of which distinguishes the streets of Rotterdam from those of London, between which some travellers find great resemblance, especially in the color of the houses and the grave aspect of the inhabitants. White faces, pallid faces, faces the color of Parmesan cheese; light hair, very light hair, reddish, yellowish; broad beardless visages, beards under the chin and around the neck; blue eyes, so light as to seem almost without a pupil; women stumpy, fat, rosy, slow, with white caps and ear-rings in the form of corkscrews; these are the first things one observes in the crowd.

But for the moment it was not the people that most stimulated my curiosity. I crossed the Hoog Straat, and found myself in the new city. Here it is impossible to say if it be port or city, if land or water predominate, if there are more ships than houses, or *vice versâ*.

Broad and long canals divide the city into so many islands, united by draw-bridges, turning bridges, and bridges of stone. On either side of every canal extends a street, flanked by trees on one side and houses on the other. All these canals are deep enough to float large vessels, and all are full of them from one end to the other, except a space in the middle left for passage in and out. An immense fleet imprisoned in a city.

When I arrived it was the busiest hour, so I planted myself upon the highest bridge over the principal crossing. From thence were visible four canals, four forests of ships, bordered by eight files of trees; the streets were crammed with people and merchandise; droves of cattle were crossing the bridges; bridges were rising in the air, or opening in the middle, to allow vessels to pass through, and were scarcely replaced or closed before they were inundated by a throng of people, carts, and carriages; ships came and went in the canals, shining like models in a museum, and with the wives and children of the sailors on the decks; boats darted from vessel to vessel; the shops drove a busy trade; servant-women washed the walls and windows; and all this moving life was rendered more gay and cheerful by the reflections in the water, the green of the trees, the red of the houses, the tall windmills, showing their dark tops and white sails against the azure of the sky, and still more by an air of quiet simplicity not seen in any other northern city.

I took observations of a Dutch vessel. Almost all the ships crowded in the canals of Rotterdam are built for the Rhine and Holland; they have one mast only, and are broad, stout, and variously colored like toy ships. The hull is generally of a bright grass green, ornamented with a red or a white stripe, or sometimes several stripes, looking like a band of different colored ribbons. The poop is usually gilded. The deck and mast are varnished and shining like the cleanest of house-floors. The outside of the hatches, the buckets, the barrels, the yards, the planks, are all painted red, with white or blue stripes. The cabin where the sailors' families are is colored like a Chinese kiosk, and has its windows of clear glass, and its white muslin curtains tied up with knots of rose-colored ribbon. In every moment of spare time, sailors, women, and children are busy washing, sweeping, polishing every part with infinite care and pains; and when their little vessel makes its exit from the port, all fresh and shining like a holiday-coach, they all stand on the poop and accept with dignity the mute compliments which they gather from the glances of the spectators along the canals.

From canal to canal, and from bridge to bridge, I finally reached the dyke of the Boompjes upon the Meuse, where boils and bubbles all the life of the great commercial city. On the left extends a long row of small many-colored steamboats, which start every hour in the day for Dordrecht, Arnhem, Gonda, Schiedam, Brilla, Zealand, and continually send forth clouds of white smoke and the sound of their cheerful bells. To the right lie the large ships which make the voyage to various European ports, mingled with fine three-masted vessels bound for the East Indies, with names written in golden letters—Java, Sumatra, Borneo, Samarang—carrying the fancy to those distant and savage countries like the echoes of distant voices. In front the Meuse, covered with boats and barks, and the distant shore with a forest of beech trees, windmills, and towers; and over all the unquiet sky, full of gleams of light, and gloomy clouds, fleeting and changing in their constant movement, as if repeating the restless labour on the earth below.

Rotterdam, it must be said here, is, in commercial importance, the first city in Holland after Amsterdam. It was already a flourishing town in the thirteenth century. Ludovico Guicciardini, in his work on the Low Countries, already cited, adduces a proof of the wealth of the city in the sixteenth century, saying that in one year nine

ROTTERDAM.   47

hundred houses that had been destroyed by fire were rebuilt. Bentivoglio, in his history of the war in Flanders, calls it "the largest and most mercantile of the lands of Holland." But its greatest prosperity did not begin until 1830, or after the separation of Holland and Belgium, when Rotterdam seemed to draw to herself everything that was lost by her rival, Antwerp. Her situation is extremely advantageous. She communicates with the sea by the Meuse, which brings to her ports in a few hours the largest merchantmen; and by the same river she communicates with the Rhine, which brings to her from the Swiss mountains and Bavaria immense quantities of timber—entire forests that come to Holland to be transformed into ships, dykes, and villages. More than eighty splendid vessels come and go, in the space of nine months, between Rotterdam and India. Merchandise flows in from all sides in such great abundance that a large part of it has to be distributed through the neighbouring towns. Meantime, Rotterdam is growing; vast store-houses are now in process of construction, and the works are commenced for an enormous bridge which will cross the Meuse and the entire city, thus extending the railway which now stops on the left bank of the river, if not to the port of Delph, at least to its junction with the road to the Hague.

Rotterdam, in short, has a future more splendid than that of Amsterdam, and has long been regarded as a rival by her elder sister. She does not possess the wealth of the capital; but is more industrious in increasing what she has; she dares, risks, undertakes, like a young and adventurous city. Amsterdam, like a merchant grown cautious after having made his fortune by hazardous undertakings, begins to doze over her treasures. At Rotterdam fortunes are made; at Amsterdam they are consolidated; at the Hague they are spent.

It may be understood from this that Rotterdam is regarded somewhat in the light of a *parvenu* by the other two cities; and also for another reason: that she is simply a trader, occupied only in trade, and has but little aristocracy, and that little modest and not rich. Amsterdam, on the contrary, contains the flower of the mercantile patriciate; Amsterdam has picture galleries, protects art and literature; but notwithstanding her superiority, each is jealous of the other; what one does the other tries to do; what the Government accords to one the other wants also. At this very moment (1874) both are cutting canals to the sea. It is not yet quite certain what use can be made of these two canals; but that does not matter. So children act: Peter has a horse, I want a horse too, and Grandpapa Government must content both big and little.

Having visited the port, I traversed the dykes of the Boompjes, along which extends an uninterrupted line of big new houses, in the style of Paris and London, houses which, as is usual, the inhabitants admire, and the stranger never looks at, or looks at them with dislike; then returning, I re-entered the city and came to the corner formed by the Hoog Straat and one of the two long canals that bound the city on the east. It is the poorest quarter of the town; the streets are narrow, and the houses smaller and more crooked than in other parts;

ROTTERDAM. THE OLD HARBOR. (*Page* 48.)

in some you can touch the roof with your hand. The windows are about a foot from the ground, and the doors so low that you must stoop to enter them. Nevertheless, there is no appearance of misery. Even here the windows have their small looking-glasses—spies, as they are called in Holland—their flower-pots, and their white curtains; and the doors, painted green or blue, stand wide open, giving a view of the bed-room, the kitchen, all the internal arrangements; tiny rooms like boxes, but everything in them ranged in order, and clean and bright as in gentlemen's houses. There is no dirt in the streets, no bad smells, not a rag to be seen, or a hand held out to beg; there is an atmosphere of cleanliness and well-being which makes one blush for the miserable quarters where the poor are crowded in our cities, not excepting Paris, which has its Rue Mouffetard.

On my way back to my hotel I passed through the great market-place in the middle of the city, not less peculiar than all its surroundings.

It is both a public square and a bridge, and connects the Hoog Straat, or principal dyke, with another quarter of the city surrounded by canals. This airy place is bordered on three sides by old buildings and a long, dark, narrow canal, like a street in Venice; the fourth side is open upon a kind of basin formed by the largest canal, which communicates with the river Meuse.

In the middle of the market-place, surrounded by heaps of vegetables, fruit, and earthenware pots and pans, stands the statue of Desiderius Erasmus, the first literary light of Holland; that Gerrit Gerritz—for he assumed the Latin name himself, according to the custom of writers in his day—that Gerrit Gerritz belonged, by his education, his style, and his ideas, to the family of the humanists and erudite of Italy; a fine writer, profound and indefatigable in letters and science, he filled all Europe with his name between the fifteenth and sixteenth centuries; he was loaded with favours by the popes, and sought after and entertained by princes; and his "Praise of Folly," written in Latin like the rest of his innumerable works, and dedicated to Sir Thomas More, is still read. The bronze statue, erected in 1622, represents Erasmus dressed in a furred gown, with a cap of the same, a little bent forward as if walking, and in the act of reading a large book, held open in the hand; the pedestal bears a double inscription, in Dutch and Latin, calling him, "*Vir sæculi sui primarius*" and "*Civis omnium præstantissimus.*" In spite of this pompous eulogium, however, poor Erasmus, planted there like a municipal guard in the market-place, makes but a pitiful figure. I do not believe that there is in the world another statue of a man of letters that is, like this, neglected by the passer-by, despised by those about it, commiserated by those who look at it. But who knows whether Erasmus, acute philosopher as he was, and must be still, be not contented with his corner, the more that it is not far from his own house, if the tradition is correct? In a small street near the market-place, in the wall of a little house now occupied as a tavern, there is a niche with a bronze statuette representing the great writer, and under it the inscription, "*Hæc est parva domus magnus qua natus Erasmus.*"

In one corner of this square there is a little house known as the "House of Fear," upon the wall of which may be seen an ancient painting whose subject I have forgotten. The name of the "House of Fear" was given to it, says the tradition, because when the Spaniards sacked the city the most conspicuous personages took refuge in this house and remained shut up in it three days without food. And this is not the only memorial of the Spaniards at Rotterdam. Many edifices, built during their domination, show the style of architecture which was then in use in Spain; and some still bear Spanish inscriptions. In Holland inscriptions upon houses are very common. They glory in their old age like bottles of wine, and bear the date of the year of their construction inscribed in large characters on the façade.

In the market-place I had a good opportunity for observing the ear-rings of the women, which are well worthy of remark.

At Rotterdam I saw only the ear-rings in use in South Holland; but even so, their variety is very great. They are all alike, however, in one particular, that instead of being in the ears, they are attached to the two extremities of an ornament in gold, silver, or gilt copper, which encircles the head like a diadem and ends on the temples. The commonest form of ear-ring is a spiral of five or six rows, often very large, and setting out on either side of the face in a very conspicuous fashion. Many of the women wear ordinary ear-rings attached to these spiral ornaments, which dangle over their cheeks and fall down upon the bosom. Some have a second circlet of gold, much chased and ornamented with flowers and buttons in relief, that passes over the forehead. Almost all wear the hair smooth and tight, and covered with a night-cap like head-dress of lace and muslin, falling in a sort of veil over the neck and shoulders. This Arab-like veil and their extravagant and preposterous ear-rings give them a mixed regal and barbaric aspect, which, if they were not as fair as they are, might cause them to be mistaken for the women of some savage country who had preserved the head-dress of their ancient costume. I do not wonder that some travellers, seeing them for the first time, should have believed that their ear-rings were a combination of ornament and implement, and asked their purpose. But we may also suppose that they serve as defensive arms, since any impertinent person, who should put his face too near that of the wearer, would find his approach warded off by these impediments. Worn chiefly by the peasants, these ear-rings and their accessories are generally in gold, and cost a large sum; but I saw still greater riches among the Dutch peasantry.

Near the market-place is the cathedral, founded towards the end of the fifteenth century, at the time of the decline of Gothic architecture, then a Catholic church dedicated to Saint Lawrence, and now the first Protestant church in the city. Protestantism, that vandal of religion, entered the ancient churches with a pick and a white-wash brush, and with pedantic fanaticism eradicated everything that was beautiful and splendid, reducing it to a naked whiteness and coldness, such as in the times of the *false and lying gods* might have suited a temple sacred to the god-

ROTTERDAM. 53

dess of Ennui. An immense organ, with about fifty thousand pipes, giving among other sounds the effect of an echo; some tombs of admirals adorned with long inscriptions in Dutch and Latin; numerous benches; a few boys with their caps on their heads; a group of women chattering together in loud voices; an old man in a corner, with a cigar in his mouth; this was all I saw. That was the first Protestant church in which I set my foot, and I confess that it made a disagreeable impression upon me. I was half saddened, half scandalised. I compared its desolate and bare interior with the magnificent cathedrals of Spain and Italy, where, amid the soft mysterious light and through clouds of incense, the eye encounters the loving looks of saints and angels on the walls, pointing us to heaven; where we see so many images of innocence that calm our souls, and of pain that help us to suffer, while they inspire resignation, peace, the sweetness of forgiveness; where the homeless and the hungry, driven from the rich man's door, may pray amid marble and gold, as in a kingdom where he is not disdained, amid a pomp and splendor that does not humiliate him, that even honours and comforts his misery; those cathedrals where we knelt as children at our mother's side, and felt for the first time a sweet security of living again one day with her in those azure depths depicted upon the domes above our heads. Comparing the church with those cathedrals, I discovered that I was a better Catholic than I had thought, and I felt the truth of those words of Emilio Castelar: "Well, yes, I am a rationalist; but if one day I should wish to return into the bosom of a religion, I would go back to that splendid one of my fathers, and not to this squalid and naked religion that saddens my eyes and my heart!"

From the top of the tower, the whole of Rotterdam can be seen at a glance, with all its little sharp red roofs, its broad canals, its ships scattered among houses, and all about the city a vast green plain, intersected by canals bordered by trees, sprinkled with windmills, and villages hidden in masses of verdure, showing only the tops of their steeples. When I was there, the sky was clear, and I could see the waters of the Meuse shining from the neighbourhood of Bois-le-Duc, nearly to its mouth; the steeples of Dordrecht, Leyden, Delft, the Hague, and Gouda were visible, but neither far nor near was there a hill, a rising ground, a swell to interrupt the straight and rigid line of the horizon. It was like a green and motionless sea, where the steeples represented masts of ships at anchor. The eye roamed over that immense space with a sense of repose, and I felt for the first time, that indefinable sentiment inspired by the Dutch landscape, which is neither pleasure, nor sadness, nor ennui, but a mixture of all three, and which holds you for a long time silent and motionless.

Suddenly I was startled by the sound of strange music coming from I knew not where. It was a chime of bells ringing a lively air, the silvery notes now falling slowly one by one, and now coming in groups, in strange flourishes, in trills, in sonorous chords, a quaint dancing strain, somewhat primitive like the many-colored city, on which its notes hovered like a flock of wild birds, or like the city's natural voice, an echo of the antique life of her people, recalling the sea, the solitudes, the huts, and making one smile and sigh at the same moment. All at once the music ceased, and the clock struck the hour. At the same moment other steeples took up the airy strains, playing airs of which only the higher notes reached my ears, and then they also struck the hour. This aerial concert is repeated every hour of the day and night, in all the steeples of Holland, the tunes being national airs, or from German or Italian operas. Thus in Holland the passing hour sings, as if to distract the mind from sad thoughts of flying time, and its song is of country, faith, and love, floating in harmony above the sordid noises of the earth.

The Hollanders eat a great deal. Their greatest pleasures, as Cardinal Bentivoglio says, are those of the table. Their appetites are voracious, and they care more for quantity than quality. In the old time they were laughed at by their neighbours, not only for the rudeness of their manners, but for the simplicity of their nutriment, and were called milk and cheese eaters. They eat, in general, five times a day; at breakfast, tea, coffee, milk, bread, cheese, and butter; a little before noon a good luncheon; before dinner, what might be called a bite, a biscuit and a glass of wine; then a large dinner; and late in the evening, supper, just so as not to go to bed with an empty stomach. They eat together on every occasion. I do not speak of birth and marriage feasts, which are customary in all countries; but, for example, they have funeral feasts. It is the custom for the friends and acquaintances who have acccompanied the funeral procession, to return with the family of the defunct to their house, and there to eat and drink, doing in general great honor to their entertainer. If there were no other witnesses, the Dutch painters all bear testimony to the large part which the table holds in the life of the people. Besides the infinite number of pictures of domestic subjects, in which it might be said that the plate and the bottle are the protagonists, almost all the great pictures that represent historical subjects, burgomasters, civic guards, show them seated at table in the act of biting, cutting, pouring out. Even their great hero, William the Taciturn, the incarnation of new Holland, was an example of this national fondness for eating, and his cook was the first artist of his time; so great a one that the German princes sent beginners to perfect themselves in his school, and Philip II., in one of his periods of apparent reconciliation with his mortal enemy, asked for the cook as a present.

But, as has been said, the character of Dutch cookery was rather abundance than refinement. The French, who understand the art, found much to criticise. I remember a writer of certain "Memoirs sur la Hollande," who inveighs with lyric force against the Dutch kitchen, saying: "What is this beer soup? this mingling of meats and sweets? this devouring of meat in such quantity without bread?" Other writers have spoken of dining in this country as of a domestic calamity. It is superfluous to say that all this is exaggeration. An ultra-delicate palate can in a short time become accustomed to Dutch cookery. The foundation of the dinner is always a dish of meat, with which are served four or five dishes of vegetables or salted meats, of which each one takes and comoines as he likes with the principal dish. The meat is very good, and the vegetables are exquisite, and cooked in a great variety of ways; the potatoes and cabbages are worthy of special mention, and the art of making an omelet is perfectly understood.

I say nothing of game, fish, milk, and butter, because all these are already known to fame; and I am silent, not to be carried away by enthusiasm, on the subject of that celebrated cheese, wherein when once you have thrust your knife you can never leave off until you have excavated the whole, while desire still hovers over the shell.

A stranger dining for the first time in a Dutch tavern sees a few novelties. First of all he is struck by the great size and thickness of the plates, proportionate to the national appetite; and in many places he will find a napkin of fine white paper, folded in a three-cornered shape, and stamped with a border of flowers, a little landscape in the corner, and the name of the hotel or café, with a *Bon appetit* in large blue letters. The stranger, to be sure of his facts, will order roast beef, and they will bring him half-a-dozen slices, as large as cabbage-leaves; or a beefsteak, and he is presented with a sort of cushion of bleeding meat, enough to satisfy a family; or fish, and there appears a marine animal as long as the table; and with each of these comes a mountain of boiled potatoes and a pot of vigorous mustard. Of bread, a little thin slice about as big as a dollar, most displeasing to us Latins, whose habit it is to devour bread in quantities; so that in a Dutch tavern one must be constantly asking for more, to the great amazement of the waiters. With any one of these three dishes, and a glass of Bavarian or Amsterdam beer, an honest man may be said to have dined. As for wine, whoever has the cramp in his purse will not talk of wine in Holland, since it is extremely dear; but as purses here are pretty generally robust, almost all middle-class Dutchmen and their betters drink it; and there are certainly few countries where so great a variety and abundance of foreign wines are found as in Holland, French and Rhine wines especially.

It is unnecessary to say that Holland is famous for its liquors, and that the most famous of all is that called, from the little town where it is manufactured, Schiedam. There are two hundred manufactories of it at Schiedam, which is distant but a few miles from Rotterdam; and to give an idea of the quantity made, I need only mention that thirty thousand swine are fed yearly with the refuse of the distilleries. This famous liquor, when tasted for the first time, is usually accompanied by a triple oath that the taster will never drink another drop of it, if he live a hundred years; but as the French proverb says, "Who drinks, will drink again," and one begins the second time with a morsel of sugar, and then with less, and finally with none, until at last, *horribile dictu,* on pretence of damp and fog, one swallows two small glasses with the ease of a sailor. Next, in order of excellence, comes Curaçoa, a fine, feminine liquor, less powerful than the Schiedam, but very much more so than the sickly sweet stuff that is sold under its name in other countries. After Curaçoa come many more, of all grades of strength and flavor, with which an expert drinker can give himself, according to his fancy, all the shades of inebriety; the mild, the strong, the talkative, the silent, and thus dispose his brains in such a way that he may see the world according as best suits his humor, as one arranges an optical instrument, changing the colors of the lenses.

The first time one dines in Holland there is a surprise at the moment of paying the bill. I had made a repast that would have been scanty for a Batavian but was quite sufficient for an Italian, and, from what I knew of the dearness of everything in Holland, I expected one of those shocks to which, according to Theophile Gauthier, the only possible answer is a pistol-shot. I was, then, pleasantly surprised when I was told that my account was forty cents, *quarante sous*; and as in the great cities of Holland every kind of coin is current, I put down two silver francs, and waited for my friend to discover that he had made a mistake. But he looked at the money without any sign of reconsideration, and remarked with gravity: "Forty sous more, if you please."

The explanation was simple enough. The monetary unit in Holland is the florin, which is worth two Italian lire (*francs,*) and four centimes; consequently the Dutch sou and centime, are worth just double the Italian *soldo* and centime; hence my delusion and its cure.

Rotterdam in the evening presents an unusual aspect to the stranger's eye. Whilst in other northern cities at a certain hour of the night all the life is concentred in the houses, at Rotterdam at that hour it expands into the streets. The Hoog-straat is filled until far into the night with a dense throng, the shops are open, because the servants make their purchases in the evening, and the cafés crowded. Dutch cafés are peculiar. In general there is one long room, divided in the middle by a green curtain, which is drawn down at evening and conceals the back part, which is the only part lighted; the front part, closed from the street by large glass doors, is in darkness, so that from without only dark shadowy forms can be seen, and the burning points of cigars, like so many fire-flies. Among these dark forms, the vague profile of a woman who prefers darkness to light may be detected here and there.

Next in interest after the café come the tobacco shops. There is one at almost every step, and they are without exception the finest in Europe, even surpassing the great tobacco shops of Madrid, where Havanna tobacco is sold. In these shops, resplendent with lights like the Parisian cafés may be found cigars of every form and flavor; and the courteous merchant hands you your purchase neatly done up in fine thin paper, after having cut off the end of one cigar with a little machine.

Dutch shops are illuminated in the most splendid manner; and although in themselves they differ but little from those of other European cities, they still have a peculiar aspect at night because of the contrast between the ground-floor and the rest of the house. Below all is light, color, splendor, and crystal; above, the dark house-front, with its strange angles, steps, and curves The upper part is old Holland—simple, dark and silent; the lower part is the new—life, fashion, luxury, elegance. Besides this, as all the houses are very narrow, and the shops occupy the entire ground-floor, and are set closely one beside the other, at night, in streets like the Hoog-straat, there is not a bit of wall to be seen, the houses seem to have their ground-floors built of glass, and the street is bordered on either side by two long lines of brilliant illumination, inundating it with light, so that anyone can see to pick up a pin.

Walking through Rotterdam in the evening, it is evident that the city is teeming with life and in process of expansion; a youthful city, still growing, and feeling herself every year more and more pressed for room in her streets and houses. In a not far distant future, her hun-huundred and fourteen thousand inhabitants will have increased to two hundred thousand. The smaller streets swarm with children; there is an overflow of life and movement that cheers the eye and heart; a kind of holiday air. The white and rosy faces of the servant-maids, whose white caps gleam on every side; the serene visages of shopkeepers slowly imbibing great glassfuls of beer; the peasants with their monstrous ear-rings; the cleanliness; the flowers in the windows; the tranquil and laborious throng: all give to Rotterdam an aspect of healthful and peaceful content, which brings to the lips the chant of *Te Beata,* not with the cry of enthusiasm, but with the smile of sympathy.

When I came back to my hotel, I found a French family occupied in the hall admiring the nails in a door, which looked like so many silver buttons.

The next morning, looking out of my window on the

second floor, and observing the roofs of the opposite houses, I recognised, with astonishment, that Bismarck was excusable when he imagined that he saw spectres on the roofs of the Rotterdam houses. From every chimney of all the older buildings rise tubes, curved or straight, crossing and recrossing each other like open arms, like enormous horns, forked, and in every kind of fantastic attitude, and looking very much as if they had a mutual understanding and might fly about at night with brooms.

Upon descending into the Hoog-straat, I found it was a holiday and very few shops were open; but even those few, I was told, would have been closed not many years ago: the observance of religious forms, which had once been very rigorous, beginning to relax. I saw signs of holiday in the dress of the people, especially the men, who—above all, those of the inferior classes—have a manifest sympathy for black clothes, and generally wear them on a Sunday: black cravat, black trousers, and a long black surtout reaching to the knee—a costume which, combined with their slow motions and grave faces, gives them rather the look of a village mayor on his way to assist at an official *Te Deum*.

But what astonished me was to see, at that early hour, almost everyone, rich and poor, men and boys, with a cigar in their mouths. This ill-omened habit of "dreaming with the eyes open," to quote Emile de Girardin in his attack upon smokers, occupies so large a part in the lives of the Dutch people, that I must devote a few words to it.

The Hollanders are, perhaps, of all the northern peoples,

those who smoke the most. The humidity of their climate makes it almost a necessity, and the very moderate cost of tobacco renders it accessible to all. To show how deeply rooted is the habit, it is enough to say that the boatmen of the *treschknit*, the aquatic diligence of Holland, measure distances by smoke. From here, they say, to such and such a place, it is, not so many miles, but so many pipes. When you enter a house, after the first salutations, your host offers you a cigar; when you take leave, he hands you another, and often insists upon filling your cigar-case. In the streets you see persons lighting a fresh cigar with the burning stump of the last one, without pausing in their walk, and with the busy air of people who do not wish to lose a moment of time or a mouthful of smoke. Many go to sleep with pipe in mouth, relight it if they wake in the night, and again in the morning before they step out of bed. " A Dutchman," says Diderot, "is a living alembic." It really does appear that smoking is for him a necessary vital function. Many people think that so much smoke dulls the intelligence. Nevertheless, if there be a people, as Esquiroz justly observes, whose intellect is of the clearest and highest precision, it is the Dutch people. Again, in Holland the cigar is not an excuse for idleness, nor do they smoke in order to dream with their eyes open; everyone goes about his business puffing out white clouds of smoke, with the regularity of a factory chimney, and the cigar, instead of being a mere distraction, is a stimulant and an aid to labour. "Smoke," said a Hollander to me, "is our second breath." Another defined the cigar as the sixth finger of the hand.

Here, *apropos* of tobacco, I am tempted to record the life and death of a famous Dutch smoker; but I am a little afraid of the shrugs of my Dutch friends, who, relating to me the story, lamented much that when foreigners wrote about Holland they were so apt to neglect things important and honorable to the country, while they occupied themselves with trifles of that nature. It appears to me, however, to be a trifle of so new and original a type, that I cannot restrain my pen.

There was, then, once upon a time, a rich gentleman of Rotterdam, of the name of Van Klaes, who was surnamed Father Great-pipe because he was old, fat, and a great smoker. Tradition relates that he had honestly amassed a fortune as a merchant in India, and that he was a kind-hearted and good-tempered man. On his return from India, he built a beautiful palace near Rotterdam, and in this palace he collected and arranged, as in a museum, all the models of pipes that had ever seen the sun in all countries and in every time, from those used by the antique barbarian to smoke his hemp, up to the splendid pipes of meerschaum and amber, carved in relief and bound with gold, such as are seen in the richest Parisian shops. The museum was open to strangers, and to everyone who visited it, Van Klaes, after having displayed his vast erudition in the matter of smoking, presented a catalogue of the museum bound in velvet, and filled his pockets with cigars and tobacco.

Mynheer Van Klaes smoked a hundred and fifty grammes of tobacco per day, and died at the age of ninety-

ROTTERDAM.

eight years; so that, if we suppose that he began to smoke at eighteen years of age, in the course of his life he had smoked four thousand three hundred and eighty-three kilogammes; with which quantity of tobacco an uninterrupted black line of twenty French leagues in length might be formed. With all this, Mynheer Van Klaes showed himself a much greater smoker in death than he had been in life. Tradition has preserved all the particulars of his end. There wanted but a few days to the completion of his ninety-eighth year, when he suddenly felt that his end was approaching. He sent for his notary, who was also a smoker of great merit, and without further preamble, "My good notary," said he, "fill my pipe and your own; I am about to die." The notary obeyed; and when both pipes were lighted, Van Klaes dictated his will, which became celebrated all over Holland.

After having disposed of a large part of his property in favour of relations, friends, and hospitals, he dictated the following article:—

"I desire that all the smokers in the country shall be invited to my funeral, by all possible means, newspapers, private letters, circulars, and advertisements. Every smoker who shall accept the invitation shall receive a gift of ten pounds of tobacco and two pipes, upon which shall be engraved my name, my arms, and the date of my death. The poor of the district who shall follow my body to the grave shall receive each man, every year, on the anniversary of my death, a large parcel of tobacco. To all those who shall be present at the funeral ceremonies, I make the condition, if they wish to benefit by my will, that they shall smoke uninterruptedly throughout the duration of the ceremony. My body shall be enclosed in a case lined inside with the wood of my old Havana cigar-boxes. At the bottom of the case shall be deposited a box of French tobacco called *caporal,* and a parcel of our old Dutch tobacco. At my side shall be laid my favorite pipe and a box of matches, because no one knows what may happen. When the coffin is deposited in the vault, every person present shall pass by and cast upon it the ashes of his pipe."

The last will and testament of Mynheer Van Klaes was rigorously carried out; the funeral was splendid and veiled in a thick cloud of smoke. The cook of the defunct, who was called Gertrude, to whom her master had left a comfortable income, on condition that she should conquer her aversion to tobacco, accompanied the procession with a paper cigarette in her mouth; the poor blessed the memory of the beneficent deceased, and the whole country rang with his praises, as it still rings with his fame.

Passing along the canal I saw, with new effects, one of those rapid changes of weather that I have mentioned. All at once the sun vanished, the infinite variety of colors were dimmed, and an autumn wind began to blow. Then to the cheerful, tranquil gaiety of a moment before succeeded a kind of timid agitation. The branches of the trees rustled, the flags of the ships streamed out, the boats tied to the piles danced about, the water trembled, the thousand small objects about the houses swung to and fro, the arms of the windmills whirled more rapidly; a wintry chill seemed to run through the whole city and moved it as if with a mysterious menace. After a moment, the sun burst out again, and with it came color, peace, and cheer. The spectacle made me think that, after all, Holland is not, as many call it, a dreary country; but rather, very dreary at times, and at times very gay, according to the weather. It is in everything the land of contrasts. Under the most capricious of skies dwell the least capricious of peoples; and this solid, resolute, and orderly race, has the most helter-skelter and disorderly architecture that can be seen in the world.

Before entering the Rotterdam Museum, a few observations upon Dutch painting seem opportune, not for " those who know," be it understood, but for those who have forgotten.

The Dutch school of painting has one quality which renders it particularly attractive to us Italians: it is of all others the most different from our own, the very antithesis, or the opposite pole of art. The Dutch and Italian schools are the two most original, or, as has been said, the only two to which the title rigorously belongs; the others being only daughters, or younger sisters, more or less resembling them.

Thus even in painting Holland offers that which is most sought after in travel and in books of travel: the new.

Dutch painting was born with the liberty and independence of Holland. As long as the northern and southern provinces of the Low Countries remained under the Spanish rule and in the Catholic faith, Dutch painters painted like Belgian painters; they studied in Belgium, Germany, and Italy; Hemskerk imitated Michael Angelo; Bloemart followed Correggio, and "Il Moro" copied Titian, not to indicate others; and they were one and all pedantic imitators, who added to the exaggerations of the Italian style a certain German coarseness, the result of which was a bastard style of painting, still inferior to the first, childish, stiff in design, crude in color, and completely wanting in *chiaroscuro*, but not, at least, a servile imitation, and becoming, as it were, a faint prelude of the true Dutch art that was to be.

With the war of independence, liberty, reform, and painting also were renewed. With religious traditions fell artistic traditions; the nude nymphs, Madonnas, saints, allegory, mythology, the ideal—all the old edifice fell to pieces. Holland, animated by a new life, felt the need of manifesting and expanding it in a new way; the small country, become all at once glorious and formidable, felt the desire for illustration; the faculties, which had been excited and strengthened in the grand undertaking of creating a nation, now that the work was completed, overflowed and ran into new channels; the conditions of the country were favourable to the revival of art; the supreme dangers were conjured away; there was security, prosperity, a splendid future; the heroes had done their duty, and the artists were permitted to come to the front; Holland, after many sacrifices and much suffering, issued victoriously from the struggle, lifted her face among her people and smiled. And that smile is Art.

What that art would necessarily be, might have been guessed, even had no monument of it remained. A pacific, laborious, practical people, continually beaten down, to quote a great German poet, to prosaic realities by the occupations of a vulgar, burgher life; cultivating its reason at the expense of its imagination; living, consequently, more in clear ideas than in beautiful images; taking refuge from abstractions; never darting its thoughts beyond that nature with which it is in perpetual battle; seeing only that which is, enjoying only that which it can possess, making its happiness consist in the tranquil ease and honest sensuality of a life without violent passions or exorbitant desires; such a people must have tranquillity also in their art, they must love an art that pleases without startling the mind, which addresses the senses rather than the spirit, an art full of repose, precision, and delicacy, though material like their lives: in one word, a realistic art in which they can see themselves as they are, and as they are content to be.

The artists began by tracing that which they saw before their eyes—the house. The long winters, the persistent rains, the dampness, the variableness of the climate, obliged the Hollander to stay within doors the greater part of the year. He loved his little house, his shell, much better than we love our abodes, for the reason that he had more need of it, and stayed more within it; he provided it with all sorts of conveniences, caressed it, made much of it; he liked to look out from his well-stopped windows at the falling snow, and the drenching rain, and to hug himself with the thought, " Rage, tempest, I am warm and safe!" Snug in his shell, his faithful housewife beside him, his children about him, he passed the long autumn and winter evenings in eating much, drinking much, smoking much, and taking his well-earned ease after the cares of the day were over. The Dutch painters represented these houses and this life in little pictures proportionate to the size of the walls on which they were to hang: the bed-chambers that make one feel a desire to sleep, the kitchens, the tables set out, the fresh and smiling faces of the house-mothers, the men at their ease around the fire; and with that conscientious realism which never forsakes them, they depict the dozing cat, the yawning dog, the clucking hen, the broom, the vegetables, the scattered pots and pans, the chicken ready for the spit. Thus they represent life in all its scenes, and in every grade of the social scale—the dance, the *conversazione*, the orgie, the feast, the game; and thus did Terburg, Metzu, Netscher, Dow, Mieris, Steen, Brouwer, and Van Ostade become famous.

After depicting the house, they turned their attention to the country. The stern climate allowed but a brief time for the admiration of nature, but for this very reason Dutch artists admired her all the more; they saluted the spring with a livelier joy, and permitted that fugitive smile of heaven to stamp itself more deeply on their fancy. The country was not beautiful, but it was twice dear because it had been torn from the sea and from the foreign oppressor. The Dutch artist painted it lovingly; he represented it simply, ingenuously, with a sense of intimacy which at that time was not to be found in Italian or Belgian landscape. The flat, monotonous country had, to the Dutch painter's

Cows, by Paul Potter. (*Page 71.*)

eyes, a marvellous variety. He caught all the mutations of the sky, and knew the value of the water, with its reflections, its grace and freshness, and its power of illuminating everything. Having no mountains, he took the dykes for background; and with no forests, he imparted to a simple group of trees all the mystery of a forest; and he animated the whole with beautiful animals and white sails.

The subjects of their pictures are poor enough—a windmill, a canal, a grey sky;—but how they make one think! A few Dutch painters, not content with nature in their own country, came to Italy in search of hills, luminous skies, and famous ruins; and another band of select artists is the result, Both, Swanevelt, Pynacker, Breenberg, Van Laer, Asselyn. But the palm remains with the landscapists of Holland, with Wynauts the painter of morning, with Van der Neer the painter of night, with Ruysdael the painter of melancholy, with Hoffema the illustrator of windmills, cabins, and kitchen gardens, and with others who have restricted themselves to the expression of the enchantment of nature as she is in Holland.

Simultaneously with landscape art was born another kind of painting, especially peculiar to Holland—animal painting. Animals are the riches of the country; and that magnificent race of cattle which has no rival in Europe for fecundity and beauty. The Hollanders, who owe so much to them, treat them, one may say, as part of the population; they wash them, comb them, dress them, and love them dearly. They are to be seen everywhere; they are reflected in all the canals, and dot with points of black and white the immense fields that stretch on every side, giving an air of peace and comfort to every place, and exciting in the spectator's heart a sentiment of arcadian gentleness and patriarchal serenity. The Dutch artists studied these animals in all their varieties, in all their habits, and divined, as one may say, their inner life and sentiments, animating the tranquil beauty of the landscape with their forms. Rubens, Luyders, Paul de Vos, and other Belgian painters, had drawn animals with admirable mastery, but all these are surpassed by the Dutch artists Van der Velde, Berghun, Karel der Jardin, and by the prince of animal painters, Paul Potter, whose famous "Bull," in the gallery of the Hague, deserves to be placed in the Vatican beside the "Transfiguration" by Rafael.

In yet another field are the Dutch painters great—the sea. The sea, their enemy, their power, and their glory, for ever threatening their country, and entering in a hundred ways into their lives and fortunes; that turbulent North Sea, full of sinister colors, with a light of infinite melancholy upon it, beating for ever upon a desolate coast, must subjugate the imagination of the artist. He, indeed, passes long hours on the shore, contemplating its tremendous beauty, ventures upon its waves to study the effects of tempests, buys a vessel and sails with his wife and family, observing and making notes, follows the fleet into battle, and takes part in the fight; and in this way are made marine painters like William Vander Velde the elder, and William the younger, like Backhuysen, Dubbels, and Stork.

Another kind of painting was to arise in Holland, as the expression of the character of the people and of republican manners. A people which without greatness had done so many great things, as Michelet says, must have its heroic painters, if we call them so, destined to illustrate men and events. But this school of painting—precisely because the people were without greatness, or, to express it better, without the form of greatness, modest, inclined to consider all equal before the country, because all had done their duty, abhorring adulation, and the glorification in one only of the virtues and the triumph of many—this school has to illustrate not a few men who have excelled, and a few extraordinary facts, but all classes of citizenship gathered among the most ordinary and pacific of burgher life. From this come the great pictures which represent five, ten, thirty persons together, arquebusiers, mayors, officers, professors, magistrates, administrators, seated or standing around a table, feasting and conversing, of life size, most faithful likenesses, grave, open faces, expressing that secure serenity of conscience by which may be divined rather than seen the nobleness of a life consecrated to one's country, the character of that strong, laborious epoch, the masculine virtues of that excellent generation; all this set off by the fine costume of the time, so admirably combining grace and dignity: those gorgets, those doublets, those black mantles, those silken scarves and ribbons, those arms and banners. In this field stand pre-eminent Van der Helst, Hals, Govaert, Flink, and Bol.

Descending from the consideration of the various kinds

of painting, to the special manner by means of which the artist excelled in treatment, one leads all the rest as the distinctive feature of Dutch painting—the light.

The light in Holland, by reason of the particular conditions of its manifestation, could not fail to give rise to a special manner of painting. A pale light, waving with marvellous mobility through an atmosphere impregnated with vapor, a nebulous veil continually and abruptly torn, a perpetual struggle between light and shadow, such was the spectacle which attracted the eye of the artist. He began to observe and to reproduce all this agitation of the heavens, this struggle which animates with varied and fantastic life the solitude of nature in Holland; and in representing it, the struggle passed into his soul, and instead of representing, he created. Then he caused the two elements to contend under his hand; he accumulated darkness that he might split and seam it with all manner of luminous effects and sudden gleams of light; sunbeams darted through the rifts, sunset reflections and the yellow rays of lamp-light were blended with delicate manipulation into mysterious shadows, and their dim depths were peopled with half-seen forms; and thus he created all sorts of contrasts, enigmas, play and effect of strange and unexpected *chiaroscuro*. In this field, among many, stand conspicuous Gerard Don, the author of the famous four-candle picture, and the great magician and sovereign illuminator, Rembrandt.

Another marked feature of Dutch painting was to be color. Besides the generally accepted reasons that in a country where there are no mountainous horizons, no varied prospects, no great *coup d'œil*, no forms, in short, that lend themselves to design, the artist's eye must inevitably be attracted by color, and that this must be peculiarly the case in Holland, where the uncertain light, the fog-veiled atmosphere, confuse and blend the outlines of all objects, so that the eye, unable to fix itself upon the form, flies to color as the principal attribute that nature presents to it; besides these reasons, there is the fact that in a country so flat, so uniform, and so grey as Holland, there is the same need of color as in southern lands there is need of shade. The Dutch artists did but follow the imperious taste of their countrymen, who painted their houses in vivid colors, as well as their ships, and in some places the trunks of their trees and the palings and fences of their fields and gardens; whose dress was of the gayest, richest hues; who loved tulips and hyacinths even to madness. And thus the Dutch painters were potent colorists, and Rembrandt was their chief.

Realism, natural to the calmness and slowness of the Dutch character, was to give to their art yet another distinctive feature, finish, which was carried to the very extreme of possibility. It is truly said that the leading quality of the people may be found in their pictures, viz. patience. Everything is represented with the minuteness of a daguerreotype; every vein in the wood of a piece of furniture, every fibre in a leaf, the threads of cloth, the stitches in a patch, every hair upon an animal's coat, every wrinkle in a man's face; everything finished with microscopic precision, as if done with a fairy pencil, or at the expense of the painter's eyes and reason. It reality a defect rather than an excellence, since the office of painting is to represent not what *is*, but what the eye sees, and the eye does not see everything; but a defect carried to such a pitch of perfection that one admires, and does not find fault. In this respect the most famous prodigies of patience were Don, Micris, Potter, Van der Helst, and more or less, all the Dutch painters.

But realism, which gives to Dutch art so original a stamp, and such admirable qualities, is yet the root of its most serious defects. The artists, desirous only of representing material truths, gave to their figures no expression save that of their physical sentiments. Grief, love, enthusiasm, and the thousand delicate shades of feeling that have no name, or take a different one with the different causes that give rise to them, they express rarely, or not at all. For them the heart does not beat, the eye does not weep, the lips do not quiver. One whole side of the human soul, the noblest and highest, is wanting in their pictures. More, in their faithful reproduction of everything, even the ugly, and especially the ugly, they end by exaggerating even that, making defects into deformities, and portraits into caricatures; they calumniate the national type; they give a burlesque and graceless aspect to the human countenance. In order to have the proper background for such figures, they are constrained to choose trivial subjects; hence the great number of pictures representing beer-shops, and drinkers with grotesque, stupid faces, in absurd attitudes, ugly women, and ridiculous old men; scenes in which one can almost hear the brutal laughter and the obscene words. Looking at these pictures, one would naturally conclude that Holland was inhabited by the ugliest and most ill-mannered people on the earth. We will not speak of greater and worse license. Steen, Potter, and Brouwer, the great Rembrandt himself, have all painted incidents that are scarcely to be mentioned to civilised ears, and certainly should not be looked at. But even setting aside these excesses, in the picture galleries of Holland there is to be found nothing that elevates the mind, or moves it to high and gentle thoughts. You admire, you enjoy, you laugh, you stand pensive for a moment before some canvas; but coming out, you feel that something is lacking to your pleasure, you experience a desire to look upon a handsome countenance, to read inspired verses, and sometimes you catch yourself murmuring, half unconsciously:—" Oh Rafael!"

Finally, there are still two important excellences to be recorded of this school of painting—its variety, and its importance as the expression, the mirror, so to speak, of the country. If we except Rembrandt with his group of followers and imitators, almost all the other artists differ very much from one another; no other school presents so great a number of original masters. The realism of the Dutch painters is born of their common love of nature; but each one has shown in his work a kind of love peculiarly his own; each one has rendered a different impression which he has received from nature; and all, starting from the same point, which was the worship of material truth, have arrived at separate and distinct goals. Their realism, then, inciting them to disdain nothing as food for the pencil, has so acted that Dutch art succeeds in representing Holland more completely than has ever been accomplished by any other school in any other country. It has been truly said that should every other visible witness of the existence of Holland in the seventeenth century—her period of greatness—vanish from the earth, and the pictures remain, in them would be found preserved entire the city, the country, the ports, the ships, the markets, the shops, the costumes, the arms, the linen, the stuffs, the merchandise, the kitchen utensils, the food, the pleasures, the habits, the religious belief and superstitions, the qualities, and effects of the people; and all this, which is great praise for literature, is no less praise for her sister art.

But there is one great hiatus in Dutch art, the reason for which can scarcely be found in the pacific and modest disposition of the people. This art, so profoundly national in all other respects, has, with the exception of a few naval battles, completely neglected all the great events of the war of independence, among which the sieges of Leyden and of Harlem alone would have been enough to have inspired a whole legion of painters. A war of almost a century in duration, full of strange and terrible vicissitudes, has not been recorded in one single memorable painting. Art, so varied and so conscientious in its records of the country and its people, has represented no scene of that great tragedy, as William the Silent prophetically named it, which cost the Dutch people, for so long a time, so many different emotions of terror, of pain, of rage, of joy, and of pride!

The splendor of art in Holland is dimmed by that of

political greatness. Almost all the great painters were born in the first thirty years of the seventeenth century, or in the last part of the sixteenth; all were dead after the first ten years of the eighteenth, and after them there were no more; Holland had exhausted her fecundity. Already towards the end of the seventeenth century the national sentiment had grown weaker, taste had corrupted, the inspiration of the painters had declined with the moral energies of the nation. In the eighteenth century, the artists, as if they were tired of nature, went back to mythology, to classicism, to conventionalities; the imagination grew cold, style was impoverished, every spark of the antique genius was extinct. Dutch art still showed to the world the wonderful flowers of Van Huysum, the last great lover of nature, and then folded her tired hands, and let the flowers fall upon his tomb.

The actual gallery of pictures of Rotterdam contains but a small number, among which there are very few by the first artists, and none of the great *chef-d'œuvres* of Dutch painting. Three hundred pictures and thirteen hundred drawings were destroyed in a fire in 1864; and of what remained the greater part come from one Jacob Otto Boymans, who left them in his will to the city. In this gallery, therefore, one may enter to make acquaintance with some particular artist, rather than to admire the Dutch school.

In one of the first rooms may be seen a few sketches of naval battles, signed with the name of Willem Van de Velde, considered as the greatest marine painter of his time, son of Willem, called the elder, also a marine painter. Father and son had the good fortune to live in the time of the great maritime wars between Holland, England, and France, and saw the battles with their own eyes. The States of Holland placed a small frigate at the disposition of the elder Van de Velde; the son accompanied his father, and both made their sketches in the midst of the cannon-smoke, sometimes pushing their vessel so near as to cause the admiral to order their withdrawal. Van de Velde the younger greatly surpassed his father, and painted, in general, small pictures—a grey sky, a calm sea, and a sail; but so done, that when fixing your eyes upon them, you seem to smell the briny breezes of the ocean, and the frame appears changed into an open window. This Van de Velde belonged to that group of Dutch painters who loved the water with a kind of fury, and painted, it may be said, upon it. Of these also was Backhuysen, a marine painter of great repute in his own time, and whom Peter the Great, when in Amsterdam, chose for his master. Backhuysen relates of himself, that he went out in a small boat in the midst of a tempest to observe the movement of the waves, and he and his boatmen ran such fearful risks that the latter, more solicitous for their own lives than for his picture, took him back to land in spite of his orders to the contrary. John Griffier did more. He bought a small vessel at London, which he furnished like a house, and installing his wife and family on board, sailed about in search of views. A tempest having wrecked his vessel on a sand-bank and destroyed everything he possessed, he, saved by a miracle with his family, went to live at Rotterdam; but soon

LANDSCAPE, BY RUYSDÄEL. (*Page* 80.)

tiring of life on land, Griffier bought another wretched old boat, recommenced his voyages, and a second time risked his life near Dordrecht; but he still persisted in sailing about as before.

In marine painting the gallery of Rotterdam has little to show; but landscape is worthily represented by two pictures by Ruysdael, the greatest of the Dutch painters of rural scenes. These two pictures represent his favourite subjects; namely, woody and solitary places, which inspire, like all his pictures, a vague sentiment of melancholy. The great power of this artist, who stands alone among his brother painters for delicacy of mind and a singular superiority of education, lies in his sentiment. It has been justly said that he makes use of landscape to express his own bitterness and weariness, his own dreams, and that he contemplates his country with a sort of sadness, and creates groves of trees in which to hide it. The veiled light of Holland is the image of his soul; no one feels more exquisitely its melancholy sweetness; no one represents like him, with a ray of languid light, the sad smile of some afflicted creature. It follows as a matter of course that so exceptional a nature was not appreciated by his countrymen till long after his death.

Near one of Ruysdael's pictures is a group of flowers by a woman painter, Rachel Ruysch, the wife of a portrait painter of note, born in the second half of the sixteenth century, and dying, pencil in hand, at eighty years of age, after having proved to her husband and the world that a woman may passionately cultivate the fine arts and still find time to bear and bring up ten children.

And since I have mentioned the wife of one artist, it may be here noted, *en passant*, that a pleasant book might be written upon the wives of the Dutch painters, as well for the variety of their adventures as for the important part which they take in the history of art. Many of them we know by sight from their portraits, made in company with their husbands, their children, their cats, and their hens; and biographers speak of them, denying or confirming reports concerning their conduct. Some even venture to hint that the greater part of these ladies did great wrongs to painting. To me it appears that there were faults on both sides. As for Rembrandt, we know that the happiest period of his life was that between his first marriage and the death of his wife, the daughter of a burgomaster of Leuwarde; posterity, therefore, owes this lady a debt of gratitude. We know, also, that Van der Helst married, when already advanced in life, a lovely young girl against whom there is nothing to be said; and posterity has to thank her as well, for having cheered the declining years of that great artist. It is true that all the wives of the Dutch painters cannot be spoken of in the same terms. The first of the two wives of Steen, for example, was a frivolous woman who left the beershop which she had inherited from her father to fall into ruin; and the second, if all is true that is said of her, was unfaithful to him. The second wife of Heemskerk was a swindler, and her husband was obliged to go about making excuses for her misdeeds. The wife of Hondekoeter was an odd, ill-tempered woman, who obliged him to pass his evenings at a tavern in order to be rid of her. The wife of Berghem was an insatiable miser, who would wake him abruptly when he fell asleep over his brushes, and make him work to gain money, while the poor man was constrained to resort to subterfuge in order to retain a little of his own earnings, to buy himself an engraving or two. On the other hand we should never have done were we to attempt to exhaust the misdeeds of the gentlemen. The painter Griffier forced his wife to go about the world in a boat; the painter Veenir got leave of his spouse to go and spend four months in Rome, and stayed four years; Karel du Jardin married a rich old woman to pay his debts, and when they were all paid, left her; Molyn had his wife murdered that he might marry a Genoese. We leave in doubt whether poor Paul Potter was betrayed or no by the wife he loved so madly; and whether the great flower-painter, Huysum, who was devoured by jealousy in the midst of riches and honors, for a wife no longer young or handsome, had any real cause for jealousy, or was merely driven wild with suspicion by the manœuvres of his envious rivals. As an appropriate finish, let us honourably record the three wives of Eglon van der Neer, who crowned him with twenty-five children, which did not, however, prevent him from painting a great number of pictures of every kind, from making numerous journeys, and from cultivating many tulips.

There are in the gallery of Rotterdam a few small pictures by Albert Cuyp, who " gave a part of himself" to Dutch art, and who in the course of a very long life painted portraits, landscapes, animals, flowers, winter scenes, moonlight, marine subjects, figures, and left on them all the stamp of original genius; nevertheless, like all the Dutch painters of his day, he was so unfortunate, that up to 1750, or more than fifty years after his death, his best pictures sold for one hundred francs, pictures which are now valued, in England, not in Holland, at one hundred thousand. Almost all his works are now in England.

I should not say a word about Heemskerk's "Christ at the Sepulchre," if it were not that it gives occasion to make known the artist, who was one of the most singular beings that ever walked the earth. Van Veen, for that was his name, was born in the village of Heemskerk, at the end of the fifteenth century, and flourished during the period of Italian imitation. He was the son of a peasant, and although he showed some disposition towards painting, seemed destined to remain a peasant. He became an artist, like many others, by an accident. His father was a man of violent temper, and the son was terribly in fear of him. One day poor Van Veen threw down the jug of milk, his father rushed at him, and he took to flight and passed the night in hiding out of doors. In the morning his mother found him, agreed with him that it would not be prudent to brave the paternal wrath, gave him a small store of linen and a little money, and sent him off to seek his fortune. The boy went to Harlem, obtained entrance into the school of a painter of note, studied, succeeded, and went to Rome to perfect himself. He did not become a *great* artist, for imitation of Italian art was injurious to him. He treated the nude stiffly and had a mannered style; but he was a productive painter and was well paid, and never had reason to regret his peasant life.

But here comes in his peculiarity : he was, according to his biographers, incredibly, morbidly, madly timid; insomuch, that when he knew that the arquebusiers were going to pass by, he fled to the roofs and the steeples, and shook with terror even there at the distant gleam of arms. And if anyone doubt this, there is a fact recorded of him which cannot be questioned: that finding himself in the city of Harlem when the Spaniards laid siege to it, the magistrates, knowing his weakness, gave him leave to quit the city before the fight began, perhaps because they foresaw that if he did not do that, he would die of fright; and he fled to Amsterdam, leaving his fellow-citizens at their greatest need.

Other Dutch artists—since I am speaking of the men and not of their works—like Heemskerk, owed to an accident their success as painters. Everdingen, a landscape painter of the first rank, owed it to a tempest which threw his ship on the coast of Norway, where he remained and, under the inspiration of the grand natural features there, created an original type of landscape.

Cornelius Vroom also owed his fortune to a shipwreck. He had sailed for Spain with some religious pictures; his ship was wrecked off the Portuguese coast; the poor artist was saved with others on an uninhabited island. They remained two days without food, and gave themselves up for lost, when they were succoured by some monks of a convent on the coast, to whom the sea had carried, with the carcass of the ship, the pictures that were in it, and the monks had found them admirable; and so Cornelius was saved, sheltered, and encouraged to paint; and the profound emotions experienced in his shipwreck gave a new and powerful impulse to his genius, and made him a true artist.

And another, Hans Fredeman, the famous painter of deceptions—he who painted in so masterly a manner the doors of a hall in imitation of columns, that Charles V. turned back after entering, thinking that the wall had closed behind him by enchantment; the same Hans Fredeman who painted palings that turned aside the passenger, and doors which people tried to open—owed his fortune to a treatise on architecture by Vitruvius, which he received by chance from a carpenter.

There is a fine little picture by Steen, representing a doctor pretending to perform the operation for the stone upon a man who imagines himself ill. An old woman receives the stone in a basin, the patient yells at the top of his lungs, and some laughing spectators look in at a window.

When we say that this picture makes you burst into a shout of laughter, we have said all that need be said. This Steen is, after Rembrandt, the most original of the Dutch figure-painters; he is one of the few artists who, once known, whether we class him as great, or place him only in the second rank, remains a fixture in our minds for ever. After having seen his pictures, you cannot meet a drunken man, a buffoon, a cripple, a dwarf, a deformed visage, a ridiculous grimace, a grotesque attitude, without instantly remembering one of his figures.

All the gradations, all the stupidity of drunkenness, all the coarse license of an orgie, all the frenzy of the basest pleasures, the cynicism of the lowest vice, the buffoonery of the maddest ruffianism, all the most bestial emotions, all the most ignoble aspects of tavern life, he has portrayed with the insolence and brutality of a man without scruples, and with a comic force and fire, a very madness of inspiration, which cannot be expressed in words.

Many volumes have been written upon him, and many diverse judgments pronounced. His warmest admirers have attributed to him a moral intention—the purpose of making low vices hateful, by painting them in all their naked hideousness, as the Spartans showed the drunken Helots to their sons. Others see nothing in his pictures but the spontaneous and instinctive expression of the tastes and disposition of the artist, represented with coarse vulgarity. However that may be, it is beyond a doubt that Steen's pictures are to be considered as satires upon vice; and in this he is superior to almost all the other Dutch painters, who restricted themselves to a simple naturalism. Hence he is called the Dutch Hogarth, the jovial philosopher, the profoundest student of the manners of his countrymen; and among his admirers there is one who said that if Steen had been born in Rome instead of Leyden, and had had Michael Angelo instead of Van Goyen for a master, he would have been one of the greatest artists in the world; and there is another who has discovered I know not what analogy between him and Rafael. Less general is the admiration for the technical qualities of his pictures, in which the delicacy and vigor of other artists, such as Ostade, Micris, and Dow, are not to be found. But considering even the satirical character of his work, it may be said that Steen often overshot his mark, if mark he had. His burlesque fury often overpowered his sentiment of reality; his figures, instead of being only ridiculous, became monstrous, hardly human, resembling rather beasts than men; and he multiplied such figures in a way to excite nausea rather than laughter, and a feeling of anger that human nature should be so outraged.

There has always been much question as to his manner of life. Volumes have been written to prove that he was a drunkard, and other volumes to prove the contrary; and, as usual, there are exaggerations on both sides. He kept a beershop at Delft, and did badly; he then set up a tavern, and came to grief. It is said that he was himself the most assiduous customer of the latter, that he drank up all the wine, and, when the cellar was empty, took down the sign, closed the doors, set himself to painting in hot haste, then sold the pictures, bought more wine, and began again as before. It is also said that he paid directly with the pictures, and that consequently most of his work was in the possession of the wine merchants. It is difficult, truly, to explain how, being always in difficulties, he could have painted so large a number of admirable pictures; but it is not less difficult to understand why he loved such subjects if he were leading a sober and orderly life. Certain it is, that, especially in the last years of his life, he committed all sorts of extravagances. He studied at first in the school of Van Goyen, a landscape-painter of note; but genius worked in him far more than study; he divined the rules of his art; and if he sometimes painted too black, as one of his critics declares, the fault probably lay in some bottle too much at dinner.

Steen is not the only Dutch artist who is accused of drunkenness. There was a time when almost all of them passed a good part of the day at the tavern, drinking, and coming to blows, and issuing forth all bruised and bloody. In a poem upon the works of Karel van Mander, the first who wrote the history of painting in the Low Countries, there is a passage against the vice of drunkenness and the habit of fighting, which says, among other things: "Be sober, and act so that the ill-omened proverb of 'debauched as a painter' shall be changed into 'temperate as an artist.'" Mieris, to cite only the most famous, was a great drinker; Van Goyen a sot; Francis Halz, Brouwer's master, a wine sponge; Brouwer an incorrigible haunter of taverns; William Cornelis and Hondekoeter both devoted to the bottle. Of the minor lights, some died of drink; and in their deaths the Dutch painters saw strange vicissitudes. The great Rembrandt died in straitened circumstances, almost unknown to all; Hoffema died at Amsterdam in the poor quarter; Steen died in misery; Brouwer in the hospital; Andrea Both and Henry Verschuring were drowned; Adrian Bloemaert was killed in a duel; Karel Fabritius was blown up in a powder-mill; John Scotel died, brush in hand, of apoplexy; Paul Potter died of consumption; Luke of Leyden was poisoned. So what between sudden death, debauchery, and jealousy, many of the Dutch painters cannot be said to have had a very happy lot.

There is in the gallery at Rotterdam a fine head by Rembrandt; a brigand scene by Wonvermaus, the great horse and battle painter; a landscape by Van Goyen, the painter of dead sands and leaden skies; a sea-piece by Backhuysen, the painter of storms; a Berghem, the painter of smiling landscapes; an Everdingen, the painter of cascades and forests; and other works, Flemish and Italian.

Coming out of the museum I met a company of soldiers, the first Dutch soldiers I had seen, dressed in dark uniforms, without visible ornament, blonde from first to last, with long fair hair, and an air of good humour that made their arms seem incongruous. At Rotterdam, a city of more than a hundred thousand inhabitants, there are three hundred soldiers in garrison! And Rotterdam has, among the cities of Holland, the reputation of being the most turbulent and dangerous! Not long ago, indeed, there was a popular demonstration against the city government, in the course of which a few windows were broken; but in a country that goes by clock-work, as this does, it seemed a great affair, the State was much excited, and cavalry came from the Hague. It is not to be concluded, however, that the people are all sugar; on the contrary, the inhabitants of Rotterdam themselves acknowledge that the lower orders (what Carducci calls the *Santa Caraglia*) are, as in other places, of the worst possible reputation; and the scarcity of the garrison is rather a provocation to license than a proof of public morals.

Rotterdam is not, as I have said, a literary or artistic city; indeed, it is one of the few Dutch cities that have never produced any great painter; a sterility which it shares with the interior of Zealand. But Erasmus is not its sole literary glory. In a small park which lies to the right of the city on the shore of the Meuse, stands a marble statue of the poet Tollens, born towards the end of the last century, and who died not long since. This Tollens, rather audaciously called by some the Dutch Béranger, was a popular poet of the country; one of those poets, simple, moral, full of good sense, with rather more good sense than inspiration, treating poetry very much as a matter of business, never writing a word that could give umbrage to their wise relations and friends, singing their good God and their good king, expressing the character of their tranquil, practical, fellow-citizens, and aiming to say just things rather than great things; and, above all, cultivating poetry at an advanced age, like prudent fathers of families, without abstracting a moment from the duties of their profession. Like many other Dutch poets (but of another nature and another genius than his), as, for example, Vandel, who was a hatter, Hooft, governor of Muyden, Van Leunep, procurator-fiscal, Gravenswaert, Councillor of State, and others, Tollens was an apothecary at Rotterdam, and passed his days in his drug-shop. He was a loving father to his children, as he has demonstrated in numerous verses celebrating the cutting of their first, second, and third teeth. He wrote " Canzoni," and odes upon familiar and patriotic subjects, among them the national hymn of

Holland—a very mediocre affair, which is, however, sung about the streets and in the schools—and a little poem, which is, perhaps, his best, upon the expedition attempted by the Dutch, towards the end of the sixteenth century, to the Polar seas. The people have all his verses by heart, and consider him their most faithful friend and interpreter. But for all that, Tollens is not considered, even in Holland, a poet of the first order; and some even refuse him the sacred laurel altogether.

For the rest, if Rotterdam is not a literary or artistic city, she has instead an extraordinary number of philanthropic institutions, splendid reading-rooms where all the journals of Europe can be found, and all the conveniences and amusements of a rich and prosperous city.

On the morning that I left Rotterdam, I saw a new and very Dutch spectacle in the street through which I passed to go to the Delft railway-station. The house-cleaning that goes on twice a week in the early morning was in progress. All the maid-servants in the city, in lilac-cotton gowns, white caps, white aprons, stockings, and *sabots*, were busy, with their sleeves turned up, washing doors, walls, and windows. Some courageously seated upon the window-sills, half in, half out, were cleaning the panes with sponges; others, kneeling on the step, rubbed the pavement with a cloth; others, with syringes, and long flexible tubes such as we use to water gardens, directed vigorous jets of water against the second-floor windows, that fell again in heavy showers; some, with sponges and rags tied on the ends of long canes, mopped the upper windows; some polished the knobs and metal plates upon the doors, some cleaned the stairs, some the furniture, brought out into the street for the purpose; the door-steps were encumbered with buckets, pans, brushes, brooms, and benches; water dripped from the walls, ran into the gutters, and splashed and sparkled everywhere. And, what is singular, whilst labour in Holland is slow and deliberate in all other forms, in this one it is quite different. All these women have flushed faces, they go in and come out, spring and push about with a sort of fury, taking acrobatic attitudes, with startling results sometimes, unheeding of the passer-by, except in so far as it may be necessary to drive him off, with jealous looks, from the pavement. In short, there was a rage and fury of cleanliness, a sort of general ablution of the city, that had a sort of festive puerility about it, and might have been some strange religious rite, prescribed to purge the place from the infection of unclean spirits.

DELFT.

In going from Rotterdam to Delft I saw for the first time the open country of Holland. It is all one plain, a succession of green and flowery meadows, crossed by long files of willows, and sprinkled with groups of poplars and elders. Here and there are seen tops of steeples, whirling wings of windmills, scattered herds of large black and white cows, with their herdsmen, and immense tracts that are completely solitary. There is nothing to strike the eye, nothing salient, nothing sloping. Every now and then, in the distance, the sail of a ship glides by, and being in a canal invisible from that distance, it seems to be gliding over the grass of the meadows, appearing and disappearing behind the trees. The pale light gives to the country a certain soft and melancholy aspect. A slight mist makes every object appear afar off. There is a kind of visible silence, a peace of line and color, a repose of all things, looking on which the eye grows dreamy and the imagination is lulled.

WINDMILLS FOR DRAWING OFF WATER. (*Page* 95.)

At a short distance from Rotterdam is the town of Schiedam, surrounded by very lofty windmills that give it the look of a fortified place crowned with towers; and in the distance appears the village of Vlaardingen, which is one of the principal stations for the great herring-fishery.

From Schiedam to Delft I gave myself up to the study of windmills. The Dutch mills do not at all resemble those decrepit objects which I had seen the year before in La Mancha, that stretched their meagre arms as if imploring succour from earth and heaven. The Dutch mills are large, strong, and full of life; and Don Quixote would have thought twice before attacking them. Some are made of stone, round and octagonal, like mediæval towers; others are of wood, and present the form of a box stuck upon the apex of a pyramid. The greater part have thatched roofs, a wooden gallery running round the middle, windows with white curtains, green doors, and the use they serve inscribed upon the door. Besides the absorption of water, they do a little of everything: they grind flour, wash rags, crush lime, break stone, saw wood, crush olives, pulverise tobacco. A mill is equivalent to a farm; and to build it, provide it with grain, colza, flour, oil, to keep it going, and send its product to market, requires a considerable fortune. Consequently, in many places, the wealth of proprietors is measured by the number of their mills; hereditary property is calculated by mills. They say of a girl that she has one or two windmills for a dowry, or two steam-mills, which is better; and speculators, who are everywhere, marry the girl in order to get her mills. This myriad of winged towers scattered over the country give it a peculiar aspect and animate its solitude. At night, among the trees, they have a fantastic appearance, like fabulous birds watching the heavens; by day, in the distance they look like enormous frames for fire-works; they whirl round, stop, go fast, go slowly, breaking the silence with their low, monotonous tic-tac; and when they catch fire, which they do sometimes, especially the grain-mills, they make a wheel of flame, a tempest of burning meal, a whirl of fiery clouds, which is quite infernal in its tumultuous splendor.

In the carriage, although there were many passengers, no one spoke. All were men of mature years, with grave faces, who looked at one another in silence, and emitted clouds of smoke at regular intervals, as if they were measuring time by their cigars. When we reached Delft I bowed as I got out, and one or two responded by a slight motion of the lips.

"Delft," says Messer Ludovico Guicciardini, "is so called from the ditch, or water-canal, which leads to it from the Meuse—a ditch being vulgarly called *delft*. It is two leagues distant from Rotterdam, and is truly great and beautiful in every part, with large and handsome edifices, and streets wide and cheerful. It was founded by Godfrey, surnamed the Gobbo (hunchback), Duke of Lotharingia, who for nearly four years occupied the country of Holland."

Delft is the city of misfortune. Towards the middle of the sixteenth century it was almost entirely destroyed by fire; in 1654 the blowing-up of a powder-magazine ruined more than two hundred houses; and in 1742 another catastrophe of the same kind occurred. William the Silent was assassinated at Delft in 1584. And here decayed and almost disappeared an industry that was its riches and its glory—the manufacture of majolica, in which the Dutch artisans had begun by imitating the forms and designs of Chinese and Japanese porcelain, and had succeeded in producing admirable work, uniting the Asiatic with the Dutch character, and extending it all over northern Europe; and even now these objects are sought for eagerly by amateurs of the art, and almost as highly prized as the finest Italian work.

Delft now is no longer a manufacturing or commercial city; its twenty-two thousand inhabitants live in profound peace. But it is one of the prettiest and most Dutch of the cities of Holland. The streets are broad, crossed by canals shaded by two rows of trees, flanked by houses, red, crimson, and rose color, picked out with white, which look glad to be so clean; and at every crossing meet and join two or three bridges of stone or wood, with white railings; here and there a large boat lying motionless as if enjoying its idleness; very few people, closed doors, and no noise of any kind.

I directed my steps towards the new church, looking about me for the famous storks' nests; but I could not see any. The tradition of the storks of Delft is, however, still alive, and no traveller writes about the city without remembering them. Guicciardini calls it " a memorable thing, and such as there is no similar record of, antique or modern." The fact occurred at the time of the great fire which ruined almost all the city. There were in Delft innumerable storks' nests. It must be understood that the stork is the favorite bird of Holland; the bird of good fortune, like the swallow; welcome to all, because it makes war upon toads and frogs; that the peasants plant poles with round pieces of wood on top to attract them to make their nests; and that in some towns they may be seen walking in the streets. At Delft then they were in great numbers. When the fire broke out, which was on the 3rd of May, the young storks were fledged, but could not yet fly. Seeing the fire approach, the parent storks attempted to carry their young ones out of danger, but they were too heavy; and after having tried all sorts of desperate efforts, the poor birds were forced to give it up. They might have saved themselves and have abandoned the little ones to their fate, as human creatures often do under similar circumstances. But they stayed instead upon their nests, gathered their little ones about them, covered them with their wings as if to retard as long as possible the fatal moment, and so awaited death, and so remained in that loving and noble attitude. And who shall say if, in the horrible dismay and flight from the flames, that example of self-sacrifice, that voluntary maternal martyrdom, may not have given strength and courage to some weak soul who was about to abandon those who had need of him!

In the great square where the new church stands I saw again those shops which had attracted my attention at Rotterdam, where every object that can possibly be attached one to the other is suspended in long garlands within and without, sometimes completely hiding the back of the shop. The signs are the same as in Rotterdam—a bottle of beer hung on a nail, a paint-brush, a box, a broom, and the usual carved head with wide-open mouth.

The new church, founded in the latter part of the fourteenth century, is for Holland what Westminster Abbey is for England. It is a large edifice, dark without and naked within; a prison rather than the House of God.

My eyes were at once attracted by the splendid mausoleum of William the Silent; but the custodian stopped me at the simple tomb of Ugo Grotius, *Prodigium Europæ,* as he is called in his epitaph, the great jurisconsult of the seventeenth century; that Grotius who at nine years of age wrote Latin verses, at eleven composed Greek odes, at fourteen philosophic theses, and three years later accompanied the illustrious Barneveldt in his embassy to Paris, where Henry IV., presenting him to the Court, said: "Behold the miracle of Holland!" that Grotius who at eighteen was distinguished as poet, theologian, commentator, and astronomer, and had written a prose epic on the city of Ostend, which Casaubon translated into Greek, and Malesherbe into French verse; that Grotius who, in his twenty-fourth year, exercised the office of Advocate-General of Holland and Zealand, and wrote a celebrated treatise on the "Liberty of the Seas"; who at thirty was Councillor of the city of Rotterdam; then partisan of Barneveldt, persecuted, condemned to perpetual imprisonment, and shut up in the Castle of Loevesteen, where he wrote the treatise of the "Right of Peace and of War," which was for a long time the codex of all the publicists of Europe; then saved miraculously by his wife, who caused herself to be introduced into his prison in a box believed to contain books, which box went out again with the prisoner in it, while the wife remained a prisoner in his stead; then the guest of Louis XIII., and sent ambassador from France to Christina of Sweden; and finally returning triumphantly to his own country, where he died, at Rostock, full of years and honors.

The mausoleum of William the Silent is in the middle of the church. It is a sort of small temple in black and white marble, loaded with ornament, and sustained by columns, between which are four statues representing Liberty, Prudence, Justice, and Religion. Upon the sarcophagus lies the figure of the prince, in white marble, and at his feet the effigy of the little dog that saved his life at the siege of Malines, waking him by its barkings one night in his tent, when two Spaniards were creeping upon him to assassinate him. At the feet of this figure rises a fine bronze statue of Victory, with outspread wings, and supported only upon the toes of the left foot; and opposite, on the other side of the little temple, another bronze statue, representing William, seated, dressed in his armour, with uncovered head, the helmet lying at his feet. A Latin inscription sets forth that the monument was raised by the States of Holland, " to the eternal memory of that William of Nassau, whom Philip II., scourge of Europe, feared, and never overcame or conquered, but killed by atrocious guile." His sons are sepulchred beside him, and in the crypt below lie all the princes of his dynasty.

In the presence of this monument the lightest and most frivolous mind feels itself constrained to stop and ponder, recalling the tremendous struggle whose hero and conqueror lies below.

On one side is Philip II., on the other William of Orange. Philip, shut up in the gloomy solitudes of the Escorial, lord of an empire that embraced all Spain, the north and south of Italy, Belgium, and Holland; in Africa, Oran, Tunis, the Cape de Verde and Canary islands; in Asia, the Phillipine islands; in America, the Antilles, Mexico, Peru; married to the Queen of England; nephew of the Emperor of Germany, who obeyed him almost as a vassal; sovereign, it may be said, of Europe, since his nearer neighbors are all weakened by political and religious dissensions; having under his hand the best soldiers in Europe, the greatest captains of the time, the gold of America, the industry of Flanders, the science of Italy, an army of informers chosen from all nations, fanatically devoted to himself, the blind instruments of his will; the most astute, the most mysterious of the princes of his time; having on his side everything that enchains, corrupts, terrifies, and moves the world: arms, riches, glory, genius, religion. Before this formidable being, around whom all creatures prostrate themselves, rises William of Orange.

This man, without a kingdom and without an army, is more powerful than he. Like Philip, he has been a disciple of Charles V. and has learned the art of founding thrones, and the art of overturning them as well. Like Philip, he is astute and impenetrable; but he sees more clearly with the eyes of his intellect, into the future. He possesses, as does his enemy, the faculty of reading the souls of men; but he has also what his enemy has not, the power of gaining their hearts. He has a good cause to sustain; but he knows how to make use of all the arts by which bad ones are supported. Philip, who spies out and reads all men, is himself spied out and read by him. The designs of the great king are discovered and circumvented before they are put in action; mysterious hands search his caskets and his pockets, and mysterious eyes read his secret papers; William in Holland reads the thoughts of Philip in the Escorial; foresees, unravels, overturns all his plots; mines the earth under his feet, provokes, and flies before him, but returns again perpetually, like a phantom that he sees but cannot clutch, or clutching cannot destroy. And when at last he dies, victory remains with him dead, and defeat with his living enemy. Holland is without her head, but the Spanish monarchy is shaken to its fall, and never will recover.

In this prodigious struggle, in which the figure of the king becomes smaller and smaller until it finally disappears, that of the Prince of Orange grows and grows, until it becomes the most glorious figure of the century. On that day when, hostage with the King of France, he discovered the design of Philip to establish the Inquisition in the Low Countries, he consecrated himself to the defence of the liberties of his country, and never in his life did he hesitate for one moment in the path he had chosen. The advantages of noble birth, a royal fortune, the peaceful and splendid existence that he loved by

WILLIAM THE SILENT. (*Page* 103.)

nature and habit, he sacrificed all for his country; proscribed and reduced to poverty, he constantly rejected the offers of pardon and favor that were made to him, under a thousand forms and a thousand ways, by the enemy who hated him and feared him. Surrounded by assassins, the mark for the most atrocious calumnies, accused even of cowardice before the enemy, and of the murder of the wife whom he adored; looked upon sometimes with suspicion by the very people whom he was defending: he bore all with calmness, and in silence. He went about his chosen work, confronting infinite peril with tranquil courage. Never did he flatter or bend before the people, never was he blinded by their passion; he was their guide, their chief, their leader always; he was the mind, the conscience, and the arm of the revolution: the beacon-fire whence irradiated the heat by which his country lived. Great in audacity as in prudence, he preserved his integrity in the time of perjury and perfidy; calm in the midst of violence, he kept his hands immaculate when all the courts in Europe were stained with blood. With an army gathered up here and there, with allies weak and doubtful, harassed by the internal discords of Lutheran and Calvinist, noble and burgher, magistrates and people, with no great captains under him, he had to struggle against the municipal spirit of the provinces that scoffed at his authority and slipped from under his hand, and he triumphed in a cause that seemed above human control; he tired out the Duke of Alva, he tired out Requescens, he tired out Don John of Austria, he tired out Alexander Farnese; he brought to nought the plots of foreign princes who wished to succour his country in order to subjugate it; he conquered sympathy and aid from every part of Europe; and completing one of the most splendid revolutions in history, founded a free state in spite of an empire that was the terror of the universe.

This man, so tremendous and grand a figure before the world, was also a loving husband and father, a kind friend and affable companion, fond of gaiety and festivals, a magnificent and polished host. He was accomplished; knowing, besides the Flemish tongue, French, German, Spanish, Italian, Latin; and could discourse learnedly of most things. Although surnamed William the Silent (more for having kept so long the secret discovered at the French Court than because he was habitually taciturn) he was one of the most eloquent men of his day. He was simple in his manners, plain in his dress; loved, and was beloved by, the people.

He frequently walked in the streets of the city alone, and with his head uncovered; conversing with the workmen and the fishermen, who offered him drink in their own cups; he listened to their grievances, settled their differences, and entered their houses to re-establish peace in families, and they called him Father William. He was, indeed, the father, rather than the son of his country. The sentiments of admiration and gratitude that still live for him in the hearts of the Hollanders, have all the intimate and tender character of filial affection; his venerated name may still be heard in their mouths; his greatness, despoiled of every veil or ornament, remains entire, clear, firm, and solid, like his work.

DELFT.

After visiting the tomb, I went to see the place where the Prince of Orange was assassinated. But after having related how he lived, it is necessary to tell how he died.

In the year 1580, Philip II. had published an edict by which he promised a reward of twenty-five thousand gold crowns, and a title of nobility, to anyone who should kill the Prince of Orange. This infamous edict, which stimulated at once both cupidity and fanaticism, had caused assassins to swarm on every side about the prince, concealing themselves under false names, and hiding their arms and their purpose, while they waited their opportunity.

A young Biscayan, named Jauregny, a fervent Catholic, to whom a Dominican monk had promised the glory of martyrdom, was the first to make the attempt. He prepared himself with fasting and prayer, heard mass, took the Communion, covered himself with sacred relics, penetrated into the palace of William of Orange, and, approaching the prince under pretext of presenting a petition, fired a pistol-shot at his head. The ball passed through the jaw, but the wound was not mortal, and the prince recovered.

The assassin was struck down in the act, with blows of swords and halberds; and afterwards quartered in the public square, and his limbs were put up over one of the gates of Antwerp, where they remained until the Duke of Parma took that city, when the Jesuits gathered them together and presented them as relics to the veneration of the faithful.

A little while afterwards another conspiracy was discovered against the life of the prince. A French gentleman, an Italian, and a Walloon, who had been following him for some time with the intention of killing him, were discovered and arrested. One of them stabbed himself and died in prison, the second was strangled in France, and the third succeeded in escaping, after having confessed that all three were acting under the orders of the Duke of Parma.

In the meantime Philip's agents were going about the country instigating persons to become assassins with promises of large reward, and priests and monks were encouraging fanatics with the promise of aid and recompense in heaven. Other attempts were made. A Spaniard, discovered and arrested, was quartered at Antwerp; a rich merchant, by name Hans Jansen, was executed at Flushing. Several persons had offered their arms to Alexander Farnese, and had received money and encouragement from him. The Prince of Orange, who knew everything, nourished a vague presentiment of his approaching end, spoke of it to those in his intimacy, and refused to take any measures to preserve his own life, saying to those who advised him to do so: "It is useless. God knows the number of my years. He will dispose of me according to His will. If there be a wretch who fears not death, my life is in his hands, however I may seek to guard it."

Eight attempts to murder him were made before the successful one.

At the time when the last was consummated, in 1584, four villains, each unknown to the other—an Englishman, a Scotchman, a Frenchman, and a native of Lorraine—were at Delft, where the Prince of Orange then was, all awaiting their opportunity to assassinate him. Besides these, there had been there for some time a young man of twenty-seven years, from Franche Comté, a Catholic, but passing for a Protestant, Guyon by name, son of Peter Guyon, who had been executed at Besançon for having embraced Calvinism. This so-called Guyon, whose real name was Balthazar Gerard, gave out that he had fled from the persecution of the Catholics; he led an austere life, and assisted at all the exercises of the Protestant faith; in a short time he was regarded as a saint. Saying that he had come to Delft to obtain the honor of being admitted into the service of the Prince of Orange, he was presented to him through the recommendation of a Protestant minister; the prince had faith in him, and appointed him to accompany M. de Schonewalle, envoy from the States of Holland to France. A little while after he returned to Delft to bring to William of Orange the news of the death of the Duke of Anjou, and presented himself at the convent of Saint Agatha where the prince and his court were then sojourning. It was the second Sunday in July. William received him in his chamber, being then in bed. They were alone. Balthazar Gerard was then tempted to kill him; but he had no arms, and concealing his impatience, quietly answered the questions put to him. William gave him a small sum of money, told him to prepare to return to Paris, and ordered him to come back the following day for letters and passports. With the money given him by the prince, Gerard bought two pistols from a soldier (who afterwards killed himself when he knew the use to which they had been put), and the next day he again presented himself at the convent of Saint Agatha. The prince, accompanied by several ladies and gentlemen of his family, was coming downstairs to dinner on the ground-floor, and the Princess of Orange, his fourth wife, was leaning on his arm; she was that gentle and unfortunate Louisa de Coligny, who on the night of St. Bartholomew had seen the Admiral her father and the Sieur de Teligny her husband murdered before her eyes. Gerard advanced to meet the prince, stopped him, and asked him to sign his passport. William told him to come back later, and passed on into the hall. Not a shadow of suspicion had crossed his mind; but Louisa de Coligny, made cautious and suspicious by experience, was disturbed. That pale-faced man, wrapped in a long mantle, had made an unpleasant impression upon her; it seemed to her that his voice was agitated and his visage convulsed. During the dinner she spoke to William of her suspicions, and asked him who was this man, "who had the worst countenance that she had ever seen." The prince smiled, told her that it was Guyon, reassured her, was cheerful as usual throughout the meal, and when it was over passed quietly out to go upstairs again. Gerard was lurking under a dark archway beside the staircase, hidden by the shadow of a door. The moment the prince appeared, he came out, sprang upon him as he placed his foot upon the second step, discharged a pistol loaded with three balls into his chest, and took to flight. The prince staggered and fell into the arms of an attendant; everybody rushed. He said in a faint voice, "I am wounded. My God, have mercy on me, and on my poor people!" He was covered with blood. His sister, Catherine of Schwartzburg, said to him, "Do you recommend your soul to Jesus Christ?" He answered faintly, "Yes." It was his last word. They placed him sitting on a step of the stairs, and asked him some questions; but his senses were gone. He was carried into a room near by, and there expired.

Gerard, meanwhile, had passed through the stables, left the convent, and reached the city bastion, where he intended to jump down into the moat and swim over to the opposite shore, where a saddled horse was waiting for him.

But in his flight he dropped his hat and his second pistol. One of the prince's servants and a halberdier, seeing these traces, started in pursuit. At the very moment when he was about to take the leap from the bastion they seized him. "Infernal traitor!" they cried. He answered calmly, "I am not a traitor; I am the faithful servant of my lord." "Of what lord?" they demanded. "Of my lord and master the King of Spain," answered Gerard. Other halberdiers and pages now came up, and they dragged him into the city, striking him as they went with fists and sword-hilts. Believing from what he heard that the prince was not dead, the wretch exclaimed with gloomy tranquillity, "Accursed be the hand that missed its stroke!"

This deplorable security of soul never abandoned him for a moment. Before the tribunal, under long interrogations, in his dungeon, loaded with irons, he maintained the same unalterable calm. He bore the torture without a groan. Between the torments, while the jailors were resting, he spoke quietly and without ostentation. Whilst on the rack, lifting now and then his bloody head, he said, "Ecce Homo." He thanked his judges for the food that they permitted to be brought him, and wrote his confession with his own hand.

He was born at Vuillafaus, in Burgundy, had studied law under an advocate of Dôle, and had there for the first time manifested a desire to kill William of Orange, striking a dagger into a door, and saying, "Thus would I like to plant a poignard into the breast of the Prince of Orange!" Three years later, hearing of Philip's edict, he went to Luxembourg with the intention of committing the murder, but was stopped by a false report of the death of William after the attempt of Jauregny. A little while after, learning that the prince was still alive, he resumed his purpose, and went to Malines to ask counsel of the Jesuits, who encouraged him in his design and promised him that, if his attempt succeeded, and he lost his life, he should have the glory and the honors of a martyr. Then he went to Tournai, was presented to Alexander Farnese, received a confirmation of Philip's promise, was approved and encouraged by the confidants of the Prince of Parma, and the ministers of God; fortified himself with readings of the Bible, and with fasting and prayer, and so, seized with a divine exaltation, dreaming of Paradise and the angels, he departed for Delft, and there fulfilled " his duty as a good Catholic and a faithful subject."

He repeated his confession more than once before his judges ; pronounced not one word of regret or repentance, boasted of his deed; called himself a new David who had slain a new Goliath; and declared that if he had not already killed the Prince of Orange, he should be ready to do it; his courage, his calmness, his profound conviction of having accomplished a holy mission and a glorious death, amazed his judges, who believed him to be possessed of an evil spirit.; an examination was made; he himself was interrogated, but he always insisted that he had never had any relations other than with God.

The sentence was read to him on the 14th of July. " It was a crime," says an illustrious historian, " against the memory of the great man whom it purposed to avenge; a sentence to strike into insensibility anyone without the superhuman fortitude of the prisoner."

He was condemned to have his right hand encased in a case of red-hot iron; his arms, legs, and thighs torn with hot pincers; his chest cut open, his heart torn out and thrown in his face; the head severed from the body and stuck on a pike; the body quartered, and each part placed over a gate of the city.

Listening to the reading of this horrid sentence, the wretched man never changed color, or gave any sign of terror, or grief, or astonishment. He only opened his doublet, laid bare his chest, and in a firm voice, fixing his eyes steadily on the face of his judges, repeated the words: " Ecce Homo ! "

What was this man? Only a fanatic, as many believed, or a monster of wickedness, or both together, with the addition of an insatiable ambition?

The sentence was executed on the following day. The

preparations were made under the eyes of the prisoner, who looked on with indifference. The executioner's assistant began by crushing the pistol, instrument of the crime, with blows of a hammer. At the first blow, the head of the hammer flew off and wounded another assistant in the ear; the people laughed, and Gerard laughed also. When he appeared on the scaffold, his body was horrible to see. Whilst his hand crackled and smoked in the burning tube, he stood mute; nor did he utter a cry while the red-hot pincers tore his flesh; when the last act came, he dropped his head, murmured some incomprehensible words, and expired.

The news of the death of the Prince of Orange had spread consternation throughout the country. His body was exposed for one month on a bier, around which the people flocked, kneeling and in tears. His funeral was worthy of a king; there came the States General of the United Provinces, the Council of State, the States of Holland, the magistrates, the ministers of religion, the princes of the house of Nassau. Twelve gentlemen carried the body; four great nobles held the cords of the pall; the prince's horse followed, splendidly caparisoned, and led by a groom; and there was seen, in the middle of the cortége of nobles, a youth of eighteen years, whose hands were to receive the glorious heritage of the dead, who was destined to humiliate the Spanish armies, to constrain Spain to plead for truce and recognise the independence of the United Provinces. That youth was Maurice of Orange, the son of William, under whom a short time after his father's death, the States of Holland conferred the dignity of Statholder, and confided to him the supreme command of the forces by land and sea.

Whilst Holland wept her loss, in all the cities subject to the King of Spain the Catholic clergy glorified the murderer and his deed; the Jesuits exalted him as a martyr; the university of Louvain published his apology; the canons of Bois-le-Duc chanted a *Te Deum*. Some years afterwards, the family of Gerard received from the King of Spain a title of nobility, and the confiscated lands of the Prince of Orange in Burgundy.

The house where the Prince of Orange was assassinated still exists; it is a gloomy-looking edifice, with arched windows and a narrow door, forming part of the cloister of the ancient church of St. Agatha, and it still bears the name of Prinsenshof, although it now serves as a cavalry barrack. I asked leave of entrance from the soldier on guard; a corporal, who knew a little French, accompanied me; we crossed a court full of soldiers, and reached the memorable spot. I saw the staircase, the dark corner where Gerard crouched, the door of the room where William dined for the last time, and the traces of the balls on the wall, isolated in a white space, with an inscription in Dutch setting forth that here the father of his country died.

The corporal pointed out the way by which the murderer had fled. Whilst I looked about with that thoughtful curiosity that one feels under such circumstances, soldiers went up and down; they stopped to look at me, and went off whistling and singing; loud laughter rang from the courtyard; and all that youthful life and gaiety contrasted touchingly with the sad and solemn memories of the place, like the frolic of children in a room where some dear parent died.

Opposite the Prinsenshof is the oldest church in Delft, which contains the tomb of that famous Admiral Tromp, the veteran of the Dutch navy, who saw thirty-two sea-fights, scattered the English fleet under Blake at the battle of the Dunes, in 1652, and returned into port with a broom fastened to his mainmast, to indicate that he had swept the English from the seas. There is the tomb of Peter Hein, who, from a simple fisherman, rose to be Grand Admiral, and made that memorable haul of Spanish ships that carried in their sides more than eleven millions of florins. There is the tomb of Leuwenhoek, the father of the science of the "infinitely little," he who, as Parini says, "saw with his investigating glass the embryo man floating in the genital sea."

The church has a tall steeple, surmounted by four small conical towers, which leans like the tower of Pisa, in consequence of the sinking of the ground. In a cell in this tower Gerard was confined on the night following the assassination.

At Rotterdam they had given me a letter for a citizen of Delft, requesting him to show me his house. "He desires," said the letter, "to penetrate the mysteries of an old Dutch house: lift for a moment, for his benefit, the curtain of the sanctuary." I had no difficulty in finding the house, and when I saw it, I exclaimed: "This is what I want."

It was a small house at the end of a street opening on

the fields, of one storey only, red, with a pointed façade, planted on the edge of the canal as if looking at itself in the water, with a fine spreading linden-tree before it, and a drawbridge directly in front. There were the white curtains, the green door, the flowers, the little mirrors; it was a small model of a Dutch house.

The street was deserted; before knocking at the door I stood a moment to look and muse. That house gave me a better idea of Holland than I could get from any book. It was at once the cause and the effect of the family affection, the modest desires, the independent character of the Dutch people. In my own country the real home does not exist; there is nothing but an apartment, a portion of a great barrack, in which one lives concealed, but not alone, hearing a thousand noises of strange people, who disturb our grief with echoes of their joy, or our joy with rumours of their grief. The true house and home is in Holland, the personal house, distinct from others, modest, discreet, and, precisely because it is distinct from others, inimical to mystery and intrigue; cheerful when the family that inhabits it is cheerful, and sad when they are sad. In these houses, with the canals and drawbridges before them, every modest citizen feels a little of the solitary dignity of the castellan, or the commander of a fortress, or a ship; and sees, indeed, from his windows, as from the deck of a vessel at anchor, a uniform and boundless plain, which inspires him with the same sentiments and thoughts, grave and free, as are inspired by the sea. The trees surrounding his habitation, almost like a garment of verdure, allow only a broken and discreet light to penetrate it; the bark laden with merchandise floats before his door; he hears no sound of horses' feet, nor crack of whip, nor songs, nor shouts; around him all the movements of life are slow and silent; everything breathes peace and gentleness; and the neighbouring steeple announces the hour with a flood of harmony sweet and constant as his affections and his labor.

I knocked; the door was opened by the master of the house in person, who, having read my letter, gave me a scrutinising glance, and invited me to enter. Dutchmen, as a rule, are diffident. With us, the first comer who brings a letter of introduction is received with open arms, as if he were our most intimate friend; and very often we do nothing for him. The Hollanders, on the contrary, receive you coldly, so much so as to be sometimes rather mortifying; but then they offer you all sorts of service, with the best will in the world, and without the least appearance of laying you under an obligation.

The inside of the house corresponded perfectly with the outside; it seemed like the interior of a ship. A winding staircase of wood that shone like ebony led to the upper rooms. Mats and carpets covered the stairs and landing-places, and lay before all the doors. The rooms were as small as cells; the furniture exquisitely clean; all the knobs and bolts and ornaments of metal shone as if they had just been made; and on every side there were quantities of china jars, vases, and cups; lamps, mirrors, little pictures, brackets, toys, and objects of every use and form, attesting the thousand small needs created by a sedentary life, the provident activity, the

INTERIOR OF A HOUSE IN HOLLAND. (*Page* 116.)

constant care, the love of small things, the taste for order and the economy of space; the residence, in short, of a quiet, home-loving woman.

The goddess of this temple, who did not or would not speak French, was hidden somewhere, in some *penetralia* which I could not guess at.

We went down to see the kitchen; it was splendid. When I returned to Italy and gave a description of it to my mother and the servant, who piqued herself on her neatness, they were annihilated. The walls were as white as untouched snow; the saucepans reflected objects like mirrors; the mantelpiece was ornamented by a species of muslin curtain, like the canopy of a bed, without a trace of smoke; the fire-place beneath was covered with china tiles that looked as bright as if no fire had ever been lighted there; the shovel, tongs, and poker, and the chains and hooks, seemed made of polished steel. A lady in a ball-dress might have gone into every hole and corner of that kitchen and come forth without a smirch upon her whiteness.

The maid-servant, meanwhile, was cleaning up, and her master commented thus: "To have an idea of what cleanliness is with us, you should watch one of these women for an hour. Here a house is soaped, and sponged, and rubbed, like a person. It is not cleaning, it is making a toilette. She blows in the cracks between the bricks, pokes in the corners with finger and pin, makes a minute supervision enough to fatigue the eye as well as the arm. It is truly a national passion. These girls, who are in general phlegmatic enough, become quite frantic on cleaning days. We are not masters in our own houses then. They invade the chambers, and turn everything upside down; they are real cleaning *Bacchantes;* they excite themselves in washing and sweeping."

I asked him whence this mania for which Holland is remarkable was supposed to come. He gave me the same reasons that are given by others: the atmosphere of the country, which injures wood and metal; the dampness, the smallness of the houses, and the multiplicity of small objects favoring dust; the superabundance of water; a certain need of the eye, that eventually finds beauty in simple cleanliness; and finally, that emulation which pushes things to extremes. "But this is not," he added, "the cleanest part of Holland: the excess, the delirium of cleanliness is to be found in the northern provinces."

We went out for a turn through the city. It was not yet noon; and the servant-maids were out on all sides as at Rotterdam. It is a singular thing that all over the country, from Rotterdam to Gröningen, and from Harlem to Nimeguen, they are all dressed exactly alike—in a lilac print gown, with a white cap and white wooden shoes. I thought at first that they formed a sort of national corporation and wore a uniform. They are generally very young, middle-aged women not being able to endure the fatigues that they go through, blonde and plump, with the posterior curves (to quote Diderot) enormous, and an appearance of perfect health shown in their clear white and red complexions.

All at once I remembered a certain entry made in my note-book before leaving Italy, and I asked my companion: "Are servants in Holland the eternal torments of their mistresses?"

Here comes in a parenthesis. It is acknowledged that ladies not too highly placed to have to do directly with their female servants generally talk, in their visits to each other, of nothing but these servants. It is always the same complaint of insupportable defects, of insolence endured, of profiting on their purchases, of shameless pretensions, and of other similar calamities, which all end with the same refrain: that honest and faithful servants, such as once gained the affection of the family and grew old in their service, are no more to be found; that one must change continually, and that there is no way of remedying the evil.

Is this true, or is it not true? Is it a consequence of the liberty and equality of classes, rendering service harder and servants more exacting? Is it an effect of the relaxation of manners and public discipline, felt also in the kitchen? However it may be, it is a fact that in my own house I heard the same ever-recurring complaint, until one day, when I was about to leave for Madrid, I said to my mother: "If anything in Madrid can console me in my absence from my family, it will be that I never shall hear this question discussed."

On my arrival at Madrid, the very first thing my landlady said to me was that she had been obliged to change her servants three times in one month, that it was really a desperate state of things, and that she did not know which way to turn, and every day there was the same lamentation.

At home again I related this anecdote, and my mother, laughing, said that it was probably an annoyance which existed in all countries. "No," I answered, "in the north it cannot be so." I went to Paris, and asked the first acquaintance that I met, whether there, as in Italy and Spain, ladies' lives were made miserable by their servants. "*Ah! mon cher Monsieur!*" she replied, with clasped hands and upturned eyes; "do not speak of it!" and then followed a long and lamentable story. Let us see in London, I thought. Entering into conversation with an English lady, and asking the same question, she covers her eyes with her hands, and responds with emphasis: "They are *flagellum Dei!*"

Some hope still remained to me in Holland, and I questioned my cicerone at Delft; and awaited with anxiety his reply. "Sir," he answered, after a moment's reflection, "we have in Holland a proverb which pronounces that servants are a cross sent from God." My last hope was annihilated. "First of all," he continued, "there is the trouble that if your house is of any size you must keep two women-servants, one to cook and one to clean, it being impossible, with the mania which possesses them for washing the very air, that one can serve for both. Then they are all mad for liberty; they choose to stay out until ten o'clock in the evening; to have one day in the seven completely free. Then their betrothed lover must be tolerated as a visitor; and they must be allowed to dance in the streets, and to go and raise the very devil at the Kermesse. More, when you dismiss them, you must wait until they find it convenient to go, and often that is not for months. Their wages amount to ninety or one hundred florins a year; and besides this, so much percentage on all the house expenditure; presents, rigorously exacted, from all invited guests; extra presents of money and clothes; and always and above all, patience, patience, and again patience."

Passing through a quiet side-street, I saw two ladies, one after the other, stop and read a placard appended to a door, make a gesture of sorrow, and pass on. My companion explained, in answer to my question, a singular custom of the country. Upon that bit of paper was written that such or such a sick person was worse. When any one of a family is ill, a bulletin is affixed every morning to the door, so that inquiring friends may not have to knock and enter. The same sort of announcement is made on other occasions. In some towns the birth of a boy baby is made known by hanging to the door a pink silk ball covered with lace, which is called in Dutch "a proof of birth." If the baby is a girl, there is a small bit of paper attached above it; if twins, the lace is double; and for several days after the birth there is a written paper setting forth that the child and mother are doing well, that they have passed a good night, or the contrary, as the case may be. At one time the announcement of birth over a door kept off the family creditors for nine days; but I think this custom is fallen into disuse, although it must have been conducive to an increase of population.

In that short walk about Delft, I met again certain funereal figures which I had seen in Rotterdam, without being able to tell whether they were priests, or magistrates, or undertakers, for they had a look of all three. They wore three-cornered hats, with a long black weeper, a black swallow-tailed coat, black small-clothes, and stockings, black cloaks, pumps with ribbons, white cravats and gloves, and a black-edged paper always in their hands. My companion informed me that they were called *aanspreckers*, and that their office was to carry the announcement of death to parents and friends, and to proclaim it in the streets. Their dress is modified in different cities, or according to whether they be Protestant or Catholic. In some places they wear an enormous hat *à la Don Basilio*. They are in general very carefully dressed and are got up with a certain elegance which contrasts irreverently with their character of announcers of death, or, as some traveller calls them, living mortuary letters.

We saw one standing in front of a house, and my companion called my attention to the fact that the shutters were half closed, which was a sign that someone was dead in the family. I asked who. "I do not know," he answered, "but judging by the shutters it cannot be a very near relative."

This argument puzzling me somewhat, he explained that in Holland when anyone died in a family, they closed one, or two, or three of the folding shutters, according to the degree of relationship of the deceased. Each fold of the shutter denoted a degree. For a father or mother, they closed all save one; for a cousin, one only; for a brother, two; and so on. This custom is apparently an ancient one, still enduring because in this country changes are slow and difficult, only occurring when they are unavoidable.*

I should have liked to see at Delft the house where the beer-shop of the painter Steen once existed, but my host assured me that there was no remembrance of it remaining. Apropos of painters, however, he gave me the agreeable intelligence that I was then in that part of Holland which is comprised between Delft, the Hague, the sea, the town of Alkmar, the gulf of Amsterdam, and the ancient lake of Harlem, which may be called properly the country of Dutch painting, both because the great artists were born there, and because, being singularly picturesque, they loved it and studied it much. I was therefore in the bosom of Holland, and leaving Delft should enter her very heart.

Before my departure I took a hasty glance at the military arsenal, occupying a large building which served first as a storehouse to the East India Company, and communicates with an artillery-barrack and a large powder-magazine placed outside the city. There is also at Delft the great Polytechnic School of Engineering, the true military school of Holland, whence issue the officers for the army of defence against the sea, and it is these youthful warriors of the dykes and cataracts, about three hundred, who give life to the quiet city of Grotius. Whilst I was going on board the vessel that was to take me to the Hague, my Dutchman was describing to me the last

---

* A custom analogous to this existed in Philadelphia twenty-five years ago, and perhaps exists still.—*Trans.*

festival celebrated by the students of Delft; one of those festivals peculiar to Holland, a kind of historical masquerade, like a reflection of past grandeur, which serves to maintain alive in the minds of people the traditions of illustrious personages and events of others times. One great cavalcade represented the entrance into Arnhem in 1492 of Charles d'Egmont, Duke of Gueldres and Count of Zutfen; of that family of Egmont which gave in the noble and unfortunate Count Lamoral the first great victim for the liberty of Holland to the Duke of Alva's axe. Two hundred students on horseback, in armour, with gilded and emblazoned coats of arms, with tall plumes and long swords, formed the cortége of the Duke of Gueldres. Then came halberdiers, archers, and lansquenechts, dressed in all the showy splendor of the fifteenth century; the bands played, the city glowed with lights, and an immense crowd from all parts of Holland thronged the streets and looked on at that splendid vision of a past age.

THE HAGUE.

THE vessel lay near a bridge, in a little basin formed by the canal that goes from Delft to the Hague, and shaded by trees like a garden lakelet.

The boats which carry passengers from one city to another are called *trekschuyten*. The *treckshuyt* is the traditional bark, emblematic of Holland, as the gondola is of Venice. Esquiroz calls it the genius of old Holland floating on the water. And, in fact, whoever has not travelled in a *treckshuyt* does not know the most original and most poetic side of Dutch life.

It is a large boat almost entirely occupied by a sort of house, in the form of a diligence, divided into two compartments: that at the prow for second-class passengers, and that at the poop for the first. Upon the prow is planted an iron bar with a ring through which is passed a long cord, which is fastened at one end near the helm, and at the other is attached to a horse ridden by one of the boatmen. The windows of this little house have their white curtains; the walls and doors are painted; in the first-class compartment there are cushioned seats, a table with a few books, a closet, a looking-glass; everything shining with polish. As I put down my valise I dropped some cigar-ash under the table; when I came in again a moment after, it was gone.

I was alone, and had not long to wait; the helmsman gave a sign, the horseman mounted, and the *treckschuyt* moved quietly through the water.

It was about one o'clock in the day and the sun was shining brilliantly, but the boat was in the shade. The canal was bordered by two rows of lindens, elms, and willows, and high hedges that hid the country. We seemed to be sailing through a wood. At every turn we saw a deep distance, green, and closed in, and a windmill on the bank. The water was covered with a carpet of marine plants, in some places studded with white star-flowers, lilies, and the marsh-lentil. The high verdant wall that bordered the canal was open here and there, and we could see as through a window the distant horizon, hidden again in an instant.

At intervals we came to a bridge. It was fine to see the rapidity with which the manœuvre of passing the bridge was performed, and to watch two *treckschuyten* meet and pass, without a word or smile being exchanged between the two conductors, as if gravity and silence were obligatory. All along the water-way we heard no sound save the rustle of the sails of windmills.

We met large boats loaded with vegetables, with peat, with stones, with casks, towed by a man with a long rope, sometimes assisted by a large dog. Some were towed by a man, a woman, and a child, one behind the other, with the cord attached to a sort of leathern or linen bellyband—all three bending forward at such an angle that it seemed a miracle how they kept their feet at all. Other large boats were towed by one old woman alone. On some there was a woman with a child at her breast, at the elm; other children about her, a cat seated on a sack, a dog, a hen, flower-pots, and a bird-cage. On others the woman was rocking a cradle with her foot while her fingers were knitting a stocking, or cooking the dinner; and in others, the whole family was assembled eating and chattering, while one steered. No words can describe the air of peace and tranquillity that seemed to surround these people, in their aquatic homes, with their animals, become, as one may say, amphibious; the placidity of that floating existence, the apparent security and freedom of those wandering families. Thousands of people in Holland have no other home than their boats. A man takes a wife, between them they buy a boat, and installing themselves on board, live by carrying goods to and from the markets. The children are born and grow up on the water; the boat carries all their small belongings, their domestic affections, their past, their present, and their future. They labor and save, and after many years they buy a larger boat, selling the old one to a family poorer than themselves, or handing it over to the eldest son who in his turn instals his wife taken from another boat, and seen for the first time in a chance meeting on the canal. And so, from boat to boat, from canal to canal, life flows on mild and tranquil as the wandering house that shelters it or the silent water that accompanies it.

For a time there was nothing to be seen on the banks but some small peasant-houses; then we began to see villas, summer-houses, and cottages half hidden among the trees; and in a shady nook some blonde lady, seated, dressed in white, and with a book in her hand; or some stout gentleman enveloped in a cloud of smoke, bearing the satisfied air of a wealthy merchant. All these villas are painted rose-color or blue, and have varnished roofs, terraces supported by columns, little gardens in front and around them, with tiny alleys and walks; miniature gardens, clean, smooth, and dainty. Some of the houses are on the edge of the canal with their feet in the water, which reflects the flowers and vases and shining toys in the windows. Almost all have an inscription over the door—a sort of aphorism of domestic felicity, the formula of its master's philosophy—such as: "Peace is money," "Repose and pleasure," "Friendship and society," "My desires are satisfied," "Without annoyance," "Tranquil and content," "Here are enjoyed the pleasures of horticulture," &c.

Here and there a handsome black and white cow lay couched on the grass, her muzzle projected over the water, turning her head placidly as the boat glided by. We met flocks of ducks that parted to let us go by. At intervals on our right and left opened small canals whose high green hedges sent out branches that met overhead, forming an arch of verdure under which we could see peasants' boats vanishing in the distance. Here and there, in the midst of the greenery, started forth a group of houses—a small many-colored village—with mirrors and tulips in the windows; without a living soul; but the profound silence at times broken by a lively air from the bells of some unseen steeple. It was a pastoral paradise, an idyllic landscape, full of freshness and mystery; a Chinese Arcadia, with small surprises, innocent artifices and prettinesses, affecting one like the low sound of voices of invisible people, murmuring " We are content."

At a certain point the canal branched off, one part leading to Leyden, while the other continued on to the Hague. Beyond this point the *treckschuyt* began to make short halts, now at a house, now at a garden-gate, to receive packages, letters, and messages for the Hague.

An old gentleman came aboard from one of the villas. He seated himself by me; and we fell into conversation in French. He had been in Italy, knew a few words of Italian, had read the " Promessi Sposi"; he asked me for some particulars of the death of Allessandro Manzoni. In ten minutes I adored him. From him I had much information about the *treckschuyten*. To understand all the poesy of the national boat, one should make a long voyage in company with the native people. Then everyone instals himself as if in his own house, the women work, the men sit and smoke on the top; people become intimate and form one family. Night falls; and the *treckschuyt* glides like a shadow through the sleeping villages, skimming the canal in the silvery moonlight, hiding herself in the dark shadows, emerging into the open country, grazing solitary houses in which shines the peasant's lamp, and meeting fishermen's barks which fleet by like phantoms. In that profound peace, in that slow and equal motion, the voyagers fall asleep side by side, one after the other, and behind the boat follow the confused murmur of the water and the sound of deep-drawn breathings.

More and more numerous as we advanced grew the gardens and the villas. My companion pointed out a distant steeple and named the village of Ryswijk, where, in 1697, the famous treaty of peace was signed between England, France, Spain, Germany, and Holland. The castle of the Prince of Orange where the signers met is no longer in existence, and an obelisk has been erected on its site. Suddenly the *treckschuyt* came out from among the trees, and I saw a vast plain, a great wood, and a city crowned with towers and windmills. It was the Hague.

The boatmen asked and received my passage-money in a leathern bag. The horseman touched up his steed. In a few minutes we arrived, and I soon found myself established in a brightly-shining chamber in the Hotel Turenne. Who knows? perhaps the very room where the great marshal slept when he was a lad and in the service of Holland.

The Hague—in Dutch, s'Gravenhage, or s'Hage—the political capital, the Washington of Holland, Amsterdam being the New York—is a city half Dutch and half French, with broad streets and no canals; vast squares full of trees, elegant houses, splendid hotels, and a population mostly made up of the rich, nobles, officials, artists, and *literati,* the populace being of a more refined order than that of the other Dutch cities.

In my first turn about the town what struck me most were the new quarters, where dwells the flower of the wealthy aristocracy. In no other city, not even in the Faubourg St. Germain at Paris, did I feel myself such a very poor devil, as in those streets. They are wide and straight, flanked by palaces of elegant form and delicate color, with large shutterless windows, through which can be seen the rich carpets and sumptuous furniture of the first floors. Every door is closed; and there is not a shop, nor a placard, nor a stain, nor a straw to be seen if you were to look for it with a hundred eyes. The silence was profound when I passed by. Only now and then I encountered some aristocratic equipage rolling almost noiselessly over the brick pavement, or the stiffest of lackeys stood before a door, or the blonde head of a lady was visible behind a curtain. Passing close to the windows and beholding my shabby travelling dress ruthlessly reflected in the plate-glass, I experienced a certain humiliation at not having been born at least a *cavaliere,* and imagined I heard low voices whispering disdainfully: "Who is that low person?"

Of the older portion of the city, the most considerabl part is the Binnenhof, a group of old buildings of different styles of architecture, which looks on two sides upon vast squares, and on the third over a great marsh. In the midst of this group of palaces, towers, and monumental doors, of a mediæval and sinister aspect, there is a spacious court, which is entered by three bridges and three gates. In one of these buildings resided the Stadtholders, and it is now the seat of the Second Chamber of the States General; opposite is the First Chamber, with the ministries and various other offices of public administration. The Minister of the Interior has his office in a little low black tower of the most lugubrious aspect, that hangs directly over the waters of the marsh.

The Binnenhof, the square to the west, called the Bintenhof, and another square beyond the marsh, called the Plaats, into which you enter by an old gate that once formed part of a prison, were the theatres of the most sanguinary events in the history of Holland.

In the Binnenhof was decapitated the venerated Van Olden Barneveldt, the second founder of the republic, the most illustrious victim of that ever-recurring struggle between the burgher aristocracy and the Statholderate, between the republican and the monarchical principle, which worked so miserably in Holland. The scaffold was erected in front of the edifice where the States General sat. Opposite is the tower from which it is said that Maurice of Orange, himself unseen, beheld the last moments of his enemy.

In the prison between the two squares Cornelis de Witt, unjustly accused of having plotted against the life of the Prince of Orange, was tortured. In the Plaats, Cornelis and the grand pensionary John de Witt were dragged by the furious populace, and there, all bloody and torn, were spat upon, beaten, and at last killed with pike and pistol; after which their corpses were insulted and mutilated. In the same Plaats, Adelaide de Poelgest, mistress of Albert,

Count of Holland, was stabbed to death on the 22nd of September 1392; and they still show the stone where she fell and breathed her last.

These dismal memories, these low and massive doors, these disorderly groups of gloomy buildings, which at night, when the moon shines on the waters of the stagnant pool, present the aspect of an enormous and inaccessible citadel, standing in the midst of the gay and pleasant city, awake a sentiment of solemnity and sadness.

In the evening the court is lighted by only a few dim lamps; the few passengers hasten their steps as if in fear; there are no lighted windows, no sounds of life and movement; you enter with a vague feeling of anxiety, and come out with a sense of relief.

Excepting these, the Hague has no considerable monuments either modern or antique. There are a few mediocre statues of different Princes of Orange; a vast and bare cathedral, and a modest royal palace. On many of the public buildings is sculptured the image of a stork, which is the heraldic crest of the city. Several of these birds walk about at liberty in the fish-market, maintained at the expense of the municipality, like the bears of Berne and the eagles of Geneva.

The finest ornament of the Hague is its forest; a true wonder of Holland, and one of the most magnificent promenades in the world. It is a wood of alder-trees, oaks, and the largest beeches that are to be found in Europe, on the eastern side of the city, a few paces from the last fringe of houses, and measuring about one French league in circuit; a truly delightful oasis in the midst of the melancholy Dutch plains. As you enter it, little Swiss châlets and kiosks, scattered here and there among the first trees, seem to have strayed and lost themselves in an endless and solitary forest. The trees are as thickly set as a cane-brake, and the alleys vanish in dark perspective.

There are lakes and canals almost hidden under the verdure of their banks; rustic bridges, deserted paths, dim recesses, darkness cool and deep, in which one breathes the air of virgin nature, and feels oneself far from the noises of the world.

This wood, like that of Harlem, is said to be the remains of an immense forest that covered, in ancient times, almost all the coast, and is respected by the Dutch people as a monument of their national history. Indeed, in the history of Holland may be found numerous references to it, proving that there has always been a jealous care for its preservation. Even the Spanish generals respected the national feeling, and preserved the sacred wood from the soldiery. On more than one occasion of grave financial distress, when the government showed a disposition to decree its destruction in order to sell the timber, the citizens saved it by voluntary subsidies. A thousand memories are bound up in this delicious grove; recollections of frightful hurricanes, of princely loves; celebrated festivals, and romantic adventures. Some of the trees bear the names of kings or emperors, others of the German Electors; a beech has the fame of having been planted by the Grand Pensionary and poet, Jacob Katz; other three, by the Countess of Holland, Jacqueline of Bavaria; and the spot where she used to repose is still pointed out. Even M. de Voltaire 'has left his record in the legend of some gallant adventure with the daughter of a barber.

In the very heart of the wood, where the smaller vegetation seems seized with a sort of fury of conquest, climbing the trees, weaving bowers overhead, and stretching its tendrils over the water, as if it would draw a verdant veil over the abode of some sylvan divinity, is hidden a royal *palazzetto* called the " Forest House," built in 1647 by the Princess Amelia de Solens, in honor of her husband the Stadtholder Frederick Henry.

When I went to visit this palace, whilst seeking for the entrance gate, I saw a lady of a noble and benevolent presence come out and get into her carriage, whom I took for an English traveller, sight-seeing like myself. I raised my hat as the carriage passed, and received a bow in return. A moment after I learned from the housekeeper who showed the place that my English traveller was no other than Her Majesty the Queen of Holland.

In the Forest House there is, among other notable things, an octagon hall, covered from floor to ceiling with pictures by the most celebrated artists of the Rubens school, among them an enormous allegorical work by Jordoens, representing the apotheosis of Frederick Henry. There is a room full of precious presents from the Emperor of Japan, the Viceroy of Egypt, and the East India Company ; and an elegant little room decorated in *chiaroscuro* in admirable imitation of bas-reliefs, by Jacob de Witt, a painter who acquired renown in the beginning of the last century. The other rooms are small, pretty but without pretension, and full of treasures that do not make much show, as befits the great and modest house of Orange.

It seemed to me singular to allow the entrance of strangers into the palace so immediately upon the exit of the queen; but it astonished me no longer when I became acquainted with other customs and popular traits, the characters, in short, of the royal family of Holland.

The king is considered rather as stadtholder than king. There is in him, as was said of the Duke d'Aosta* by some Spanish republican, "the least quantity of king possible." The sentiment which the Dutch people nourish towards the royal family is not so much devotion towards the monarch as affection for that house of Orange which participated in all its triumphs, as in all its misfortunes, and lived, it may be said, in the life of the nation for the space of three centuries. The nation, at bottom, is republican, and its monarchy is a sort of crowned presidency, without royal state. The king makes speeches at banquets and public festivals as our ministers do; and he enjoys the fame of an orator, because he speaks extempore, with a powerful voice and a certain soldierly eloquence that excites immense enthusiasm among the people. The hereditary prince, William of Orange, studied at the University of Leyden, passed a public examination, and took the laureate of advocate. Prince Alexander, the second son, is now a student in the same university, and a member of a students' club, where

---

* The second son of Victor Emmanuel, who filled the Spanish throne for a few months.

he invites his professors and fellow-students to dinner. At the Hague, Prince William enters the cafés, talks with his neighbors, and goes about with his young men friends. In the forest the queen often sits down on the same bench with some poor woman. And it cannot be said that these things are done to gain popularity, for the family of Orange can neither gain nor lose it, there not being among the people, who are by nature and tradition republicans, a grain of the spirit of faction. On the contrary, this people, who love and venerate their king, and on holidays insist that everybody shall wear an orange cockade in homage to his family name, in general never trouble themselves about him or his doings. At the Hague I had some difficulty in getting information as to the rank the Prince of Orange holds in the army; nobody seemed to know or care.

The seat of the court is at the Hague; but the king passes a great part of the summer at his castle in Gueldres, and goes once every year to Amsterdam. The people say that there is a statute which obliges the king to pass ten days in every year at Amsterdam, and for those ten days the municipality is obliged to pay his expenses; but when the clocks strike the hour of noon on the eleventh day, his majesty lights a match for his cigar, and this is at his own charge.

Returning from the royal villa to the city, the day being Sunday, I found the forest all animation; music, carriages, a crowd of ladies and children, and the cafés open everywhere. Then for the first time I had an opportunity for observing the fair sex in Holland.

Beauty is a rare flower here as everywhere; but in one turn about the wood of the Hague, I saw more pretty women than I had seen in all the picture galleries in Holland. There is not among these ladies either the sculpturesque beauty of the Roman, nor the brilliant complexion of the Englishwoman, nor the vivacity of expression of the Andalusian; but there is a fineness of feature, an innocent, tranquil grace and prettiness, which is very pleasing. They are rather tall than short, and plump; their features are irregular, their skin smooth and of a clear red and white; their cheek-bones rather prominent; clear blue eyes, sometimes so light in color as to appear glassy, and without expression. It is said that they have bad teeth, but of that I cannot speak, for they smile seldom. They walk less lightly than the French, and less stiffly than the English; wear dresses from Paris, better chosen than at Amsterdam; and display with pardonable vanity their wealth of blonde hair.

It looked odd to see great girls, who with us would have the dress and airs of women, still in short dresses and regarded as children. But here a young girl is seldom married before twenty years of age. In Holland the natives of more southern lands who marry at fifteen, are regarded as most surprising creatures. Here girls of that age are going to school, with their hair flowing or braided down their backs, and nobody dreams of looking at them.

Here I may remark that that equivocal society known in Paris under the name of the *demi-monde* does not, to all appearance, have any existence here. "Take care," said certain Dutch free-thinkers to me, "this is a Protestant country, and there is a great deal of hypocrisy." It may be so, but that cannot be a very marked feature of society which can be so easily hidden. There is not a shadow of it in public, nor an idea of it in their literature; the language itself is rebellious against the translation of the infinite forms of expression which belong to that society in the countries where it exists. And again, parents do not shut their eyes to the conduct of their sons, even after they are come to man's estate; family discipline makes no exceptions even for the bearded ones; and this discipline is aided and abetted by a cold temperament, the habit of economy, and respect for public opinion.

To presume to speak authoritatively of the character and life of the women of Holland, after having passed a few months in their country, would be not only ridiculous, but impertinent; I shall therefore content myself with quoting from books and the opinions of friends.

Many writers have spoken discourteously of the Dutch women. One calls them childish puppets; another apathetic housewives; an anonymous writer of the last century pushes impertinence so far as to say that, as men in Holland generally prefer to choose their mistresses among the servant-maids, so the women (that is the ladies) do not look higher in their aspirations. But this is probably the judgment of some disappointed suitor. "Daniel Stern," who, as a woman, has peculiar authority in the matter, says that they are proud, loyal, active, and chaste. Someone emits a doubt as to the pretended placidity of their affections. "They are still waters," says

Esquiroz, "and we know what is said of still waters." "They are frozen volcanoes," says Heine, "and when they thaw——" But of all that has been written, the words of Saint Evremont seem to me the most noticeable: " that the Dutch women are not sufficiently vivacious to trouble any man's repose; that there are some among them who are pleasing; yes, but either their wisdom or their coldness stands them instead of virtue."

One day in a company of young men, a certain rather ridiculous personage being under discussion, I asked in the sacramental phrase, " Does he disturb the repose of families?" " *Che!*" was the reply, "to disturb the repose of families in Holland would be to undertake one of the twelve labors of Hercules." "The Dutch woman," said another, "does not marry a husband, she espouses matrimony."

It may be thought that I wish to have it understood that I know the Dutch language. I hasten to say that I do not know it, and to excuse my ignorance. A people like the Dutch, grave and taciturn, richer in hidden qualities than in those that shine on the surface, who live more within than without, who act more than they speak, and are worth more than they spend, can be studied without knowing their language. Also, in Holland, French is almost universally known. In the great cities there is no person of culture who does not speak French fluently; there is not a shopkeeper who cannot express himself more or less easily in that tongue; there is scarcely a lad, even among the lower orders of the people, who does not know ten or twenty words of it, enough to help a stranger out of a difficulty. This diffusion of a language so different from their own, is the more to be admired when we know that it is not the only foreign tongue that is spoken in Holland. English and German are almost equally well known. The study of all three of these languages is obligatory in the middle-class schools. The Dutch have a peculiar facility for languages, and an extraordinary frankness in conversation.

We Italians, before attempting to speak a foreign language, must know enough of it not to make gross mistakes we blush when they escape us; we remain silent rather than converse unless we are sure of being complimented; and so we prolong for ever the period of our philological noviciate. In Holland there are quantities of people who speak French with a capital of a hundred words or so, and twenty phrases; but they talk and keep up a conversation without showing the least anxiety as to what you may think of their mistakes and their audacity. Porters, servants, lads, questioned as to their knowledge of French, answer with perfect security, "*Oui*," or "*Un peu*," and have a hundred ways of making themselves understood, the first to laugh at their own linguistic contortions, and rounding out every sentence with a "*S'il vous plait*," or a "*Pardon, Monsieur*," often so drolly out of place that it is impossible not to laugh.

As for the Dutch language, for those who do not know German it is impenetrable; and even knowing German, you may understand a little in reading it, but to hear it spoken it is utterly dark. If I might describe its effect upon the ear of a foreigner, it sounds like German spoken by a man with a hair in his throat, which is due to the frequency of a guttural aspirate, something like the Spanish *jota*. The Dutch themselves do not think their language harmonious, and will often ask a foreigner what he thinks of it, with an air expecting an unfavorable reply. And yet a book was once written to demonstrate that Adam and Eve spoke Dutch in the terrestrial paradise. But although they are so accomplished in other tongues, the Hollanders hold fast to their own, and are very indignant when a stranger, as not unfrequently happens, betrays his belief that it is a German dialect.

It is almost superfluous to recall the history of the language. The first settlers of the country spoke the Teutonic dialects. These were fused together and formed the ancient Netherlandish tongue, which, like the other languages of Europe in the middle ages, passed through the different German, Norman, French phases, and came out in its present form, the primitive idoms still remaining in the foundation, with some influences of Latin.

Certainly there is a great resemblance between the Dutch and German tongues, and particularly there are a number of radicals in common; but the syntax is different, being much more simple in Dutch. The pronunciation also differs. And because of this very resemblance, the Hollanders speak both French and English better than German.

But it is time to go to the picture gallery, the finest jewel of the Hague.

Immediately upon entering, the visitor finds himself in front of the most celebrated of painted beasts: Paul

Potter's "Bull"; that immortal bull which, as we have said, at the time when there was a mania for classifying pictures in a sort of hierarchy of celebrity, hung in the gallery of the Louvre side by side with the "Transfiguration" of Raphael, the "St. Peter, Martyr" of Titian, and the "Communion of St. Jerome" of Domenichino; that bull for which England would give a million of francs, and Holland would not part with for double that sum; that bull, in short, about which there have certainly been more pages written than the painter gave strokes of the brush, and which is still discussed and written about, as if instead of an image it was a new creation of some animal not heretofore existent.

The subject of the picture is of the simplest: a bull life size, standing, with its muzzle turned towards the spectator, a cow lying down, a few sheep, a shepherd, and a distant landscape.

The supreme merit of this bull can be given in one word: he is alive. The grave, astonished eye, expressing such a vigorous vitality and such a savage fierceness, is rendered with a fidelity that at the first aspect makes one inclined to move out of his path, as in a country road meeting the real creature. The moist black nostril seems to smoke and absorb the air with a deep inspiration. The hide is painted with all its wrinkles and the traces of rubbings against trees and earth, so that it looks like reality. The other animals are not inferior: the head of the cow, the wool of the sheep, the flies, the grass, the leaves and fibres of the plants, all are rendered with prodigious truth to nature. And whilst you appreciate the infinite care and study of the artist, you see no marks of fatigue or patient labor; it seems a work of inspiration, in which the painter, influenced with a sort of fury, has not had an instant of hesitation or discouragement. Many censures were passed upon this "incredible piece of audacity in a youth of twenty-four." They blamed its great size, and the vulgar nature of the subject; the absence of luminous effects, the light being everywhere equal and without contrast of black shadows; the rigidity of the bull's legs; the dry coloring of the plants and more distant animals; the mediocrity of the figure of the shepherd. But in spite of it all, Paul Potter's bull remains crowned with the glory of an acknowledged *chef d'œuvre*, and Europe considers it as the most majestic work of the prince of animal painters. "With his bull," says justly an illustrious critic, "Paul Potter has written the true idyl of Holland."

This is the great merit of the Dutch animal painters, and of Potter above all. He has not only represented the animals, but has made visible, and celebrated in the poetry of color, the delicate, almost maternal affection which is felt for them by the Dutch agriculturist. He has made use of the animals in order to reveal the poetic side of rustic life. With them he has expressed the peaceful silence of the fields, the pleasure of solitude, the sweetness of repose, and the satisfaction of tranquil labor. One would say that he had succeeded in being understood by them, and that they had taken certain attitudes on purpose for him to copy. He has known how to give them all the variety and attraction of personages. Gravity, the quiet contentment that follows the satisfaction of some need, the sentiments of health and strength, love and gratitude to man, all the flashes of intelligence and all the varieties of character—he has caught them all, and fixed them with loving fidelity on his canvas, causing the spectator to feel the sentiment that moved him. Paul Potter is the greatest of animal painters. Berghem is more refined, but not so natural; Van de Velde has more grace, but less energy; Du Jardin is more amiable, but wanting in depth.

And to think that the architect, his father-in-law, would not at first grant him his daughter's hand, because he was a "painter of beasts"! and that, if we are to believe the tradition, his famous bull was painted for a butcher's sign, and sold for twelve hundred francs!

Another *chef d'œuvre* of the gallery of the Hague is a small picture by Gerard Dow, the painter of the celebrated "Dropsical Woman" in the Louvre, and which hangs between the Raphaels and the Murillos. The picture represents merely a woman seated near a window, with a cradle beside her; but in this simplest of all scenes there is such a sweet and holy atmosphere of domestic peace, a repose so deep, a harmony so perfect, that the most obstinate of earthly bachelors could not fix his eyes upon it long without an irresistible desire to be that one who is evidently expected in the quiet room, or at least to enter it a moment, even with the condition of remaining hidden in a dark corner, in order to breathe a breath of that perfume of innocent and secret felicity. This, like all Dow's works, is painted with that extraordinary minuteness which almost reaches an excess, which does reach it in Slingelandt, who took three years of constant labor to paint the Meerman family; a manner which, still later, degenerated into that smooth and labored style, where the figures were ivory, the skies enamel, and the fields velvet, and of which the painter Van der Werff was the most renowned master. Among other objects in this picture of Dow's, there is a broom-handle, about as large as a pen, upon which it is said the artist worked assiduously for three days; a thing that does not astonish you when you see that all the minutest veins, knots, stains, and filaments are minutely represented. Almost incredible things are related of his superhuman patience. It is said that he occupied five days in copying the hand of a certain Madame Spirings whose portrait he was painting: who knows how much time he spent upon the head! Those sitters who were so ill-judging as to come to him, were reduced to desperation. It is related of him that he ground his own colors, made his own brushes, and kept everything hermetically closed that no grain of dust might reach it. When he entered his studio he opened the door very carefully, sat down quietly, and waited until every bit of agitation produced by motion was calmed down. In painting he made use of concave glasses to diminish objects; which ended by weakening his sight so that he was obliged to paint with a lens. Notwithstanding all this, however, his coloring never grew weak or cold, and his pictures are as vigorous seen from a distance as near by. They are, with justice, likened to natural scenes diminished in a *camera obscura*. Dow was one of the many disciples of Rembrandt who divided among them the inheritance of his genius. He had from him his finish, and the art of imitating light, especially that of candles and lamps, in which he rose to the height of his master. Among the painters of his time he was peculiar in having no pleasure in ugly or trivial subjects.

Van Ostade—called the Rembrandt of familiar subjects, because he imitated the great master's *chiaroscura*, his *spumature*, or delicate blending of colors, the transparency of his shadows, and the richness of his coloring—has two small pictures here, representing the interior and the exterior of a rustic house, with figures; both full of poetry, in spite of the vulgarity of the subjects, which he shares in common with the other painters of his school. But he has this peculiarity: that the remarkably ugly young women in his pictures are portraits of his own family, who, it is said, formed a group of little monstrosities whom he has thus pilloried before the world. So have almost all the Dutch painters chosen to paint the least handsome of the women who fell under their notice, as if they had all agreed to discredit the feminine type of their own country. The "Susanna" of Rembrandt, to instance a subject that absolutely demands beauty, is always an ugly Dutch servant-wench; and it is not necessary to allude to the women of Steen, Brouwer, and others. And yet their country was not wanting in models of noble and graceful beauty.

Francis van Mieris the elder, the first of Gerard Dow's disciples, and, like him, minute and faithful, has three fine pictures, one of which represents the artist and his wife. Of Steen there is, among others, one of his favorite subject—a physician feeling the pulse of a young girl sick for love, with an older woman standing by; an admirable play of mischievous and cunning looks and smiles which, in the physician, say, "I think I understand," in the girl, "I want another medicine than yours," and in the governess, "I know well enough what she wants."

In the way of landscapes and marine views there are the finest gems of Ruysdael, Berghem, Van de Velde, Van du Neer, Buckhuysen, Everdingen, beside a good number of pictures by Philip Wonvermaan, the horse and battle painter. There are two by Van Huysum, the great flower painter; he who, born in a time when Holland was seized by a sort of mad love for flowers, and possessed the finest in Europe, celebrated the madness with his pencil, and made it live for ever. No one has so marvellously rendered the infinite secrets of the loveliness of flowers, those pearls of vegetation and chromos of loving nature. The Hollanders carried the wonders of their gardens to him that he might copy them; all the kings of Europe wanted his pictures, and the sums he received were, for that time, very large. He was jealous of his wife, and of his art, and worked alone, invisible even to his own brothers, that they might not discover the secrets of his coloring; and so he lived and died, glorious and melancholy in the midst of petals and perfumes.

But the greatest picture in the gallery is the celebrated "Lesson in Anatomy," by Rembrandt.

This picture was inspired by a sentiment of gratitude towards the physician Tulp, professor of anatomy at

Amsterdam, who had protected Rembrandt in his youth. Dr. Tulp is represented, with his disciples, grouped about a table on which is stretched a naked corpse, with one arm opened by the anatomic knife. The professor, with his hat on his head, and standing, points out to the students with his forceps the muscles of the body. Of the other figures, some are seated, some standing, some bending over the corpse. The light, striking from left to right, illuminates the faces and one side of the dead body, leaving in obscurity the dresses, the table, and the walls of the room. The figures are life size.

It is difficult to express the effect produced by this picture. The first feeling is that of horror and repulsion from the corpse. The forehead is in shadow, the eyes open with the pupils turned upwards, the mouth half-open as if in astonishment, the chest sunken, the legs and feet stiff, the flesh livid, and looking as if, should you touch it with your hand, it would feel cold. With this rigid body a powerful contrast is produced by the vivacious attitudes, the youthful faces, the bright, attentive eyes, full of thought, of the disciples, revealing in different degrees the avidity for knowledge, the joy of learning, curiosity, wonder, the strength of intelligence, the suspense of the mind. The master has the tranquil face, the serene eye, and the almost smiling lip of one who feels the complacency of knowledge. There is in the complexion of the group an air of mystery, gravity, and scientific solemnity which inspires reverence and silence. The contrast between the light and shadow is as marvellous as that between life and death. It is all done with extraordinary finish; one can count the folds of the ruffs, the lines of the faces, the hair of the beards. It is said that the foreshortening of the corpse is wrong, and that in some points the finish runs into dryness; but universal judgment places the "Lesson in Anatomy" among the greatest triumphs of human genius.

Rembrandt was only twenty-six years old when he painted this picture, which, therefore, belongs to his first manner, in which there are not yet apparent that fire and audacity, that sovereign security in his own genius, which shine in the works of his maturer years; but there is already that luminous potency, that marvellous *chiaroscuro*, that magic of contrasts, which form the most original trait of his genius.

However one may be profane in art, and have made a vow never more to offend in too much enthusiasm, when one is in the presence of Rembrandt van Rhijn, one can but raise a little, as the Spaniards say, the key of one's style. Rembrandt exercised a particular prestige. Fra Angelico is a saint, Michael Angelo a giant, Raphael an angel, Titian a prince; Rembrandt is a supernatural being. How otherwise shall we name that son of a miller? Born in a windmill, rising unheralded, without master, without examples, without any derivation from schools, he became a universal painter, embraced all the aspects of life painted figures, landscapes, marine views, animals, saints in paradise, patriarchs, heroes, monks, wealth and misery, deformity and decrepitude, the ghetto, the tavern, the hospital, death; made, in short, a review of heaven and earth, and rendered all things visible by a light from the arcana of his own imagination. He is, at the same time, grand and minute, idealist and realist, painter and engraver; transfiguring everything and dissimulating nothing; changing men into phantoms, the most vulgar natural scenes into mysterious apparitions; this world, I may say, into another world, which seems no more this world and yet is so still. Where did he find that indefinable light, those shafts of electric rays, those reflections of unknown stars, making one muse as over an enigma? What did he see in the darkness, dreamer, visionary that he was? What was the arcanum that his genius yearned for? What was he saying with his eternal conflict of light and shadow, this painter of the air?

It was said that the contrast of light and shadow corresponded in him to diverse movements of thought. Schiller before beginning a work, heard within himself a harmony of indistinct sounds, which were like a prelude to inspiration; in like manner Rembrandt, when in the act of conceiving a picture, had a vision of rays and shadows, which spoke to his soul before he animated them with his personages. There is in his pictures a life, and what may almost be called a dramatic action, quite apart from the human figures. Vivid rays of light break into the darkness like cries of joy; the darkness flies in terror, leaving here and there fragments of shadow full of melancholy, tremulous reflections that seem like lamentations; profound obscurity full of dim threatenings; spurts of light, sparkles, ambiguous shadows, doubtful transparencies, questionings, sighs, words of a supernatural language, heard like music and not understood, and remaining in the memory like the vague relics of a dream. And in this atmosphere he plants his figures, of which some are clothed in the dazzling light of a theatrical apotheosis, others veiled like phantoms, others revealed by one stroke of light upon the face; dressed in habits of luxury or misery, but all with something strange and fantastic; without distinctness of outline, but loaded with powerful colors, sculptural reliefs, and bold touches of the brush; and everywhere a warmth of expression, a fury of violent inspiration, the superb, capricious, and profound imprint of a free and fearless genius.

For the rest, everyone is free to form his own opinion; but who knows if Rembrandt, reading the endless pages that have been written to explain the inner meaning of his works, would not burst into a shout of laughter!

Such is the fate of a man of genius; everybody, to show that he understands better than the rest, explains him in his own way; he is a theme given by God, which men turn and twist in a thousand ways; a canvas upon which human imagination paints and embroiders according to its bent or fancy.

I left the museum of the Hague with one desire unsatisfied; I had found there no picture by Jerome Busch, born at Bois-le-Duc in the fifteenth century. That diabolical brain, that terror of bigots, that great sorcerer of art, had made my flesh shrink in the gallery at Madrid, with a picture representing an army of living skeletons, sprinkled over an immense space, and engaged in a struggle with a various, confused, and desperate crowd of men and women, whom they were dragging into an abyss where death awaited them. Only from the diseased imagination of a man agitated by the terrors of damnation could such a monstrous extravagance have issued. Such were the subjects of all his pictures: tortures of the damned, spectres, abysms of fire, dragons, supernatural birds, filthy monsters, devilish furnaces, sinister landscapes. One of these terrible pictures was found in the cell where Philip II. breathed his last; others are scattered about Spain and Italy. Who was this chimerical painter? How did he live? What strange mania tormented him? No one knows. He passed over the earth wrapped in a cloud, and vanished like a vision of hell.

On the ground-floor of the museum there is a "Royal Cabinet of Curiosities," which contains, among a great variety of objects from China, Japan, and the colonies of Holland, some precious historical relics. There is the sword of that Ruyter who began life as a rope-maker at Flessingnen, and became Grand Admiral of Holland; there is the cuirass of Admiral Tromp, perforated by a ball; a chair from the prison of the venerable Barnevelt; a box containing some of the hair of that Van Spoyk, who in 1831, on the Scheldt, blew up his own ship to save the honor of the Dutch flag. There is besides the complete dress worn by William of Orange on the day of his murder at Delft: the shirt stained with blood, the waistcoat of buffalo-skin pierced by the balls, the wide trousers, the broad felt hat; and in the same glass case, the bullets, with the pistol of the assassin, and the original sentence of death.

That more than modest costume, worn in the height of

his power and glory by the chief of the Republic of the Netherlands, is a fine testimony to the patriarchal simplicity of Dutch customs. There is not, perhaps, another modern nation that has shown, at an equal height of prosperity, less vanity and luxury. It is related that when the Earl of Leicester came to Holland as ambassador from Elizabeth, and when Spinosa was there treating for peace in the name of the King of Spain, their magnificence almost created a scandal. It is said that the Spanish ambassadors sent to the Hague in 1608 to stipulate for the famous truce, saw the deputies from the States of Holland, meanly dressed, seated in a field, and making their breakfast off some bread and cheese which they had brought with them in a bag. The Grand Pensionary John de Witt, the adversary of Louis XIV., had but one servant. Admiral Ruyter lived at Amsterdam like a poor man, and swept out his own bedroom.

Another very curious object in this museum is a case opening in front like a cupboard, and representing in the minutest particulars the interior of a rich man's house at Amsterdam in the beginning of the eighteenth century. The Czar Peter the Great during his sojourn at Amsterdam had given to a rich burgher of the place the commission for this toy-house, intending to carry it to Russia as a memorial of Holland. The rich burgher, who was named Brandt, did the thing like a brave Dutchman, slowly and well. The cleverest workmen in Holland made the furniture, the most expert goldsmiths made the plate, the most accurate typographers printed the little books, the most delicate miniature-painters executed the pictures, the linen was made in Flanders, the carpets and hangings at Utrecht. After twenty-five years of labor all the rooms were completed. The nuptial-chamber had everything necessary for the approaching confinement of the little mistress; in the dining-room there was a microscopic tea-service upon a table as big as a silver dollar; the gallery of pictures was complete; the kitchen contained the utensils necessary for a dinner for a lilliputian company; there was the library, a cabinet of Chinese curiosities, cages with birds, tiny prayer-books, carpets, linen for all the family, with finest lace and embroidery; nothing was wanting but a conjugal couple, with maids and a cook a little smaller than an ordinary puppet. But there was one great fault: the house cost one hundred and twenty thousand francs. The Czar, who, as all the world knows, was an economical man, refused to take it; and Brandt, to shame the imperial avarice, made a present of it to the museum of the Hague.

From the first day of my arrival at the Hague, I had remarked in the streets certain women dressed in so extraordinary a manner that I had followed one of them in order to observe the particulars of her costume. At first I imagined that they belonged to some religious order, or that they were hermits, or pilgrims, or perhaps the women of some nomadic people passing through Holland. They wore a preposterous hat of straw lined with printed muslin, a monkish mantle of chocolate-colored serge, lined with red; a short white petticoat also of serge, and set out as if by crinoline; black stockings, and white wooden shoes. In the morning I saw them going to market, with a basketful of fish on their heads, or with a cart drawn by two great dogs. In general, they were alone, or two women together, but never with a man. They walked in a peculiar manner, with long strides, and a certain heaviness, like people accustomed to walk in sand; and in their faces and bearing there was something of sadness, which agreed with the cenobitic austerity of their garb.

A citizen to whom I applied for information concerning these odd figures, answered simply: " Go to Scheveningen."

Scheveningen is a village about two miles from the Hague, and approached by a straight road bordered by a double row of beautiful elms that allow no ray of sun to penetrate them. This road, which is gay on either side with villas and gardens, is the favorite promenade of the people of the city, but on other days is almost solitary. You meet no one but one of the figures described above, or a carriage, or the diligence that plies between the city and the village. With its deep shade, rich vegetation, and solitude, it reminds one of the grove of the Alhambra at Grenada, and one forgets that he is in Holland, and thinks no more of Scheveningen.

But arrived at the end, an instant change of scene dissipates the image of Grenada, and nothing remains but a desert of sand; the salt breeze blows in your face with a low continuous murmur, and if you mount a little hillock, you see spread out before you the North sea.

THE HAGUE.

For anyone who has never seen any sea but the Mediterranean the spectacle is a very striking one. The beach is composed of sand as fine and light as ashes, and upon it the spreading waves for ever fold and unfold themselves like a carpet. This sandy beach extends to the feet of the downs, which are composed of little hillocks of sand—steep, broken, and corroded, deformed by the eternal flagellation of the sea. Such is the entire Dutch coast, from the mouths of the Meuse to Helder. There are no mollusks, nor star-fish, nor living shells, nor crabs, nor a shrub, nor a blade of grass. Nothing but water and sand, sterility and solitude.

The sea is no less melancholy than the coast, and answers truly to the image we have formed of the North sea, in reading of the superstitious terrors of the ancients who fancied it lashed by eternal winds and peopled by gigantic monsters. Near the shore it is of a yellowish color, beyond, a pallid green, and still further off, a dull blue. The horizon is in general veiled in mists which often descend to the shores and hide the sea, like an immense curtain, leaving visible only the wave that dies upon the beach, or some specimen of a fisherman's bark not far distant. The sky is almost always grey, traversed by great clouds which cast dense and moving shadows on the water; at some points it is black with a darkness like night, raising in the mind images of tempest and horrid shipwreck; at others, illuminated by streaks of vivid light, serpentine, and like motionless lightning, or rays from some mysterious planet. The wave, always agitated, rushes to bite the shore with impetuous rage, and gives forth a prolonged cry of grief and menace, as from a crowd of lamenting creatures. The sea, the sky, and the earth turn sinister looks upon each other, like three implacable enemies, and the spectator shudders under the dread of some great convulsion of nature.

The village of Scheveningen is posted on the downs, which defend it from the sea, and hide it, so that looking from the beach you can see nothing but the sugar-loaf church-steeple standing like an obelisk in the midst of the sand. The village is divided into two parts. One part is composed of elegant little houses of all the forms and colors usual in Holland, built for the use of strangers, and having "To Let" upon them in several languages; the other portion, in which the native population lives, consists of small black cottages and narrow lanes, where strangers never set their feet.

The population of Scheveningen, which counts a few thousand souls, is almost all made up of fishermen, for the most part very poor. The village is also one of the stations for the herring fishery, that celebrated fish to which Holland owes so much of her wealth and power; but the fruits of this industry go to the owners of the fishing vessels, and the men of Scheveningen, enrolled as mariners, earn hardly enough to live. On the beach in front of the village lie many of these vessels, broad and robust, with one mast and a great square sail; they lie one beside the other in a row upon the sand, like the Greek galleys on the shores of Troy, safe from the winds and waves. The herring flotilla leaves in the early days of June, accompanied by a steam corvette, and takes its course towards the coast of Scotland. The first herrings taken are sent at once to Holland, where they are conveyed in a car all decorated with flags to the King, who gives in return five hundred florins. These boats also pursue other kinds of fish, which are in part sold at auction on the shores of the sea, and in part left to the fishermen of Scheveningen, who send them by their women to the market at the Hague.

Scheveningen, like all the other villages of the coast—Ratwijk, Wlardingen, Maasluis—is a place fallen from its once flourishing condition, in consequence of the decline of the herring fishery, caused, as everybody knows, by the rivalry of England and by disastrous wars. But poverty, instead of weakening, invigorates the character of this people—without doubt the most original and the most poetic of the inhabitants of Holland. The people of Scheveningen seem by their aspect, character, and costume, like a foreign tribe in their own country. They are at only two miles distance from a great city, and yet preserve intact their primitive manners and customs, and their love of solitude. Such as they were centuries ago, such are they now. Not one abandons his native village, and no one who is not born there penetrates it; they marry among themselves; they speak a peculiar dialect; and they dress in the same fashion and colors as their fathers and grandfathers before them. In the fishing season only the women and children remain in the village: the men are all at sea. When they leave they carry their Bibles with them, and on board there is no drunkenness or profanity, and no laughter. When the tempestuous seas toss their little boats, they close every aperture and await death with resignation; while their women, shut up in their storm-beaten cottages, sing hymns and psalms. Those small habitations, that have witnessed such mortal anxieties, heard the sobs of so many widows, seen the holy joy of return, and the inconsolable grief of parting, represent the freedom and dignified poverty of their inhabitants. From those houses come no vagabonds or abandoned women; no native of Scheveningen has ever deserted the sea, and no young girl has ever disdained the hand of a fisherman. Men and women have in the carriage of the head and the expression of the eye a something of gravity and dignity that imposes respect. They salute without bending the head, looking you straight in the eye, with an expression which implies: "We have need of no one."

Even in this small village there are two schools, and at certain hours the narrow lanes are alive with children with slate and book in hand.

Scheveningen is not only a village famous for the originality of its inhabitants, which strangers visit and artists paint; there are two great bathing establishments there, where, in the summer, come English, Russians, Germans, and Danes; the flower of the northern aristocracy; princes and ministers; half the Almanach de Gotha; and there are balls, fantastic illuminations, and fireworks on the water. The two establishments are on the downs. At every hour in the day, certain carriages in the form of caravans at a fair, each drawn by one strong horse, advance from the beach into the sea, turn round, and ladies with golden locks floating on the breeze issue from thence and plunge into the sea. At night there is music, the bathers promenade the beach, in festive array, and all the languages as well as all the beauties of Europe are to be heard and seen. The melancholy stranger wanders in the obscure solitudes of the downs, where the music reaches his ear like a distant echo, and the lights in the fishermen's houses make him think of home and peace.

The first time I went to Scheveningen, I walked over these downs, illustrated by so many painters, the only heights that intercept the view over the immense flats of Holland, rebellious daughters of the sea disputing its advance, and at once prisoners and guardians of the country. There are three ranges of downs which form a triple bulwark against the sea; the exterior ones are the most arid, those in the midst the highest, and the interior ones the most cultivated. The average height of these hills of sand is not more than fifteen metres; and altogether they do not enter more than a French league into the land. But having no greater heights near them or about them, they deceive the eye with the aspect of a mountainous region. Seen from above they present the image of a yellow, angry, and motionless sea. The dreariness and sadness of this desert is increased by a savage vegetation, which seems in mourning for nature dead and abandoned; a little thin scattered grass, flowers whose petals are almost diaphanous, broom, rosemary, and the like, through which, here and there, one may see the flight of a terrified rabbit. For long distances there is no house, nor tree, nor human being to be seen.

From time to time flocks of crows, curlews, and gulls sweep by, and their cries, with the rustle of the shrubs tossed by the wind, are the only sounds that disturb the silence of those solitudes. When the sky is black, the dull color of the earth takes on a sort of sinister light, like those fantastic gleams in which objects seen through a colored glass appear. At such times, alone in the midst of the downs, the stranger feels a sense of awe, as one in an unknown land, immeasurably far away from any inhabited country, and looks anxiously round for the shadow of a steeple wherewith to comfort his soul.

In all my walk I met only one or two peasants. It is a notable thing in a northern country, that the Dutch peasant almost always salutes the stranger whom he meets by the way. Some touch the hat with an odd gesture, hastily, and as if by mistake; generally they say " Good evening," or " Good morning," without looking in your face. If they meet two persons they say, " Good evening to both of you"; if more than two, " Good evening to altogether." I encountered in a path on the downs several of those poor fishermen who pass nearly the whole day in water up to their waists, gathering shells which are used to make a certain kind of cement, or are sprinkled in the garden-paths instead of sand. The operation which they are obliged to go through to remove the enormous leather boots which they wear in the water, takes at least half an hour of trouble and fatigue, which would give an Italian a pretext for calling all the saints out of heaven. These, on the contrary, go about it with phlegmatic patience, allowing no sign of annoyance to escape them, and never lifting their heads until the operation is completed, not even if a cannon were to explode near them.

Standing on the downs, near a stone obelisk which records the return of William of Orange from England after the fall of the French domination, I saw, for the first time, one of those sunsets which are peculiar to this country. The sun, in consequence of the refraction of the vapory mists with which the air of Holland is filled, appears of an extraordinary size, and diffuses through the clouds and over the sea a veiled and tremulous splendor like the reflection of a great conflagration. It seemed another sun, unexpectedly appearing on the horizon, and sinking, never to rise again upon this world. In Holland, says the poet, the sun does not set; he dies.

Since I have spoken of my visit to Scheveningen, I will record two other excursions that I made from the Hague during the winter.

The first was to the village of Naaldwijk and to the point of the shore where the new canal of Rotterdam is being opened. At Naaldwijk, thanks to the courtesy of a school-inspector who accompanied me, I satisfied my desire to see an elementary school; and I may say at once that my expectations were more than fulfilled. The school-house, built purposely for that use, stands alone, and has only the ground-floor. We entered a small vestibule, where there was a small mountain of wooden shoes belonging to the scholars, and which they resumed when they went out. In schools they sit with stockings only, but the stockings are very thick, and the schoolroom is warmed thoroughly.

When we came in, the scholars rose and the master came forward to meet the inspector. Even this poor village schoolmaster spoke French, so that we could enter into conversation. There were about forty scholars present, half male, half female, and the sexes divided; all were blonde and plump, with broad, good-tempered faces, and a certain precocious air of fathers and mothers of families that made one smile. The building is divided into five rooms, separated one from the other by a glazed partition; so that if the master of one class is absent, the master of the nearest one can oversee it without leaving his place. All the rooms are spacious and have very large windows extending from floor to ceiling, so that it is as light as in the street. The benches, walls, floors, stoves, and glass partitions were all as clean and bright as in a ballroom. Having a lively recollection of the pestiferous condition of certain retired spots in the schools that I had frequented when a boy, I inspected these places here, and found them in excellent condition. On the walls of the rooms there were small pictures, landscapes, and figures, and groups of animals, to which the master referred in his teaching; maps in vivid colors with the names printed large; sentences, grammatical rules, and moral precepts in large characters. One thing only seemed to be open to criticism : personal cleanliness.

In some schools in Switzerland there are washing-rooms where the pupils are obliged to wash themselves before entering the school, and also when they go away. I should have liked to see the same thing in Holland, and then there would have been nothing more to be desired.

I said "poor schoolmaster," merely as a common mode of expression, for I learned that he had a stipend of more than two thousand two hundred francs, and a home in a good house in the village. In Holland the *minimum* for the head master of an elementary school is eight hundred francs. But there are masters who have the salary of one of our university professors.

The question of instruction in Holland, as in almost all other countries, is a religious question, which, in its turn, is the most serious, if not the only, question which agitates the nation.

Of the three millions and a half of inhabitants that Holland counts, one third are Catholics; about one hundred thousand Jews, the rest Protestants. The Catholics, who for the most part inhabit the southern provinces of Limbourg and Brabant, are not, as in other countries, politically divided, but constitute one solid legion, clerical, papistical, and ultramontane, the most faithful of the Roman legions, as the Hollanders themselves say; among whom they sell the straw on which the Pontiff has slept in his dungeon, and fulminate Italy from the pulpit and through the journals. This Catholic party, not very powerful in itself, is made so by the division of the Protestants into seven sects: Orthodox Calvinists; Protestants who believe in revelation but reject certain dogmas of the Church; others who deny the divinity of Christ, without separating from the Protestant Church; others believing in God, but belonging to no church; and others, among whom are many men of great ability, who make open profession of atheism. In this state of things the Catholic party has for its natural allies the Calvinists, who, as fervent believers and inflexible conservatives of the faith of their fathers, are much less divided from the Catholics than from a large part of their co-religionists, and form, as it were, the clerical party of Protestantism. Now, in the States General there are on one side the Catholics and Calvinists, on the other side the Liberal party, and between them a wavering party that consents to the absolute supremacy of neither. The principal field of battle between the extreme parties is the question of primary instruction, reduced, on the part of the Catholics and Calvinists, to the determination that for the so-called mixed schools (where no special religious instruction is given, in order to facilitate the coming together of pupils of all religious sects) should be substituted others where dogmatic instruction should be given, and maintained by the commune under the direction of the State.

It is easy to understand the gravity of the consequences that would ensue from such a schism in popular education, the germs of discord and religious hatred, the perturbations that would in time result from the dividing the youth of the country into two groups of different faiths. At present the principle of mixed schools still prevails, but the Liberals maintain with difficulty their ascendancy; the Catholics and Calvinists obtain concessions, and will obtain more; in a word, the Catholic party, more powerful than the Calvinist, solid, resolute, and united, are gaining ground every day; and it is not improbable that they will succeed in obtaining a victory, which, although it may be only temporary, will produce a violent reaction in the country. To such a condition is Holland now reduced, which for eighty years carried on a desperate struggle against Catholic despotism, and which now has grave reasons to fear a not distant religious war.

Notwithstanding, however, this state of things, which prevents the institution, desired so ardently by the Liberals, of obligatory instruction, and which keeps a large number of Catholic children out of the schools, the state of popular instruction in Holland is so flourishing that many European states might envy it. Proportions considered, there are fewer persons ignorant of the alphabet than in Prussia. "In all Europe," says a Dutch writer (who, in other respects, judges his own country rather severely), "it is the country where the knowledge indispensable to a civilised man is most universally diffused." I once asked a Hollander whether, among the class of women-servants, there were any who could not read. "Oh, yes," he said; "I remember about twenty years ago my mother had a maid who did not know her letters; but it was considered a very unusual thing." And it is pleasant for a stranger in a Dutch city, and who does not know the language, to find that any street-boy can read a name and tell him where a street is by gestures.

Discoursing of Catholics and Calvinists, my friend and I reached the downs, and although we were not a stones-throw from the beach, we could not see the sea. "Holland is an odd country," said I, "everything in it seems to be playing at hide and seek. The façades of the houses hide the roofs, the trees hide the houses, the city hides the ships, the dykes hide the canals, the fog hides the fields, the downs hide the sea." "And one day or another," responded my friend, "the sea will hide everything else, and the game will be over."

Crossing the downs we reached the point where the preparatory works for the opening of the Rotterdam canal are in progress.

Two dykes, one more than twelve hundred metres in length, the other about two thousand, with the distance of one kilometre between them, advance into the sea in a direction perpendicular to the shore. These two dykes, constructed to protect the entrance of vessels into the canal, are formed of several rows of enormous piles, great blocks of granite, fascines, stones, and earth, and have the width of ten men standing shoulder to shoulder. The sea, which continually beats upon them, and covers them almost entirely at high tide, has clothed the surface with a thick coating of shells, black as ebony, looking at a distance like a velvet carpet, and giving to these gigantic bulwarks a severe and magnificent aspect, as if Holland had hung out a warlike drapery to celebrate her victory over the ocean. At the moment, the tide was rising and the battle raged about the distant extremities of the dykes. The livid waves raged around two granite horns that stretch, as if in mockery, into the bosom of their superb enemy. The piles and masses of masonry were beaten and gnawed and buffeted on every side, overwhelmed by angry billows, spit upon by a vaporous rain which fell about them in powdery clouds; enveloped as in the folds of furious serpents; struck, even those farthest from the struggle, by unexpected and lengthened spurts of water like impatient advance guards of that infinite army; and the waters, steadily advancing, drove back the workmen step by step.

On the longest of the two dykes, not very far from the beach, they were driving in piles. Some, with tremendous efforts, raised the great blocks of granite by means of pulleys; others, ten or fifteen together, removed the old beams to make room for new. It was fine to see the contrast between the fury of the waves and the calm impassibility of those men, which seemed almost like disdain. A bitter wind waved about their brave Dutch faces the long locks of their light hair, and covered them with flecks of foam; foolish provocations which obtained not even a glance.

I saw them plant a pile in the middle of the dyke, a monstrous trunk of a tree sharpened at the extremity, and raised between two parallel beams under an enormous steam hammer. The pile had to make its way through several strata of stones and fascines; but at every blow of that formidable hammer it sank into the dyke as if penetrating the soft earth. Nevertheless the operation for that one pile alone lasted one hour. I thought of the thousands that had been driven, and of the thousands that were yet to be driven, of the interminable dykes that defend Holland, of the infinite numbers of them that have been destroyed and reconstructed, and embracing for the first time in my thought the grandeur of the work, I stood dumb with amazement.

A dear friend of mine at the Hague had invited me to dine with him at the house of a relation, who had manifested a courteous desire to make my acquaintance. In answer to my question as to where the gentlemen lived, I was told " Far from the Hague," and was directed to be next morning at the railway station, where my friend would meet me. Having obeyed this direction, we took our tickets for Leyden, and arriving there in due time, did not enter the city, but struck off by a road across country. I asked my companion then to reveal the secret, but he declined to do so. Knowing that when a Dutchman has once said a thing, no power on earth can make him change it, I resigned myself to the inevitable. It was in February. There was a cloudy sky, but no snow; and a cold, impetuous wind, that in about five minutes made my nose of a fine purple. It was Sunday, and the country was deserted. We went on and on, passing windmills, canals, meadows, houses half hidden in trees, with tall thatched roofs tapestried with moss. We reached a village; Dutch villages are all closed by a sort of barrier. We entered. Nobody there. The doors all shut, windows with blinds drawn down, not a voice, not a step, not a breath stirring. Going through the village, we passed a church, covered with ivy like a garden-house, in which, through an opening in the door, we could see the Protestant minister, in a white cravat, preaching to a congregation of peasants whose faces were all streaked with gold and green and crimson from the windows of stained glass. Proceeding by a fine brick-paved street, we saw frames for the storks' nests, posts planted by the peasants for the cows to rub themselves against, palings painted of a celestial blue, small houses with tiles of various colors forming letters and words, basins with little boats, tiny bridges, kiosks of unknown purpose, little chapels with great gilded cocks upon the tops of their steeples; and no living soul far or near.

We go on and on. The sky clears a little and relapses into clouds again; the sun illumines for an instant a canal, glistens on the roof of a house, gilds a distant steeple, flies, returns, promises, and coquets in a hundred ways; and long oblique streaks of rain are seen on the horizon. We begin to meet a few country women with gold bands round their heads, a veil over the band, a hat on that, a bunch of flowers on the hat, and broad floating ribbons; also some carriages of the antique form of the time of Louis XV., with gilded bodies, adorned with sculpture and small mirrors; peasants in large black coats and white wooden shoes; boys with stockings of every color of the rainbow. We arrive at another village, like the first, and getting into a carriage, go on in that way. A fine cold rain wets and chills us to the bone. Wrapped in our dripping blankets, we reach the border of a broad canal; a man comes out of a hut, runs our vehicle upon a raft, and ferries us over to the other side. The carriage goes down a wide road, and we are at the bottom of the old lake of Harlem, the horse trotting where fish once glided, and our coachman smoking where shipwrecked men breathed their last and naval battles were fought. We catch glimpses of canals, villages, cultivated fields—a new world, where thirty years ago there was a waste of waters. The rain ceased, and it began to snow with a fury such as I had never seen—a real tempest of snow, hard and thick, which an impetuous wind blew straight in our faces. We pulled over us the oil-cloth cover, opened our umbrellas, and screwed ourselves into the smallest compass, all in vain. The wind blew away all our defences, froze us from head to foot, and whitened us with snow. After a long time we came out of the basin of the lake, reached a village, when we left the carriage and proceeded again on foot. On and on we went, past bridges, mills, closed houses, solitary roads, immense fields, and not a creature moving. We passed an arm of the Rhine, arrived at another barren and silent village, with here and there a dim face looking at us through the window-panes, and passing this, came out upon the downs. The sky began to grow dark, and I began to get anxious. I asked my companion where we were going, and he responded, "Wherever chance may lead us." "But who is this relative of yours?" I said. "Where does he live? What does he do? What is there under all this devilry? He cannot be a man like others. Tell me where you are taking me."

My companion made no reply, but stopped and looked before him. I looked also, and saw far off something that resembled a house, alone in the midst of a desert, and half hidden by a rise in the ground. We hastened our steps, the house appearing and disappearing before us like a shadow. Around it were visible tall objects that looked like gallows, but my companion insisted that they were frames for the storks' nests. When within about a hundred paces we came upon a long wooden water-conduit, which seemed to me to be stained with blood, but my friend assured me that it was only painted red. The house is small, surrounded by a paling; the doors and windows closed. "Do not go in!" I cried; "we can yet turn back. There is some witchcraft in that house; take care what you do. Look up; I never saw so black a sky." My friend paid no heed to me, but advanced courageously, and I followed. Instead of making for the entrance-door, he took a short cut. A ferocious barking of dogs was heard. We ran, breaking our way through a forest of shrubs, and jumping over a low wall, knocked at a door. The door opened; there was no creature visible. We mounted a small crooked staircase, and entered a room. Oh, pleasant wonder! The solitary, the sorcerer, was a gay and gentle youth, and the diabolical house a little villa, full of conveniences, warm, light, and luxurious—a real enchanted palace in miniature, in which our host retired for a few months of every year to make studies for the fertilisation of the downs.

We soon found ourselves seated at a table sparkling with crystal and silver, on which smoked a princely dinner, guarded by a small army of gilded and emblazoned bottles. The snow beat against the windows; the moaning voices of the sea were heard; the winds raged about the house, which seemed like a ship in the midst of a tempest. We drank to the fertilisation of the downs, to the conquerors of Atchin, to the prosperity of the colonies. But I still had some anxieties. Our host, to call his servant, touched a concealed knob; to order his coachman to get ready the carriage, he spoke some words into a hole in the wall; and these proceedings did not please me.

"Reassure me," said I; "tell me that this house does really exist; promise me that it shall not vanish, leaving nothing but a hole in the ground, and a smell of sulphur in the air! Will you swear that you say your prayers every night?"

I cannot relate the extravagant talk and the laughter that went on to a late hour of the night, accompanied by the clinking of glasses, and the howling of the winds without. But the moment of departure came at last, and we descended, to hide ourselves in a large vehicle and begin our crossing of the desert. The land was covered with snow, the white outlines of the downs were drawn upon a black and stormy sky; the carriage rolled silently forward amid strange and indistinct forms, which succeeded each other rapidly in the gleam of the lanterns, and appeared to melt one into the other; and in those enormous solitudes reigned a mortal silence that prevented speech with us.

*   *   *   *

At last I have seen winter in Holland, not as I had imagined it on leaving Italy, because it was very mild; but still very characteristic of the Holland of my dreams.

In the morning early, what first meets the eye in the white and silent streets are the innumerable prints of the wooden shoes of the children going to school—footsteps as of elephants, so large are the shoes—and succeeding each other in a straight line, plainly demonstrating that the scholars take the shortest way to school, like sedate

A VIEW OF OLD SCHEVINGEN. (*Page* 158.)

and zealous Dutch children. Files of them may be seen, all wrapped up warm, with nothing but the point of a nose or the corner of a book visible in the shapeless bundle, two and two, or three and three, or in close groups like bunches of asparagus. The children all housed, the streets remain deserted for a time, for the Hollanders are not early risers, especially in winter. You may wander about without meeting a soul or hearing the least noise. The snow, among all those red houses, seems of a more brilliant whiteness; and the houses, with all their raised points and ornaments relieved by a pure white line, and the carved wooden heads and images over the shops all decked seemingly in wigs of cotton, and the pendant chains and cords like garlands of white flowers, present a strange aspect. On days when it freezes, and the sun shines bright, everything sparkles as if sewn with silver spangles; the ice accumulated on the edges of the canals glows with the colors of the rainbow; and the trees glimmer with pearls, like the plants in the gardens of the "Arabian Nights." Then it is pleasant to walk in the forest, about sunset, on the hardened snow which creaks under the foot like marble dust, in the midst of white and leafless branches, presenting the image of a gigantic crystallization; while the alleys are illuminated by the red rays of the setting sun, and the shadows are azure and violet, sparkling with diamond dust. But nothing equals the spectacle of the open country seen in the morning after a great snowstorm from the heights of some tall steeple. Under a low grey sky there lies an immense white plain, where there is no trace of road or path, or house or canal, but only depressions and elevations, leaving one to divine vaguely the hidden forms, as under the swathing folds of a great sheet; and the infinite whiteness is unstained unless by some spirals of smoke issuing timidly here and there from distant houses, as if to announce to anyone who is looking on that even in that snowy desert human life still palpitates.

But any mention of winter in Holland would be incomplete without allusion to that which constitutes the originality and principal character of winter-life in that country. Skating in Holland is not only a delightful exercise but an ordinary way of getting about. To cite an illustrious example, everybody knows how the Hollanders made use of it in the memorable siege of Harlem. In times of hard frost the canals are changed into roads, and skates do the office of boats. The peasant skates to market, the laborer to his work, the shopkeeper to his shop; whole families go from the country to the city with bag and basket on their backs, or upon sleds. Skating is as easy and natural to them as walking, and they do it with a rapidity that makes them all but invisible. In former years bets were made among the best Dutch skaters as to which of them could keep up with the railway train that ran along the edge of the canal; and in general the skater not only kept even with the train but even outstripped it. There are people who skate from the Hague to Amsterdam and back in the same day; university students, who leave Utrecht in the morning, dine at Amsterdam, and get back to college before night. The bet of going from Amsterdam to

Leyden in a little more than an hour has often been won. And it is not only the speed which is remarkable, but the admirable security with which they traverse immense distances on skates. Many peasants skate from one city to another at night. Sometimes walking along the canal you see a human figure pass and disappear like an arrow; it is a peasant girl carrying milk to some house in the town.

There are also sleds or sledges of every size and form; some pushed from behind by a skater, some drawn by horses, some moved by two iron-shod sticks held in the hands of the person seated in the sledge; and quantities of carriages and vehicles of different sorts, deprived of their wheels, and placed on runners, flying along with all the rapidity of the others. On holiday occasions even the boats of Scheveningen may be seen sliding along the streets of the Hague. Sometimes vessels, with all sails set, move on the frozen rivers with such rapidity that persons on board are obliged to cover their eyes, unable to bear the dizzy velocity of their flight.

The finest of the festivals of Holland are held upon the ice. At Rotterdam, the Meuse becomes a place of meeting for all sorts of diversions. The snow is swept off, so that the ice is as clean as a pavement of crystal; cafés, eating-houses, pavilions, and small theatres rise on every side; all are illuminated at night; by day there is a throng of skaters of all ages, sexes, and conditions. In other cities, above all in Friesland, which is the classic land of the art, there are societies of skaters who institute public trials of skill for prizes. Masts and banners are planted along the canals, stands and railings are put up; an immense multitude assembles from all the villages round about, and the flower of the citizens are on the ground; music sounds; the skaters are dressed in peculiar costumes, the women wearing pantaloons; there are men's races and women's races, and then men and women together; and the names of the winners are inscribed upon the rolls of the society, and are famous for years after.

There are in Holland two schools of skating, which differ completely from each other: the Dutch school and the school of Friesland, each having its peculiar skate. The Frieslanders, older in the art, aim at speed only, while the Dutch are the more graceful. The former dart forward in a straight line, with the body erect and rigid, and the eyes fixed on the goal to be attained; the Hollander goes in a zig-zag, moving from right to left and from left to right, with an undulatory motion of the hips. The one is an arrow, the other a rocket. The Dutch school suits the women best. The ladies of Rotterdam, Amsterdam, and the Hague are the most fascinating skaters in all the United Provinces. They begin as babies, and go on as girls and wives; adding the height of loveliness to the apogee of art, and striking out with the irons of their skates sparks from the ice that light up many a conflagration. There are ladies among them who attain to a high grade of mastery in the art. Those who have seen them say that it is impossible to imagine the grace of the undulations, bendings, dartings, the thousand soft and charming ways in which they turn, and fly, and return, emulating the birds and butterflies, and how their tranquil beauty is animated by it. But all do not succeed, and many do not presume to show their skill in public, and some who, among us, would obtain the prize, here scarcely attract attention; to such a pitch has the art of skating attained. It is the same with the men, who go through every sort of play and prowess; some describing on the ice fantastic figures or amorous words, others making rapid pirouettes, and then darting backwards for a long distance on one leg; others twisting and twining in infinite dizzy whirls within one small space, bent, or crouching, or straight upright, like puppets moved by springs.

The first day on which the canals and basins present ice sufficiently solid for skating is a holiday for a Dutch city. Early skaters who have been experimenting at sunrise, spread the news; the journals announce it; groups of boys run about the streets with cries of joy; servants, of both sexes, ask leave to go out, with the air of people resolved to rebel in case of refusal; old ladies forget their years and pains, and go to the canals to gossip with friends and children. At the Hague, the basin in the middle of the city, near the Binnenhof, is invaded by a crowd of people who elbow each other and press and mingle as if they were all seized with dizziness; the flower of the aristocracy skates on a basin in the midst of the wood; and there, altogether in the snow, glide officers, ladies, deputies, students, old men, boys, and sometimes among them the hereditary prince, and around gathers a throng of spectators; music accompanies the festival; and the enormous disc of the sun of Holland, sinking towards the horizon, sends them, through the branches of gigantic beeches, its dazzling salutations.

When the snow is hard comes the turn of the sledges. Every family has one, and at the usual hour they come out by hundreds. They fly by in a long file, two and three together; some shaped like shells, some like swans, dragons, boats, coaches, gilded and painted in different colors, drawn by horses in magnificent trappings of rich furs, their heads ornamented by feathers and tassels, and their harness studded with glittering points; and carrying ladies wrapped in sables, marten, and the skin of the Siberian fox. The horses toss their heads in a cloud of vapor from their bodies, their manes sparkling with frost; the sleighs leap forward; the dry snow flies like a silvery foam; and the splendid pageant passes and disappears like a silent whirlwind over a field of lilies and jasmine. At night, when they are provided with torches, those thousands of little flames chasing and crossing each other through the silent city, and throwing livid reflections upon the snow, present the image of an infernal battle, presided over from the tower of the Binnenhof by the spectre of Philip II.

But alas! everything changes, even the winter, and with it the arts of skating and sledging. For many years past severe winters in Holland have alternated with winters so mild, that not only do the rivers not freeze over, but even the smaller canals in the towns. It follows that the skaters, remaining too long without practice, no longer risk appearing in public when the opportunity presents itself; and so little by little their numbers become smaller, and the fair sex especially are growing unaccustomed to the ice. In the winter of last year (1873) there was very little skating; and this year there has not been a single competition, and not one sledge has been seen. May heaven grant that this deplorable state of things may not continue, that winter may return to caress Holland with his frozen Polar bear's paw, and that the beautiful art of skating may arise once more with her owy mantle and her crown of icicles.

In the meantime let me announce the publication of a work called "The Art of Skating" (*Il Patinamento*), upon which a deputy of the States of Holland has been at work for several years, a work which will be the history, the epic, and the codex of the art, and from which all the skaters of Europe and America, male and female, can draw instruction and inspiration.

During all the time that I remained at the Hague I frequented the principal club of the city, composed of more than two thousand members, and occupying a palace near the Binnenhof; and there I made my observations upon Dutch character.

Besides the library, the dining-hall, and the card-room, there is a conversation and reading room, which is quite full of people from 4 o'clock in the afternoon until midnight. There are artists, professors, merchants, deputies, clerks, and officers. The greater part of them go there to drink a small glass of gin before dinner, and return afterwards for their coffee and another comforting glass of their favorite liquor. They almost all talk, and yet one hears only a slight murmur, so that with one's eyes shut one would fancy only about a third of the number present. You can make a dozen turns about the room without seeing an emphatic gesture or hearing one word a little louder than another; and at ten paces distance from the groups of talkers you would not notice that conversation was going on, but for the motion of the lips. There are many corpulent men to be seen, with large faces, whiskerless, and with beards under the chin, who converse without lifting their eyes from the table, or removing their hand from their glass. It is extremely rare to see among all their broad faces a fine, acute countenance like that of Erasmus, whom many, but not I, consider as the true Dutch type.

The friend who opened the doors of the club to me, presented me to several of its members. The diversity between the Dutch and Italian character is shown particularly in introductions. More than once, seeing the person to whom I had been presented make a slight movement of the head, and then remain quite silent, I have thought that my respected visage did not suit his taste, and have felt in my heart an echo of cordial antipathy. After a little the introducer would go away, leaving me face to face with my enemy. "Now," thought I, "I will burst before I speak a word to him!" But my neighbor, after a moment's silence, said with great gravity: "I hope that, if you have no other engagement, you will do me the honor to dine with me to-day." I was struck dumb with amazement. We dined together, and my Amphytrion coldly populated the table with bottles of Bordeaux, Champagne, and Hock, and we did not separate without my being constrained to accept a second invitation. Others, of whom I had asked information about various things, scarcely answered me, as if to make me understand that my questions were importunate, whilst I said to myself, "Did ever anyone see such an ill-natured person!" The next day came the answers written out, clear, minute, and satisfactory in a higher degree than I had ever hoped for. One evening I asked a person to look out for me something in that sea of figures which is called a railway guide. For a moment he made no reply, and I was humiliated. Then he took the book, put on his glasses, read, examined, made notes, summed up, and subtracted, with the patience of a saint, for the space of half an hour; and when he had finished, gave me the written reply, and put his spectacles into their case without a word.

Many of those with whom I passed the evening were in the habit of going home at 10 o'clock to work, and coming back to the club at half-past 11 to remain until 1; and when they had said "I must go," there was no possibility of changing their resolution. When the last stroke of ten was sounding, they were already outside the door; when half-past 11 struck they were on the threshold. It is not surprising that, with this chronometrical regularity, they should find time to do so many things and to do them without haste; or that those who had not given themselves to study as a means of life, had still read whole libraries. French literature in particular they had at the ends of their fingers. And what is said of literature can be said with more reason of politics. Holland is one of the countries of Europe where there is the greatest affluence of foreign journals, and perhaps the one in which the affairs of other nations are most discussed. The country is small and tranquil; the news in the papers is soon discussed; after ten minutes the conversation jumps over the Rhine and roams over Europe. I remember that I was much struck by hearing the recent fall of the ministry in Italy discussed as if it had been a family affair.

One of my first cares was to scan the religious sentiments of the people; and I found, to my astonishment, a great disorder. As a learned Hollander has lately written, ideas subversive of every religious dogma have acquired a great field in that country. It would be an error, however, to believe that while faith grows less, indifference increases. Those creatures who appeared so monstrous to Pascal,—men, that is, who lived without giving a thought to religion, who are so numerous among us in Italy,—there do not exist. The religious question, which is with us only a question, is there a battle, in which everyone brandishes his weapon. Every class of society, men and women, old and young, occupy themselves with theology, and follow the controversies of the doctors, devouring a prodigious number of writings on religious polemics. This tendency of the country is manifested even in Parliament, where it sometimes happens that the members attack each other with Biblical citations, read in Hebrew, translated and commentated, and the discussion degenerates into a theological disquisition.

All this goes on, however, in the mind rather than in the heart; passion has no part in it; and the proof of it is that Holland, which, of all European countries, has the greatest number of religious sects, is also the country in which the sects agree best, and where the greatest tolerance reigns. If this were not so, the Catholic party would not have made so much way as it has made, protected in the beginning by the Liberal party against the only intolerant sect in the country—the orthodox Calvinists.

I did not know any orthodox Calvinists, to my great regret. I never believed what I have heard as to their extravagant ideas; that there are ladies, for instance, who hide the legs of their tables lest they should remind visitors of the legs of their hostess. But it is undeniable that they do live with extreme austerity. Many never put foot in a theatre, a ball-room, or even a concert-room. There are families who eat cold meat on Sundays rather than allow the cook to transgress the law of rest. In many houses the master reads the Bible every morning in the presence of his household, and all pray together. For the rest, this sect of orthodox Calvinists, which has almost all its proselytes among the aristocracy and the peasantry, exercises no great influence on the country, as is proved by the fact that in the Parliament it is inferior in number to the Catholics, and can do nothing without them.

I have spoken of the theatre. At the Hague, as in the other cities of Holland, there are no great theatres, and no great spectacles. For the most part they represent operas of German music, sung by foreign singers, and

French comedies and operettes. Concerts are much in fashion. In this, Holland is faithful to her traditions, since it has been noted, and Guicciardini also mentions it, that in the sixteenth century her musicians were sought for by all the courts of Christendom. It was also said that the Hollanders were very clever at singing in chorus. And great, indeed, must be the pleasure which they take in singing together, if it is proportionate to the aversion they seem to have to singing alone, for I do not remember to have heard in any Dutch town, at any hour of the night or day, a voice humming a tune in the streets.

I have spoken of French comedy and opera. At the Hague, not only the public entertainments, but all public life, is almost entirely French. Rotterdam has the English stamp, Amsterdam the German, and the Hague has the Parisian stamp; so that it is just to say that the people of the great Dutch cities unite and temper the qualities and defects of the three neighboring nations. At the Hague, in many families of the higher society, French is always spoken; in others they affect Frenchified ways, as in some cities of northern Italy; the addresses of letters are generally written in French; there is, in short, a portion of society, not a rare thing in small countries, who display rather ostentatiously a certain contempt for the language, literature, and art of their native country, and pay court to an adopted country beyond the Rhine and the Meuse. Sympathies, however, are divided. The elegant and fashionable set lean towards France, the learned ones towards Germany, and the mercantile class towards England. The sympathy for

France decreased after the Commune. Against Germany a secret animosity was born and is still fermenting, generated by the fear that her conquering gaze might soon be turned on Holland; but it is tempered by the common interest against Catholic clericalism.

When it is said that the Hague is a half French city, it is understood that appearance only is meant. At bottom the Dutch character predominates. Although it is rich, elegant, and gay, it is not a city of scandals, or evil speaking, or dissipation, or duelling. The life in it, however, is more varied and animated than that in the other Dutch cities, and somewhat less tranquil. The duels which occur at the Hague can be counted on the five fingers of the hand from ten years to ten years, and in those few an officer is generally the cause. Nevertheless, to show how potent is still in Holland the ferocious prejudice, as Rousseau says, " that honor dwells on the point of the sword," I recall a discussion among some Dutch gentlemen, brought about by a question of mine. When I asked whether public opinion in Holland was hostile to duelling, they answered with one voice " Very hostile "; but when I wished to know if a young man in good society, who should refuse a challenge, would be universally praised, treated by all with the same respect and attention as before, sustained, in short, in public opinion, so as never to repent of his conduct, then the discussion began. One weakly answered Yes, another resolutely No, but the majority said No. From which, I think, I may conclude that if duelling is not frequent in Holland, it is not, as I had thought, because of the universal and absolute contempt for the ferocious prejudice, but rather from the rarity of cases in which two citizens allow themselves to be driven by passion to the arbitrament of arms, which depends rather upon nature than education. In public discussion, or in very violent private argument, personalities are rare; and in the Parliamentary battles, which are sometimes very hot, the members are dryly impertinent, but calmly, and without noise; impertinence, I may say, more in facts, which wounds silently, than in words.

In the conversations at the club, I remarked that no one talked for the sake of talking. When anyone opened his mouth it was to ask a question, or to give a piece of news, or to make an observation. That art of making a period of every idea, a story of every fact, a question of every trifle, in which Italians, French, and Spanish are masters, is completely unknown to them. Conversation is not an exchange of sounds, but a commerce in things, and no one makes the slightest effort to appear learned, or eloquent, or acute. In all the time of my stay at the Hague, I remember to have heard only one witticism, and that was from a deputy, who, speaking of the alliance between the ancient Batavians and the Romans, said: "We have always been friends with the constituted authorities." And yet the Dutch language lends itself to puns; in proof of which I have heard cited the case of a lovely foreign lady, who, wishing to ask the boatman of the *tresekuit* for a pillow, pronounced the word badly and asked for a kiss, the two words being nearly the same in Dutch, and had scarcely time to explain the *equivoque*, the boatman wiping his lips with the back of his hand.

In my study of the Dutch character, it did not appear to me true, what I had read in several books, that the Hollanders are fond of talking about their maladies, and that they are avaricious and egotistical. As to the first accusation, they deride the Germans for this very defect. In support of the second, the rather incredible fact has been adduced that during a naval battle with the English the officers of the Dutch fleet went on board the enemy's ships, which were out of ammunition, and sold them powder and projectiles at exorbitant prices; after which the battle recommenced. Against this accusation of avarice stand the facts of the wealth and ease of the citizens, and the large sums spent in books and pictures; and still more in large beneficence, in which Dutch society is incontestably the first in Europe. And it is not official beneficence which in any way receives its impulse from the Government, but spontaneous, and very liberal, exercised by a large and powerful community which founds innumerable institutes, schools, prizes, libraries, popular meetings; which aids and precedes the Government in the work of public instruction; which extends its wings from the great city to the humblest village, covering all religious sects, all ages, all professions, and all needs; a beneficence, in short, by virtue of which there is not left in Holland one poor person without shelter, or an arm without work. All writers who have studied Holland agree in saying that there is perhaps no other state in Europe in which such copious alms descend from the wealthy to the needy classes, in proportion to the population.

It is not to be said, however, that the people of Holland are faultless, for they are not so, if we are to count as faults the want of those qualities which should be like the splendor and softness of their virtues. Their firmness is sometimes obstinacy; their probity has a touch of niggardliness; in their coldness is felt the absence of that spontaneity of feeling without which it seems as if there could be no affection, no generosity, no true greatness of soul. But the better we know them, the more we hesitate to pronounce such judgments, and the more we feel the growth of sympathy and respect for them. Voltaire could say, on leaving Holland, his famous words: "*Adieu, canaux, canards canaille*"; but when he judged Holland seriously, he remembered that in her capital cities he found "neither an idle man, nor a poor man, nor a dissipated man, nor an insolent man," and that he had seen everywhere "labor and modesty." Louis Napoleon proclaimed that in no people of Europe were good sense and the sentiments of reason and justice innate as in the Dutch; Descartes gave them the highest praise that a philosopher can give to a people, saying that in no country did one enjoy greater liberty than in Holland; Charles V. said that they were "the best of subjects, but the worst of slaves." An Englishman wrote that the Hollanders inspire an esteem that never reaches to affection. Perhaps he did not esteem them enough.

I do not conceal that among the causes of my sympathy is that of having found that Italy is much better known in Holland than I had dared to hope. Not only did the revolution in Italy find there a favorable echo, as is natural among an independent people, free, and hostile to the Papacy; but Italian men and events of late years are not less well known there than those of France and Germany. The principal journals, which have correspondents among us, keep the country minutely informed as to affairs in Italy. Portraits of her chief citizens are seen in various places. Nor is literary intelligence less regarded than political matters. Leaving aside the facts that Italian music was sung at the courts of the ancient counts of Holland, that in the best century of Dutch literature the Italian tongue was held in great honor among lettered people, and that some of the most illustrious poets of the time wrote letters and verses in Italian, or imitated our pastoral poetry, the Italian language is to this day much studied; it is not rare to find those who speak it, and still less rare is it to find our books upon the tables of the ladies. The "Divina Commedia," which came much into vogue after the year 1830, has two translations, both in *terza rima*, one of which is the work of Hacke van Mijnden, who consecrated all his life to Dante. The "Jerusalem Delivered" has a translation by a Protestant pastor, Ten Kate, and had another, unpublished, and now lost, by Maria Tesseeschave, the poetess of the seventeenth century and intimate friend of the great Dutch poet Vondel, who advised and aided her in the translation. Of the "Pastor Fido" there are at least five translations by different authors; several of the "Aminta"; and, to make a leap, at least four of Silvio Pellico's "Mie Prigaoni," and one very fine one of the "Promessi Sposi," a romance which few Hollanders have not read either in their own tongue or another. And to cite yet one more thing that regards us, there is a poem entitled "Florence," written for the last centenary of Dante by one of the most distinguished of the Dutch poets of our own day.

Here it becomes appropriate to say something of Dutch literature.

Holland presents a singular disproportion between the expansive force of her political, scientific, and commercial life, and that of her literary life. While under all other forms the works of the Hollanders find their way over the borders of their country, their literary work remains circumscribed within its confines. With a remarkable fertility of literary production, which renders the fact more strange, Holland has not produced, as other small countries have done, a single book which has become European, that is, if we except the works of Spinoza, the one great philosopher of his country, or consider as Dutch literature the forgotten Latin treatises of Erasmus of Rotterdam. And yet if there is a country where nature and events have offered subjects apt to inspire some of those poetic works which strike the imagination of every people, that country is Holland. The marvellous transformations of the soil, the immense inundations, the wonderful maritime expeditions, ought to generate an original poem, powerful even when deprived of its native form. Why has it never been done? Various reasons may be adduced. The peculiar character of the Dutch mind, which sees everything on the utility side, and often wishes to bend even literature to some practical purpose; a tendency, the direct opposite of this, and perhaps derived from it, to soar too much above human nature in order not to graze the earth; a certain natural circumspection in their genius, which gives to reason a sovereign superiority over fancy; the innate love of the exact and the finished, producing a prolixity in which great ideas are diluted; the spirit of religious sectarianism, which binds within a narrow circle minds that were born to spread themselves over a vast horizon. But neither these nor other reasons can do away with the wonder that there should not be in all Dutch literature a writer who worthily represents before the world the greatness of his country; a name to place between those of Rembrandt and Spinoza.

It would be wrong, however, to say nothing of the three principal figures in that literature, two of the seventeenth century and one of the nineteenth, three poets of originality, and differing much from each other, who represent a compendium of Dutch poetry: Vondel, Catz, and Bilderdijk.

Vondel is the greatest of the poets of Holland. He was born in 1587 at Cologne, where his father, a hatter, had fled from Antwerp to avoid the persecutions of the Spaniards. While still a child the future poet returned to his native country in a cart, with his father and mother following on foot, praying and reciting verses from the Bible. He made his first studies in Amsterdam. At fifteen years of age he already enjoyed fame as a poet; but his most celebrated works date only from 1620. Up to the age of thirty he knew no language but his own;

later he learned French and Latin, and gave himself up with ardour to classical studies; at fifty he dedicated himself to Greek. His first tragedy (he was a tragic poet principally), entitled "The Destruction of Jerusalem," had not much success. The second, called "Palamede," in which was shadowed forth the pitiful and terrible story of Olden-Barneveldt, the victim of Maurice of Orange, drew upon him a criminal prosecution, in consequence of which he fled and remained in hiding until the unexpectedly mild sentence condemning him to a fine of three hundred florins was pronounced. In 1627 he made a voyage to Denmark and Sweden, where he was received with honor by Gustavus Adolphus. Eleven years afterwards he inaugurated the Amsterdam theatre with a national drama called "Gilbert d'Amstel," which is still represented once a year in homage to his memory. The last years of his life were very unhappy. The dissipation of his son having reduced him to penury, the poor old man, weary of study and worn with pain, was obliged to ask for a small employment in the *Monté di Pietà*, or government pawn-broking establishment. A few years before his death he embraced the Catholic faith, and fired by a new inspiration, he wrote his tragedy of "The Virgins," and a poem which is one of the best of his works, entitled "The Mysteries of the Altar." He died very old, and was buried in a church at Amsterdam, where, a century later, a monument was erected to his memory. Besides his tragedies, he wrote patriotic war-songs, and others addressed to illustrious Dutch sailors, and to Prince Frederic Henry. But his principal glory is the theatre.

An admirer of Greek tragedy, he preserves in his own the unities, the chorus, the supernatural, substituting Providence for destiny, demons and angels for the avenging gods, and introducing the good and bad genii of Christianity. Almost all his subjects are taken from the Bible. His *chef d'œuvre* is the tragedy of "Lucifer," represented twice in spite of the almost insuperable difficulties of representation, in the theatre of Amsterdam, and there interdicted by the influence of the Protestant clergy. This tragedy has for its subject the rebellion of Lucifer, and for personages the good and bad angels. As in it, so in others, there are fanciful descriptions, full of splendid imagery, flashes of powerful eloquence, fine choruses, vigorous thoughts, solemn phrases, rich and sounding verses, and here and there flashes and sparkles of genius. On the other side there is a mysticism sometimes obscure and cold; the want of harmony between the Christian idea and the Pagan form; the lyric overpowering the dramatic; good taste often offended; and more than all, an exaltation of thought and sentiment, which, aiming at the sublime and rising too far above the earth, leaves the human heart and intellect below. Nevertheless, historic precedence, originality, ardent patriotism, his noble, suffering life, made Vondel great and venerated in his country, where he is considered as the most eminent personification of the national genius, and placed with affectionate audacity by the side of the first poets of other literatures.

Vondel is the greatest, Jacob Catz the purest, personification of Dutch genius; and not only is he the most popular of the poets of his nation, but such is his popularity, that it may be affirmed that in no other country, not exclusive of Cervantes in Spain and Manzoni in Italy, is there a writer more generally known or more constantly read than he; and I may add that there is not, perhaps, another poet in the world whose popularity is more necessarily restricted within the confines of his own country. Jacob Catz was born in 1577, of a patrician family in Brouwershaven, a town in Zealand. He studied law, became Pensionary of Middlebourg, went as ambassador to England, was made Grand Pensionary of Holland, and executing with exemplary zeal and rectitude these high offices, cultivated poetry with a loving spirit. In the evening, after having treated of State affairs with deputies from the provinces, he withdrew into his house, and made verses. At seventy-five years of age, he asked to be relieved of his offices, and when the Stadtholder announced to him in honorable words that his demand was granted, he fell on his knees in presence of the assembly of the States, and thanked God for having always protected him in the course of his long and laborious political life. A few days afterwards he retired to one of his villas, where he continued to enjoy a tranquil and honoured old age, studying and writing verses, until 1660, when he died, more than eighty years old, wept by all Holland.

His poetry forms several large volumes. There are fables, madrigals, stories, and mythological tales, sprinkled with descriptions, citations, sentences, and precepts; full of kindness, honesty, and sweetness, and written with ingenuous simplicity and delicate wit. His volume is the book of national wisdom, the second Bible of the Dutch people, a manual for the teaching of an honest and peaceful life. He gives counsel to all; to the youth and to the old man, to the merchant as to the prince, to the mistress as to the servant, to the rich man as to the mendicant. He teaches how to spend, how to spare, how to keep a house, how to govern a family, how to educate children. He is at the same time friend, father, spiritual director, master, steward, physician, advocate. He loves modest nature, the gardens, the fields, adores his wife; he works, is content with himself and others, and desires that all should be as happy as he. His poetry is found in every house beside the Bible. There is not a peasant's hut where the head of the family does not read some of his verses aloud every evening. In days of doubt and sadness all seek and find comfort in their old poet. He is the fire-side friend, the assiduous companion of the infirm or sick; over his book the faces of betrothed lovers first approach each other; his verses are the first to be learned by the child, and the last to be pronounced by the grandfather. No poet was ever more beloved. Every Hollander smiles at the sound of his name, and no foreigner has been in Holland without learning to pronounce it with sympathy and respect.

The third, Bilderdijk, born in 1756, died in 1831, was one of the most wonderful intellects that has ever appeared in the world. Poet, historian, philologist, critic, astronomer, chemist, theologian, antiquarian, jurisconsult, draughtsman, engraver; a restless man and a wanderer, capricious, violent, his life was but an investigation, a transformation, a perpetual battle of his vast genius. Young, and already a famous poet, he left poetry, threw himself into politics, emigrated to England with the Stadtholder, and taught in London for a living. Tired of England, he went to Germany; weary of German romanticism, he returned to Holland, where Louis Napoleon loaded him with favours. But Louis descended from the throne, and Napoleon the Great took away Bilderdijk's pension, and reduced him to poverty. He asked for a chair in the University of Leyden, and was refused. Finally, he obtained a small subsidy from the Government, and continued to write and study and combat up to the last day of his life. His works are composed of more than thirty volumes of science, art, and literature. He treated every kind of subject, and succeeded in all except the drama. He enlarged the field of historical criticism, writing one of the finest national histories that his country possesses. He wrote a poem, " The Primitive World," a grandiose and obscure work, much admired in Holland. He treated every kind of question, mingling strange paradoxes and luminous truths. Finally, he raised the national literature, which had fallen before his time, and left a phalanx of elect disciples who followed his steps in politics, art, and philosophy. He excited more than enthusiasm in Holland, he excited fanaticism; and it cannot be doubted that, after Vondel, he is the greatest poet of his country. But he was injured by religious passion, a blind hatred against the new ideas, poetry made the instrument of a sect, theology intermingled with everything, so that he never rose into that region of serenity and freedom, outside of which genius gains no enduring victories or universal acknowledgment.

About these three poets, who have in them the three principal vices of Dutch literature—to lose itself in the clouds, or to graze the earth too near, or to be caught in the net of mysticism—are grouped numbers of others, epic, comic, satiric, lyric, most of them of the seventeenth century, very few of the eighteenth; many of whom enjoy great fame in Holland, but none of whom stands out in relief from the rest sufficient to draw the attention of a foreigner.

A rapid glance is due to the present day. That criticism, despoiling Dutch history of the poetic veil in which patriotic writers have dressed her, has conducted her along the wider and more fertile paths of justice; that philological studies are held in the highest honor, and that almost all the sciences have in Holland professors of European fame—are things that no studious man in Italy is ignorant of, and need only to be hinted at.

Of literature properly so called, the most flourishing kind is Romance. Holland has had her national romance-writer, her Walter Scott, in Van Lennep, who died only a few years ago, and whose historical novels were received with enthusiasm by all classes of society; a most excellent painter of costume, learned, witty, a master of description and admirable in dialogue; but who is often prolix, and makes use of old artifices, and does not always hide himself sufficiently, while he frequently forces the *dénouement* of his plot. His last novel, entitled "The Adventures of Nicoletta Zevenster "—in which, representing, in a masterly manner, Dutch society at the beginning of this century, he had the audacity to describe an unnameable house at the Hague—was commented upon, discussed, abused, and lauded to the skies; and the battle still goes on. Other historical romances were written by Schimmel, an emulator of Van Leunep; and one Madame Rosboon Toussaint, a cultivated writer, rich in study and deep genius. Nevertheless, historical romance, even in Holland, may be considered as dead. Better fortune attends romances of manners and novels, in which one Beets is first, a poet and Protestant minister, author of a celebrated book called the "Dark Chamber." There is also Koetsveld, and some young men of talent, who contend with each other in raising up that persecuting demon of the literature of the day—haste.

Holland has also a kind of romance quite her own, which may be called Indian romance, and which paints the manners and the life of the people of the colonies; and several of this kind have appeared of late years, which have been received with much applause in the country, and have been translated into various languages; among others, "The Beau monde of Batavia," by Professor Ten Briuck, a learned and brilliant writer, whom I wish I could speak of at greater length, in order to attest in some way my gratitude and admiration. But apropos of Indian romances, it is interesting to note how, in Holland, you hear and see at every step something to remind you of her colonies; how a ray of the sun of India seems to penetrate through her fogs and color her life. Besides the ships which bring a breath of that country into her ports—besides the birds, the flowers, the thousand objects, that, like scattered strains of distant music, bring to the mind fancies of another nature and another race—it is not rare to meet in the streets of the Dutch cities, in the midst of the white faces, visages bronzed by the sun, of people born in the colonies, or who have lived there for many years; merchants who talk with unusual vivacity about brunettes, bananas, groves of palms, and lakes embowered in vines; bold young men who risk their lives in the midst of the savages of Borneo and Sumatra; men of science, men of letters, and officers, who tell about the worshippers of fishes, or ambassadors who carry the heads of the vanquished suspended from their girdles, combats between bulls and tigers, the furies of opium-eaters or multitudes baptised with pomp; or a thousand other strange and wonderful things, which occasion a singular effect when uttered by the cold natives of this most tranquil land.

Poetry, after having lost Da Costa, a disciple of Bilderdijk, and a religious and enthusiastic poet, and Genestel, a satirical poet, who died very young, has but few specimens left of the past generation, who are mostly silent, or sing with faint voices. The theatre is in a worse condition. Dutch actors, declamatory and untrained, act in general only French or German dramas and comedies, which are badly translated, and which high society will not go to see. Dutch writers of talent, like Hofdijk, Schimmel, and the before-mentioned Van Leunep, wrote comedies which, in some respects, were admirable, but did not please enough to keep the stage. Tragedy is in no better condition than comedy or drama.

From what I have said it would appear that there is no great literary movement in Holland; but there is, in fact, a great deal. The quantity of books published is incredible; and so is the avidity with which they are read. Every city, every religious sect, every society has its review or its journal. There is, besides, a flood of foreign books; English novels in every hand; French works in eight, ten, twenty volumes, translated into the national tongue, an admirable thing in a country where every educated person can read them in the original, and which proves that it is usual not only to read them but to buy them, notwithstanding the fact that books in Holland are very dear. But it is precisely this superabundance of publications, and this rage for reading, which injures literature. Authors, in order to satisfy the impatient curiosity of the public, write too fast, and the mania for foreign reading suffocates and corrupts the national genius. Nevertheless, Dutch literature has still a title to the gratitude of the country; it is fallen but not perverted; it has preserved its innocence and freshness; what it lacks in fancy, in originality, in splendor, is made up in good sense, in severe respect for good taste and good manners, in benevolent solicitude for the poorer classes, in efficacious works for the promotion of beneficence and civil education. Other literatures are great plants covered with odorous flowers; Dutch literature is a little tree loaded with fruit.

On the morning that I left the Hague, the second time

that I was there, some of my dearest friends accompanied me to the railway station. The weather was rainy. In the waiting-room I thanked my kind hosts for the pleasant welcome they had given me; and as I knew I should not probably ever see them again, I expressed my gratitude in affectionate and melancholy words, which they listened to in silence. One only interrupted me to beg me to be careful against the dampness. "Should anyone belonging to you come to Italy," I continued, "it would give me the opportunity to show my gratitude. Promise me that someone will come, and I shall depart with a feeling of consolation. I will not go until someone tells me that he will come to Italy." They looked at each other, and one of them answered faintly, "Perhaps." Another gave me the advice never to change French gold in the shops.

At that moment the bell for departure rang out.

"Farewell, then," I said, in a slightly agitated voice, pressing their hands; "until we meet again. I shall never forget the pleasant days I have passed at the Hague. I shall always remember you all among the most agreeable memories of my journey; think of me sometimes." "Good-bye," they answered, in the same tone as if they expected to meet me again next day. I entered the carriage with a heavy heart, and looked out of the window until the train moved on; and they stood there mute, impassible, with their eyes fixed on mine. Waving my hand for the last time, they responded with a slight nod, and disappeared for ever from my eyes. Every time I think of them, I see them as they stood there, with grave faces and fixed eyes, and the affection I feel for them has something of the austere and sad, like their own skies, under which I saw them for the last time.

———

LEYDEN.

THE country between the Hague and Leyden is all one verdant plain, dotted by the vivid red of the roofs and streaked by the blue of the canals; with here and there groups of trees, windmills, and scattered herds of cattle. You move onwards and seem still to be at the same point, gazing at the same objects. The train glides on slowly and almost noiselessly through the silent country; in the carriage no one speaks, at the stations no voice is heard, and gradually the mind settles into a sort of doze, in which you forget where you are and whither you are going. "And yet," says Diderot, travelling in Holland, "and yet people do sleep in this country!" The remark came often to my lips as we sped along, until I heard the cry of "Leyden!" and alighted at a station, silent and solitary as a convent,

Leyden, the antique Athens of the north, the Saragossa of the Low Countries, the oldest and most illustrious of the daughters of Holland, is one of those cities which make you thoughtful upon first entering them, and are remembered for a long time afterwards with a certain impression of sadness.

I had hardly arrived when the chill of a dead city seemed to fall upon me. The old Rhine, which crosses Leyden, dividing it into many islets joined together by one hundred and fifty stone bridges, forms wide canals and basins which contain no ship or boat, and the city seems rather invaded by the waters than merely crossed by them. The principal streets are very broad and flanked by rows of old blockhouses with the usual pointed gables, and the few people seen in the streets and squares are like the survivors of a city depopulated by the plague. In the smaller streets you walk upon long tracts of grass, between houses with closed doors and windows, in a silence as profound as that of those fabled cities where all the inhabitants are sunk in a supernatural sleep. You pass over bridges overgrown with weeds, and long canals covered with a green carpet, through small squares that seem like convent courtyards; and then, suddenly, you reach a broad thoroughfare, like the streets of Paris; from which you again penetrate into a labyrinth of narrow alleys. From bridge to bridge, from canal to canal, from island to island, you wander for hours seeking for the life and movement of the ancient Leyden, and finding only solitude, silence, and the waters which reflect the melancholy majesty of the fallen city.

After a long turn, I came out into a vast square where a squadron of cavalry was going through its exercises. An old cicerone who accompanied me, stopped me under the shade of a tree, and told me that the square, called in Dutch the Ruin, commemorated a great disaster to the city of Leyden. "Before 1807," he mumbled in broken French, and in a schoolmaster's tone peculiar to all Dutch ciceroni, " this great space was all covered with houses, and the canal that now crosses it ran through the middle of a street. On the 12th of January 1807, a ship laden with gunpowder, which lay here, blew up, and eight hundred houses with several hundred people flew up in the air, and so this square was formed. Among the inhabitants who perished was the illustrious historian John Luzuc, who was afterwards buried in the church of St. Peter, with a fine inscription; and among the houses which flew up in the air was that of the Elzevir family, the glory of Dutch typography." "The house of the Elzevirs!" thought I, in agreeable surprise; and certain bibliomaniacs whom I knew in Italy came to my mind, who would have been but too happy to press with their feet the ground which had once sustained that illustrious house, whence had issued those small marvels of typography which they sought for, dreamed of, and caressed with such warm affection; those tiny books that seemed stamped in adamantine characters; those models of fineness and precision, in which a typographical error is a portent which duplicates the value of the prize; those wonders of polytype, of twists and flourishes, and tail-pieces, which they discuss in low voices and with glistening eyes!

Coming out of the square of Ruin I entered the Breede Straat, the broadest and longest of the Leyden streets, which crosses the city from one end to the other in the form of an S, and arrived in front of the City Hall, which is one of the most curious buildings of the sixteenth century. At first sight it has a theatrical appearance and contrasts unpleasantly with the grave aspect of the city. It is a long, low building, of an ash color, with a bare façade, along the top of which runs a stone balustrade, ornamented with obelisks, pyramids, and aerial frontispieces set off with grotesque statues, the whole forming a sort of fantastic embroidery around the steep roof. Opposite to the principal entrance rises a bell-tower composed of several stories, one within the other, giving it the aspect of a very tall kiosk, with an enormous iron crown upon the top in form of a reversed balloon, surmounted by a flagstaff. Above the door, which is approached by two flights of steps, there is an inscription in Dutch, commemorating the famine of 1574, composed in one hundred and thirty-one letters, corresponding to the number of days of the duration of the siege of Leyden.

Going into the palace, I wandered from room to room without encountering a living soul or hearing a sound that indicated habitation, until at last I came across an usher, who placed himself at my side, and making me cross a large room where sat some clerks, as motionless as images, he conducted me to the hall of curiosities. The first object that attracted my attention was a disjointed table, upon which, if the tradition is true, the famous tailor, John of Leyden, worked; he who, in the beginning of the sixteenth century, turned the country upside down, as had been done five centuries before by Tankelyn, of obscene memory; that John of Leyden, the leader of the Anabaptists, who held the city of Munster against the Count Bishop of Waldeck, and was there elected king by his fanatical partisans; that pious prophet, who had a seraglio of women, and who cut off the head of one of them because she complained of hunger; that John of Leyden, in short, who, at the age of twenty-six, died, torn by red-hot irons, and whose body, enclosed in an iron cage on the top of a tower, was devoured by crows. He did not succeed, however, in exciting the fanaticism which was raised by Tankelyn, to whom women prostituted themselves in the sight of their husbands and mothers, persuaded that they were doing what was grateful to God; and men drank, as a water of purification, the water in which he had washed his filthy person.

In other rooms there are paintings by Hinck, Francis Mieris, Cornelius Engelbrechsten, and a "Last Judgment" by Luca von Leyden, the patriarch of Dutch painting, the first who seized the laws of aerial perspective, a valiant colorist and engraver of great fame, to whom, it is to be hoped, will be forgiven in the next world the ignoble ugliness of the Marys and Magdalens, the burlesque saints and convulsive angels, with which he has peopled his canvas. He also, like almost all the Dutch painters, had a most adventurous life. He travelled about Holland in a boat of his own; in every city he gathered the painters together at a banquet. He was, or believed himself to be, poisoned by some slow poison administered by his rivals. He kept his bed for years, and painted in bed his *chef d'œuvre*, "The Blind Man of

Jericho cured by Christ." He died two years afterwards, on a day memorable for a prodigious heat, which killed many, and produced much illness.

Coming out of the City Hall, I went up to a castle posted upon a small hill which rises in the midst of the city, between the two principal branches of the Rhine; the most ancient part of Leyden. This castle, called by Hollanders the " Burg," is no other than a great round tower, quite empty, built, according to some authorities, by the Romans; according to others by one Hengist, Duke of the Anglo-Saxons; and recently restored and crowned with battlements. The hill is covered by tall oak trees, which hide the tower and prevent the enjoyment of the surrounding view; only here and there, looking through the branches, can glimpses be caught of the red roofs of Leyden, the plain streaked with canals, the downs, and the bell-towers of the distant city.

On the top of that tower, under the shadow of the oaks, it is usual for the stranger to evoke the memories of that siege which was " the most dismal tragedy of modern times," and which seems to have left an indelible trace of sadness upon the aspect of Leyden.

In 1573 the Spaniards, led by Valdez, laid siege to Leyden. In the city there were only some volunteer soldiers. The military command was given to Van der Voes, a valiant man, and a Latin poet of some renown. Van der Werf was burgomaster. In brief time the besiegers had constructed more than sixty forts in all the places where it was possible to penetrate into the city by sea or land, and Leyden was completely isolated. But the people of Leyden did not lose heart. William of Orange had sent them word to hold out for three months, within which time he would succour them, for on the fate of Leyden depended that of Holland; and the men of Leyden had promised to resist to the last extremity. Valdez sent to offer them pardon in the name of the King of Spain, if they would open their gates. They replied with a Latin verse: "*Fistula dulce canit, volucrem dum decipit anceps,*" and began to make sorties and to attack. Meanwhile, within the city provisions began to grow scarce, and the circle of the besiegers grew tighter from day to day. William of Orange, who occupied the fortress of Polderwaert, between Delft and Rotterdam, seeing no other way to succour the city, conceived the design of raising the siege of Leyden by breaking the dykes of the Issel and the Meuse, and driving out the Spaniards by water, since it could not be done by arms. This desperate design was forthwith put in action. The dykes being broken in sixty places, the sluice-gates of Rotterdam and Gonda were opened, the sea began to invade the land, and two hundred barges were in readiness at Rotterdam, at Deftshaven, and other points, to carry provisions into the city as soon as the great rise of the waters should take place which comes with the autumnal equinox. The Spaniards, startled at the first news of the inundation, were reassured when they understood the purpose of the Hollanders, holding it certain that the city must surrender before the waters could arrive at the first fortifications, and pushed on the siege with redoubled vigor. In the meantime, the people of Leyden, who began to feel the pressure of famine, and to despair of succour arriving in time, sent letters by means of pigeons to William of Orange, who was sick of fever at Amsterdam, to lay before him the sad condition of the city; and William responded, encouraging them to protracted resistance, promising that as soon as he was better he would fly in person to their aid. The waters advanced; the Spaniards began to abandon the lower fortifications; the inhabitants of Leyden continually climbed the tower to watch the sea, now hoping, now despairing, and never ceased to work at the walls, to make sorties, and to repulse attacks. At last the Prince of Orange got well, and preparations for the deliverance of Leyden, which during his illness had gone on but slowly, were now resumed with vigor. On the 1st of September the people of Leyden, from the top of their tower, saw appear upon the distant waters the first Dutch vessels. It was a small fleet, commanded by Admiral Boisot, and carrying eight hundred Zealanders, savage men, covered with scars, accustomed to the sea, disdainful of life, fierce in battle, wearing in their caps a crescent on which was inscribed "Rather Turks than Papists," and forming a phalanx of strange and terrible aspect, resolute to save Leyden or to perish in the waters. The ships advanced to within five miles of the city, against the outermost dyke, which was defended by the Spaniards. The battle began with the assault upon the dyke, which was taken, cut, the sea broke in, and the Dutch vessels floated triumphantly through the breach. It was a great step, but it was only the first. Behind this dyke there was another. Again the battle began; the second dyke was taken and cut, and the fleet passed on.

All at once the wind changed to the contrary quarter, and the ships were constrained to stop; it changed again, and they went on; it shifted once more, and again the fleet was arrested.

Whilst this was going on, within the city there began to be a scarcity even of the disgusting animals on which the citizens had been constrained to feed; people threw themselves on the ground to lick up the blood of the slain; women and children searched for scraps of food among the refuse in the streets; an epidemic broke out; the houses were full of corpses; more than sixteen thousand citizens died; every hope of relief had perished. A crowd of famishing people rushed to the burgomaster Van der Werff, and demanded the surrender of the city with loud cries. Van der Werff refused. The people broke into threats. Then he made a sign with his hat that he wished to speak, and in the midst of the general silence, cried: " Citizens of Leyden ! I have sworn to defend the city unto death, and with the help of God, I will maintain my oath. It is better to die of hunger than of shame. Your threats do not move me. I can die but once. Kill me, if you will, and satiate your hunger on my flesh; but while I live do not ask me to surrender Leyden !" The crowd, moved by his words, dispersed in silence, resigned to death, and the defence went on. At last, on the night of the 1st of October, a violent tempest of wind burst out; the sea rose, overwhelmed the ruined dykes, and furiously invaded the land. At midnight, when the tempest was at its height, in profound darkness, the Dutch fleet once more set sail. Some Spanish vessels came to meet them. Then began a terrible battle among the tops of trees and the roofs of submerged houses, by the light of the cannon-flashes. The Spanish ships were boarded and sunk; the Zealanders jumped overboard and pushed their vessels forward with their shoulders; the Spanish soldiers, seized with terror, abandoned the forts, fell by hundreds into the sea, were killed with daggers and grappling-irons, precipitated from roofs and dykes, destroyed, dispersed. One more fortress remained in the hands of Valdez; the besiegers wavered yet a little between hope and despair; then this fortress was abandoned; the Dutch fleet entered the city.

Here a horrible spectacle awaited them. A population of bony spectres, almost dead with hunger, crowded the banks of the canals, staggering, and falling, and stretching out their arms towards the ships. The sailors began to throw bread to them, and then ensued among these dying men a desperate struggle; many were suffocated; others died in the act of eating; others fell into the canals. The first rage of hunger satisfied, the most crying need of the city provided for, citizens, Zealanders, sailors, civic guards, soldiers, women, and children, and all that glorious and wasted crowd rushed to the cathedral, where they sang, in voices broken by sobs, a hymn of thanks and praise to God.

The Prince of Orange received the news of the safety of the city at Delft, in church, where he was present at Divine service. He sent the message at once to the preacher, and the latter announced it to the congregation, who received it with shouts of joy. Although only just recovered from his illness, and the epidemic still raging at

Leyden, William would see at once his dear and valorous city. He went there; his entry was a triumph; his majestic and serene aspect put new heart into the people; his words made them forget all they had suffered. To reward Leyden for her heroic defence, he left her her choice between exemption from certain imposts or the foundation of a university. Leyden chose the university.

The festival of the inauguration of the university was celebrated on the 5th of February 1575 with a solemn procession. First came a company of the burgher militia, and five companies of infantry from the garrison of Leyden, behind whom came a car drawn by four horses, in which was a woman dressed in white, who represented the Gospel, and around the car the four Evangelists. Justice, with her eyes bandaged, followed, carrying the scales and sword, mounted on a unicorn, and surrounded by Julius, Papinius, Ulpius, and Tribinius. After Justice came Medicine, on horseback, with a treatise in one hand and in the other a garland of medicinal herbs, and accompanied by the four great doctors—Hippocratus, Galen, Dioscoridus, and Theophrastus. Minerva followed, armed with lance and shield, and escorted by four horsemen who represented Plato, Aristotle, Cicero, and Virgil. Between all these came warriors in ancient armour; and the procession ended with halberdiers, mace-bearers, music, officials, the new professors, the magistrates, and a great crowd. It passed slowly through streets strewn with flowers, under triumphal arches, between hangings and banners, until it reached a small port on the Rhine, where it encountered a large vessel, splendidly decorated, upon which, under a canopy of laurel and orange boughs, sat Apollo, playing on the lute, surrounded by the nine muses singing, and Neptune, saviour of the city, who acted as helmsman. The vessel approached the shore; the golden-haired god and the nine sisters landed, and kissed one after another the new professors, saluting them with Latin verses; after which the procession went onwards to the building destined for the university, where a professor of theology, the Very Reverend Gaspar Kolhas, pronounced an eloquent inaugural address, preceded by music and followed by a splendid banquet.

How this university answered to the hopes of Leyden, it is superfluous to say. Everybody knows how the States of Holland with their liberal offers drew learned men from every country; how philosophy, driven out of France, took refuge there; how Leyden was for a long time the securest citadel for all men who were struggling for the triumph of human reason; how it became at length the most famous school in Europe. The actual university is in an ancient convent. One cannot enter without a sentiment of profound respect the great hall of the Academic Senate, where are seen the portraits of all the professors who have succeeded each other from the foundation of the university up to the present day. Among them are Lipseus, Vossius, Heinsius, Gronovius, Herastuhuys, Ruhncken, Valckeneer, the great Scaliger, whom the States of Holland invited to Leyden through the intervention of Henry IV.; the two famous men, Gomarius and Arminius, who provoked the great definite religious struggle of the synod of Dordrecht; the celebrated physician Boerhaave, at whose lessons Peter the Great attended, to whom came invalids from all parts of Europe, and who received a letter from a Chinese mandarin with the simple direction: *" To the illustrious Boerhaave, physician in Europe."*

Now this glorious university, although it still has illustrious professors, is declining. Its students, who in the old time amounted to two thousand, are now reduced to a few hundreds. The instruction which is given there cannot any more rival that of the universities of Berlin, Munich, or Weimar. The principal reason for this decadence is to be found in the number of Dutch universities. Besides that at Leyden, there is one at Utrecht, one at Groeningen, and an Athenæum at Amsterdam; whence it follows that the libraries, museums, and eminent professors which gathered in one city would form an excellent university, are now scattered about, and are unequal to their task. Yet Holland is none the less convinced that one single excellent university would serve her better than four inferior ones. And why is it not done? O reader, all the world is one country. It is the same in Holland as elsewhere. The three university towns cry out together, "Let us suppress them!" and each one says to the other, "You begin"; and so they go on.

But, although fallen, the Leyden University is still the most flourishing in Holland, more especially for the numerous and rich museums which belong to it. Neither of these, however, nor of the libraries, nor of the admirable botanic gardens, would it be proper to treat, as I should have to do, lightly and hastily. I cannot forget two very curious things in the Museum of Natural History, one ridiculous and one serious. The first, which is in the anatomical cabinet (one of the richest in Europe), is an orchestra formed of fifty skeletons of very small mice, some erect, some sitting on a double row of benches, all with tails in the air, and with violins and guitars in their paws, music-books before them, cigars in their mouths, handkerchiefs and snuff-boxes beside them; and the leader gesticulating from an elevated seat. The serious thing consists of some pieces of corroded wood, full of holes like a sponge, fragments of piles and sluice-gates, which recall an immense danger run by Holland towards the middle of the last century. A shell-fish, a species of wood-worm, called *taret*, brought, it is believed, by some ship returning from the tropics, and multiplying with marvellous rapidity in northern waters, had so corroded and gnawed the wood of the dykes, that had it gone on for a short time longer without discovery, the sea would have broken in and flooded the whole country. The discovery of this danger threw Holland into dismay, the people rushed to the churches, and the entire population set to work; they lined the sluice-gates with copper, they fortified the injured dykes, they strengthened the piles with nails, with stone, with sea-weed, and with masonry; and partly by these means, but especially by the rigor of the climate, which destroyed the terrible animal, the horrible calamity, feared at first as irreparable, was avoided. A worm had made Holland tremble; triumph denied to the tempests of the ocean and the anger of Philip of Spain.

Another precious ornament of Leyden is the Japanese museum of Doctor Siebold, a German by birth, physician to the Dutch colony in the Island of Detsima; who, according to a romantic tradition, first obtained permission from the Emperor of Japan to enter his mysterious empire in reward for having cured his daughter; or, according to a more credible tradition, he got into the country in disguise, and did not come out again until he had paid for his temerity with nine months of imprisonment, and caused the loss of their heads to some mandarins who had aided him in his enterprise. However this may be, Doctor Siebold's museum, is, perhaps, the finest collection of the kind that is to be found in Europe. An hour passed in the rooms is a voyage to Japan. There you can follow a Japanese family throughout the entire day; from the morning toilet to the dinner, from the theatre to visiting, from the city to the country. There are to be found houses, temples, idols, portable altars, instruments of music, household utensils, agricultural tools, costumes of laborers and fishermen; bronze candle-sticks formed of a stork standing on a tortoise; vases, jewels, poignards wrought with exquisite delicacy; birds, tigers, rabbits, buffaloes in ivory, reproduced feather by feather and hair by hair, with the patience peculiar to that ingenious and patient people. Among the objects which impressed me most, was a colossal head of Buddha, which at first made me recoil, and which is ever before me, with its monstrous contraction and inexplicable look between laughter, delirium, and spasm, which excites at once both disgust and terror.

Behind this face of Buddha I saw the puppets of the Java theatres, real creations of a delirious brain, wearying the eye and confounding the mind; kings, queens, and monstrous warriors, mixtures of man, beast, and plant, with arms ending in leaves, legs finished with ornaments, leaves spreading into hands, breasts in a state of vegetation, noses opening into flowers, faces full of holes, squinting eyes, eyeballs in the back of the neck, limbs turned hind part before, dragons' wings, Sirens' tails, hair like snakes, fishes' mouths, elephants' teeth, gilded wrinkles, zig-zag necks, and attitudes which no tongue can describe, nor any memory retain. Coming out of the museum, I seemed to awaken from some fever-dream in which I had seen something, I knew not what, continually changing with furious rapidity into some other nameless thing.

There is nothing else to be seen at Leyden. The mill where Rembrandt was born is no longer in existence. Of the houses where were born the painters Dow, Steen, Metzu, Van Goyen, and that Otto van Veen who had the honour and the misfortune to be master to Peter Paul Rubens, there is no trace or record. The castle of Endegeest may still be seen, where Boerhaave and Descartes sojourned, the last for several years, during which his principal works of philosophy and mathematics were written. The castle is on the road from Leyden to the village of Katwijk, where the old Rhine, uniting its various branches into one, throws itself into the sea.

The second time I was at Leyden I went to see the death of the marvellous river. The first time that I crossed the old Rhine, I had stopped on the bridge, asking myself whether that small and humble stream of water was really the same river that I had seen rushing in thunder over the rocks at Schaffhausen, spreading majestically before Mayence, passing in triumph under the fortress of Ehrenbreitstein, beating in sonorous cadence at the foot of the Seven Mountains; reflecting in its course Gothic cathedrals, princely castles, fertile hills, steep rocks, famous ruins, cities, groves, and gardens; everywhere covered with vessels of all sorts, and saluted with music and song; and thinking of these things, with my gaze fixed upon the little stream shut in between two flat and desert shores, I had repeated, " Is this that Rhine?"

The vicissitudes which accompany the agony and death of this great river in Holland, are such as really to excite a sense of pity, such as is felt for the misfortunes and inglorious end of a people once powerful and happy. From the neighbourhood of Emmerich, before reaching the Dutch frontier, it has lost all the beauty of its banks, and flows in great curves through vast and ugly flats, which seem to mark the approach to old age. At Millingen it runs entirely in the territory of Holland; a little farther on it divides. The main branch shamefully loses its name, and goes to throw itself into the Meuse; the other branch, insulted by the title of the Dannerden canal, flows nearly to the city of Arnehm, when it once more divides into two branches. One empties into the Gulf of Zuyder-Zee; the other still called, out of compassion, the Lower Rhine, goes as far as the village of Durstede, where it divides for the third time; a humiliation now of old date. One of these branches, changing its name like a coward, throws itself into the Meuse near Rotterdam; the other still called the Rhine, but with the ridiculous surname of " curved," reaches Utrecht with difficulty, where for the fourth time it again divides; capricious as an old man in his dotage. One part, denying its old name, drags itself as far as Muiden, where it falls into the Zuyder Zee; the other, with the name of Old Rhine, or simply the Old, flows slowly to the city of Leyden, whose streets it crosses almost without giving a sign of movement, and is finally gathered into one canal by which it goes to its miserable death in the North Sea.

But it is not many years since even this pitiful end was denied it. From the year 839, in which a furious tempest had accumulated mountains of sand at its mouth, until the beginning of the present century, the Old Rhine lost itself in the sand before reaching the sea, and covered a vast tract of country with pools and marshes. Under the reign of Louis Buonaparte the waters were collected into a large canal protected by three enormous sluice-gates, and from that time the Rhine flows directly to the sea. These sluices are the greatest monument in Holland and, perhaps, the most admirable hydraulic work in Europe. The dykes which protect the mouth of the canal, the walls, pillars, and gates, present altogether the aspect of a Cyclopian fortress, against which it seems that not only that sea, but the united forces of all seas, must break as against a granite mountain. When the tide rises the gates are closed to prevent the waters from invading the land; when the tide recedes they are opened to give passage to the waters of the Rhine which have accumulated behind them; and then a mass of three thousand cubic feet of water passes through them in one minute. On days when storms prevail, a concession is made to the sea, and the most advanced of the sluice-gates is left open; and then the furious billows rush into the canal, like an enemy entering by a breach, but they break upon the formidable barrier of the second gate, behind which Holland stands and cries, "Thus far shalt thou go, and no farther!" That enormous fortification which, on a desert shore, defends a dying river and a fallen city from the ocean, has something of solemnity which commands respect and admiration.

Again I look upon Leyden as I saw her on the evening of my return from an excursion, dark and silent like a deserted city, and speak a reverent farewell, with my mind already cheered by the thought of Haarlem, the city of landscapes and flowers.

HAARLEM.

The railway from Leyden to Haarlem runs upon a strip of land comprised between the sea and the bottom of that great lake which thirty years ago covered all the country and which lies between Haarlem, Leyden, and Amsterdam. The stranger travelling on that road with an old map printed before 1850, looks about him and can find no lake of Haarlem. This happened to myself; and the thing appearing strange, I turned to a neighbor and demanded an account of the vanished lake. My fellow travellers laughed, and my question received the following odd reply: "We have drunk it up."

The story of this wonderful work would be a subject worthy of a poem.

The great lake of Haarlem, joined by the meeting of four small lakes, and swelled by the effects of inundations, had already, at the end of the seventeenth century, a circuit of forty-four kilometres, and was called a sea. A sea indeed it was, and a tempestuous one, in which fleets of seventy ships had fought, and many vessels had been wrecked. Thanks to the downs which stretched along its shores, this great mass of water had not yet been able to join itself to the North Sea, and thus convert Southern Holland into an island; but on the other side, it threatened the country, the towns and villages, and constrained the inhabitants to be continually on the defensive. Already in 1640 a Dutch engineer of the name of Leeghwater had published a book with the design of showing the possibility and utility of draining this dangerous lake; but partly because of the difficulties presented by the method proposed by him, and more because the country was then engaged in the war with Spain, the undertaking found no promoters. The political events which followed the peace of 1648, and the disastrous wars between France and England, caused Leeghwater's project to be forgotten until the beginning of the present century. Finally, towards 1819, the question was resumed, and new studies and new proposals made; but the execution was still deferred, and, perhaps, would not even yet have been brought to a conclusion, but for an unforeseen event which gave it the final impulse. On the 9th of November 1836, the waters of the Haarlem sea, driven by a furious wind, overflowed the dykes and reached even to the gates of Amsterdam; and in the following month they invaded Leyden and all the country about the city. It was the final provocation. Holland took up the glove, and in 1839 the States General condemned the insolent sea to vanish from the face of the state. The works were begun in 1840. They commenced by the construction of a double dyke around the lake, and a broad canal destined to receive the waters, which then, by other canals, would be conducted to the sea. The lake contained seven hundred and twenty-four millions of cubic metres of water, without counting rains and filtration which, during the draining, were found to amount to thirty-three millions of cubic metres of water per year. The engineers had computed the quantity of water which would pass monthly from the lake through the canal at thirty-six millions two hundred thousand cubic metres. Three enormous steam-engines were sufficient for the work. One was placed near Haarlem, another between Haarlem and Amsterdam, the third near Leyden. This last was named Leeghwater, in honor of the engineer who had first proposed the scheme. I saw it, for not only is it preserved, but is still in use at times, to absorb and turn into the canal the rain-water and that of filtration. And so with the other two, which equal the last. The engines are enclosed in large, round, battlemented towers, each one of which is encircled by a row of windows with pointed arches, from which project eleven great arms that, rising and falling with majestic deliberation, put in motion as many pumps, capable of raising, each in its turn, the enormous weight of sixty-six cubic metres of water. The first to be set to work was the Leeghwater, on the 7th of June 1849. The other two began soon after. From that time the level of the lake sank one centimetre a day. After thirty-nine months of labor, the gigantic enterprise was completed; the engines had absorbed nine hundred and twenty-four million two hundred and sixty-six thousand one hundred and twelve cubic metres of water; the Haarlem sea was no more. This work, which cost seven million two hundred and forty thousand three hundred and sixty-eight florins, gave to Holland a new province of eighteen thousand five hundred hectares of land. Cultivators came from all parts of Holland. They began by sowing colza, which gave a wonderful return; and then every kind of produce, which succeeded perfectly well. And as the population came from different provinces, there were to be found all the different systems of cultivation rivalling one another, Zealand, Brabant, Friesland, Groningen, and North Holland were there, and there were to be heard all the dialects of the United Provinces; a smaller Holland within Holland.

As you approach Haarlem the villas and gardens become more and more numerous; but the city remains hidden among trees, above which appears only the tall bell-tower of the cathedral, surmounted by an iron ornament in the bulbous form of a Muscovite steeple. Entering the town you see on every side canals, windmills, drawbridges, fishing-boats, and houses reflected in the water; and after having walked about a hundred paces you come out into a vast square, at which you exclaim, in pleased wonder: "Oh, this is really Holland!"

In one corner is the cathedral, a bare and lofty edifice, surmounted by a roof in the form of a prism, which seems to cleave the sky like the edge of a sharp axe. Opposite the cathedral rises the ancient City Hall, crowned with battlements, with a roof like a ship bottom upwards, and a little balcony like a bird-cage stuck over the door; one part of the façade is hidden by two little houses of strange form, made up of theatre, church, and a castle of fireworks. On the other sides of the square there are houses in all the most capricious styles of Dutch architecture, here and there a little off the perpendicular, black, reddish, or vermilion, with their fronts studded with white bosses, looking like so many chess-boards, and a row of trees planted close against the walls so as to conceal all the upper windows. Next the cathedral there is an extravagant edifice, which is for public auctions; a monument of fantastic architecture, half red and half white, all steps, obelisks, pyramids, bas-reliefs, and nameless ornaments in the form of chandeliers and extinguishers and twelfth-night cakes, which seem thrown at haphazard, and all together present the effect of an Indian pagoda transformed, with a crazy look of Spain about it, and a touch of Holland, the whole done by an artist somewhat the worse for gin. But the strangest thing is an ugly bronze statue in the middle of the square, with an inscription which says: "*Laurentius Johannes filius Costerus Typographiæ litteris mobilibus e metalle fusis inventor.*" "What!" asks the ignorant stranger on the spot; "what news is this? I thought Gutenberg was the inventor of printing! What pretender have we here? Who is this Coster?

This Coster's name was Lawrence Janszoon, and was called Coster because he was a sacristan, or *coster* in Dutch. Tradition relates that this Coster, born in Haarlem towards the end of the fourteenth century, walking one day in the beautiful grove that lies to the south of the city, broke off a branch from a tree, and to amuse his children, cut with his knife some letters in relief upon it, from which grew the first idea of printing. In fact, returning home, he dipped these coarse wooden types in ink, printed them on paper, made new attempts, perfected the letters, printed entire pages, and finally, after long vicissitudes of study, fatigue, deceptions, and persecutions, brought upon him by copyists and elucidators, he succeeded in producing his *chef d'œuvre*, which was the "Speculum humanæ salvationis," printed in German, in double columns, and Gothic characters. This "Speculum humanæ salvationis," which can be seen in the Town Hall, is partly printed with wooden immovable types and partly with movable ones, and bears the date of 1440, the most remote date which can be admitted for the invention of movable types, in which the invention of printing really consists. If we accept the "Speculum," then Gutenberg is done for. But the proofs. Here begin the difficulties for the Dutch inventor. Among the objects belonging to him which are preserved in the Town Hall, there are no movable types; and there is an utter absence of written documents, or any testimony whatever which would prove beyond a doubt that the "Speculum," or at least that part of it printed with movable types, is the work of Coster. How do the supporters of the Dutch inventor supply this need? Here starts up another legend. On Christmas night 1440, whilst Coster, old and sick, was present at the midnight Mass, praying to God for strength to bear and to struggle against the persecutions of his enemies, one of his workmen—one of those who had sworn never to betray the secret of his invention—carried off his instruments, types, and books, which poor Coster discovering on his return home, he died of grief. According to the legend, this sacrilegious thief was Faust of Magonza, or the elder brother of Gutenberg; and this is the explanation, both of how the glory of the invention passed from Holland to Germany, and why the statue of poor Coster has the right to stand in the square at Haarlem, like an avenging spectre. Upon this question, which went on for centuries, an entire library has been written in Holland and Germany; until a few years ago it was doubtful before which of the statues, that at Haarlem or that at Magonza, the traveller should doff his hat. Germany rejected the pretensions of Holland with supreme disdain; Holland, although less and less positive, obstinately ignored the pretensions of Germany. But now it appears that the knot of the question is for ever undone. Doctor Von Linde, a Dutchman, has published a book entitled "The Legend of Coster," after reading which, according to the Hollanders themselves, you can put no more faith in Coster as the inventor of printing than in Tubal-Cain as the discoverer of iron, or Prometheus the robber of celestial fire. Consequently the statue of poor Coster may be melted up into a fine cannon to send against the pirates of Sumatra. But with Holland will remain for ever, in the field of typography, the incontestable glory of the Elzevirs, and the enviable honor of having printed almost all the great writers of the age of Louis XIV., of having diffused throughout Europe the French philosophy of the eighteenth century, of having gathered up, defended, and propagated human thought, when proscribed by despotism and denied by fear.

In the City Hall there is a picture gallery, which might be called the gallery of Franz Hals, because the chief works of that great artist are its principal ornaments. Born, as we know, at Malines, at the end of the sixteenth century, he lived many years at Haarlem, whilst landscape art flourished there, and among other illustrious Dutch artists, Ruysdaël, Winauts, Brouwer, and Cornelius Bega were all sojourning there. The principal room in the gallery, which is very large, is almost entirely occupied by his large pictures. As you enter you experience for a moment a singular illusion. You seem to have entered a banquet-hall, divided, as great banquets usually are, into different tables; and at the sound of your step all the guests have turned round to look at you. They are all groups of officers of archers and administrators of the hospital, of life size, some seated, some standing, about tables splendidly decorated, and all with faces turned towards the spectator, like people in the attitude of being photographed. On every side are to be seen broad faces full of health and good humor, with eyes fixed upon you, seeming to say, "Do you know me?" And there is so much truth of expression in these faces, that you really feel as if you knew them, as if you had met them many times in the streets of Leyden and the Hague. This truth of expression, the jovial character of the scene, the rich and ample costumes of the sixteenth century, the arms, the tables, and there being no other pictures to lead the mind to other times, make it seem that you are really looking at the Holland of two hundred years ago, feeling the air of the great century, living in the midst of those strong, candid, cordial people. You are not in a gallery; you are present at the representation of an historical play; and you would not be astonished to see Maurice of Orange or Frederic Henry arrive.

The most noteworthy of these pictures represents nineteen archers grouped around their colonel, and it is one of the *chef d'œuvres* of the high Dutch school, broad and free in design, warm and brilliant in color, worthy to be placed beside the famous " Banquet of the Civic Guard," by Van der Helst. Among the pictures by other artists, I remember one by Peter Brenghel the younger, which is a comic illustration of more than eighty Flemish proverbs, and which I cannot think of without a smile. But it is a picture which cannot be described for many honest reasons.

In one room of the picture gallery is preserved the banner which belonged to the famous heroine Kanan Hasselaer, the Joan d'Arc of Haarlem, who in 1572 fought at the head of three hundred armed Amazons against the Spaniards who were besieging the city. The defence of Haarlem, though not crowned with victory, was not less glorious than that of Leyden. The city was surrounded by old walls and towers falling into ruin, and had, besides the women's legion, only four thousand armed defenders. The Spaniards, after having cannonaded the walls for three days, rushed with great confidence to the assault; but repulsed by a rain of bullets, stones, boiling oil, and burning pitch, were obliged to proceed to lay siege to the place in the regular manner. The city was succoured by the country people, men, women, and children, who, sliding over the ice under favour of the December fogs, brought provisions and munitions of war on sleds. William of Orange, on his side, did all that was in his power to make the Spaniards raise the siege. But fortune did not smile upon him. Three thousand Dutch soldiers, sent forward first, were defeated, the prisoners were hung, and one officer put to death on a gibbet with his head downwards. Another attempt to aid the city had the same result: the Spaniards cut off the head of an officer whom they had taken, and threw it into the city with an insulting inscription. The citizens, in their turn, threw over into the enemy's camp a barrel containing the heads of eleven Spanish prisoners, with a note, which said: "Ten heads are sent to the Duke of Alva in payment of his tax of tenths, with one head more for interest."

The fighting became more and more desperate, accompanied by the explosion of mines and countermines in the bosom of the earth. On the 28th of January there arrived in the city by the lake of Haarlem one hundred and seventy sledges loaded with bread and powder. Don Frederick, the Spanish captain, wished to raise the siege; but his father, the Duke of Alva, ordered him to persist. Finally the thaws began, and it became difficult to get supplies into the town; the besieged began to feel the pangs of hunger. On the 25th of March they made a sortie, in which they burned three hundred tents and took seven cannon; but this success was rendered vain by a defeat sustained by the fleet of the Prince of Orange, which had given battle to the Spanish ships on Haarlem lake. This misfortune threw the besieged into despair. In the month of June they were reduced to all the last horrors of famine. On the 1st of July they made a vain attempt to come to terms with the enemy. On the 8th, five thousand volunteers sent by William of Orange to succour the city were defeated, and a prisoner was sent into Haarlem to carry the news, with nose and ears cut off. Then the besieged resolved to form a serried legion, with the women and children in their midst, and sally out of the city to cut their way through the enemy's camp. This resolution being made known to Don Frederick, he hypocritically promised pardon if the city would surrender without conditions. The city surrendered, the Spaniards entered, massacred all the soldiers of the garrison, cut off the heads of one thousand citizens, and tying two hundred more in couples, threw them into the lake. The Spanish army had paid with twelve thousand dead this victory secured by treachery and contaminated by the executioner.

From the museum I went to the cathedral, with the hope of hearing the famous organ of Christian Müller, said to be the largest in the world, and counting among its glories those of having been played by the celebrated Händel and by a boy of ten years old whose name was Mozart. The church, founded in the fifteenth century, is white and bare like a mosque, and covered by a high vaulted roof lined with cedar - wood, supported upon twenty-eight light columns. In one wall there is a cannon-ball which dates from the siege of 1573. In the middle of the church is a monument consecrated to the memory of the engineer Conrad, the builder of the sluice-gates of Katwijk, and his colleague Brunings, "*protectors of Holland against the furies of the sea and the power of the tempest.*" Behind the choir is buried the great poet Bilderdijk. Suspended from one of the arches hang some small models of ships of war, in memory of the fifth crusade, which was led by Count William I. of Holland. The tomb of Coster is near the pulpit. The organ, supported by porphyry columns, covers all one wall from roof to pavement, and has four key-boards, sixty-four registers, and five thousand pipes, some of which are twice the height of a Dutch house. At the moment there were some strangers in the church; the organist arrived promptly; and I could hear, as Victor Hugo says, "the music of God's cannon." I am unable to say, having no knowledge of the art, in what manner the organ of Haarlem differs from that of St. Paul's in London, or that in the Fribourg Cathedral, or that of the basilica of Seville. I heard the usual trumpet announcing the battle, followed by a formidable tumult of cannon, cries of the wounded, and victorious strains that grew more and more distant until they were lost among the hills; and then arose a tranquil harmony of flutes and pastoral melodies, which seemed to present all the sweetness of country life, when suddenly the lightning flashed, the hurricane was unchained, the church shook to its foundations; then the tempest was stilled, little by little, to the sound of the tremulous and solemn chant of legions of angels arriving slowly from an immense distance, and floating up among the clouds, pursued by the curses of an army of demons growling from the depths of the earth. The whole ended with an air from "*La Fille de Madame Angot*," which conveyed that it had been all a joke, and that the organist recommended himself to the courtesy of the strangers.

From the top of the steeple the eye embraces all the beautiful country about Haarlem, sprinkled with groves, windmills, and villages; the two great canals that go to Leyden and Amsterdam can be seen, skimmed by long files of boats with sails; the steeples of Amsterdam; the fields that cover what was once the lake of Haarlem; the village of Bloemendal, surrounded by gardens and villas; the desolate downs which defend this terrestrial paradise against the tempest; and beyond the downs, the North Sea, looking like a livid, luminous streak across the mists of the horizon. Coming out of the church, I chose a street and started on a tour about the city.

Although, in many respects, Haarlem resembles all other Dutch cities, still it has a character of its own by which it is stamped distinctly enough upon the memory. It is a pretty, quiet place, in which the traveller feels more acutely than in any other the need of his friend or his wife upon his arm. It is a woman's town. A broad watercourse, called the Spaarne, which serves as a canal for the drainage of the old lake of Haarlem and the gulf of Zuyder Zee, crosses it, separating into several branches, and forming a canal, which encircles it like a fortress. The internal canals are bordered by trees, which almost meet above them in a vault of verdure, so that each one seems a lakelet in a garden, and the barges and boats that float along in the shade seem there for pleasure rather than for business. All the streets are paved with bricks, and the houses are built of bricks, so that on every side, above and below, you see the same eternal red color, as if the city had been excavated out of a mountain of red jasper. A large number of the houses have their pointed façades cut into eight, ten, and even sixteen steps, like the paper churches children cut out with scissors; and there are very few mirrors, nothing hung in the windows, and signs over the shops are rare. The streets are so clean that one hesitates to let fall the ashes of one's cigar. For long distances you meet no living soul, or only some girl going alone to school, with her hair loose over her shoulders, and her books under her arm. There is no sound of labor, no roll of cart-wheels, no cry of itinerant vendor. The whole place has an appearance of aristocratic reserve and modest coquetry, which excites the curiosity in a singular way, and makes one walk on and on, insensible of fatigue, as if by dint of walking about one might discover some pleasant secret which the whole city keeps hidden from strangers.

There is a beautiful grove of beeches at the southern extremity of the town, believed to be a remnant of that immense forest which, in ancient times, covered the greater part of Holland. It is traversed by paths, and has cafés, kiosks, and society-rooms, and has, in the middle, a pretty park, stocked with deer. In one solitary shady spot is placed a small monument erected in 1823 in honor of Lawrence Coster, who, according to the legend, cut here the famous branch of a beech-tree on which he engraved the first types. Wandering about among the dark recesses of the wood I met a boy, who saluted me with a gentle "Bon jour," turning his face away; I asked my way of a girl with a gold band around her head and she blushed as red as a carnation; I requested a light from a peasant who was reading a newspaper; I passed a lady on horseback, who looked at me with two light-blue eyes, serene as the sky above us; and then returned towards the entrance of the grove, where there is a gallery of modern pictures about which I feel no remorse in being silent.

It is, however, well to observe, apropos of this gallery, that of late years Dutch art has made, under several aspects, honorable progress. The style which is preferred is still small landscapes, and in this there is no change; but painting scenes of private life has risen into higher regions. It has left the dregs of society for the middle classes, and come out of the taverns to dedicate itself lovingly to that sober, severe, and valorous people, the fishermen who labor and suffer in silence on the coast of Holland, from Helder to the mouths of the Meuse; it has forgotten the plebeian orgies and dances, to represent the sailor leaving for the herring fishery, and the wife on the shore giving her last farewell and crying, "God be with you!" or the fisherman returning from a long voyage to his beloved Scheveningen, his children running with open arms to meet him; or the sea lashed by a tempest, and the family of the poor sailor, out on the downs, and with anxious, tearful eyes watching the horizon for a black point upon its darkness. Excessive minuteness has disappeared; painting has taken a broader, freer manner. Few artists go to study out of their own country, and those who do lose their native character; but of those who remain, their work, especially landscape, is still, as formerly, a faithful mirror of their country, modest and original, and full of sadness, sweetness, and peace. Near the grove is the garden of Herr Koelage, the most famous tulip-fancier in Holland.

The word "tulip" recalls one of the strangest popular follies that has ever been seen in the world, which showed itself in Holland towards the middle of the seventeenth century. The country at that time had reached the height of prosperity; antique parsimony had given place to luxury; the houses of the wealthy, very modest at the beginning of the century, were transformed into little palaces; velvet, silk, and pearls replaced the patriarchal simplicity of the ancient costume; Holland had become vain, ambitious, and prodigal. After having filled their houses with pictures, hangings, porcelain, and precious objects from all the countries of Europe and Asia, the rich merchants of the large Dutch cities began to spend considerable sums in ornamenting their gardens with tulips—the flower which answers best to that innate avidity for vivid colors which the Dutch people manifest in so many ways. This taste for tulips promoted their rapid cultivation; everywhere gardens were laid out, studies promoted, new varieties of the favorite flower sought for. In a short time the fever became general; on every side there swarmed unknown tulips, of strange forms, and wonderful shades or combinations of colors, full of contrasts, caprices, and surprises. Prices rose in a marvellous way; a new variegation, a new form, obtained in those blessed leaves was an event, a fortune. Thousands of persons gave themselves up to the study with the fury of insanity; all over the country nothing was talked of but petals, bulbs, colors, vases, seeds The mania grew to such a pass that all Europe was laughing at it. Bulbs of the favorite tulips of the rarer varieties rose to fabulous prices; some constituted a fortune, like a house, an orchard, or a mill; one bulb was equivalent to a dowry for the daughter of a rich family; for one bulb were given, in I know not what city, two carts of grain, four carts of barley, four oxen, twelve sheep, two casks of wine, four casks of beer, a thousand pounds of cheese, a complete dress, and silver goblet. Another bulb of a tulip named *Semper Augustus* was bought at the price of thirteen thousand florins. A bulb of the *Admiral Enkhuyzen* tulip cost two thousand dollars. One day there were only two bulbs of the *Semper Augustus* left in Holland, one at Amsterdam and the other at Haarlem, and for one of them there were offered, and refused, four thousand six hundred florins, a splendid coach, and a pair of grey horses with beautiful harness. Another offered twelve acres of land, and he also was refused. On the registers of Alkmaar it is recorded that in 1637 there were sold in that city, at public auction, one hundred and twenty tulips for the benefit of the Orphanage, and that the sale produced one hundred and eighty thousand francs. Then they began to traffic in tulips, as in State bonds and shares. They sold for enormous sums bulbs which they did not possess, engaging to provide them for a certain day; and in this way a traffic was carried on for a much larger number of tulips than the whole of Holland could furnish. It is related that one Dutch town sold twenty millions of francs' worth of tulips, and that an Amsterdam merchant gained in this trade more than sixty-eight thousand florins in the space of four months. These sold that which they had not, and those that which they never could have; the market passed from hand to hand, the differences were paid, and the flowers for and by which so many people were ruined or enriched, flourished only in the imaginations of the traffickers. Finally matters arrived at such a pass that, many buyers having refused to pay the sums agreed upon, and contests and disorders following, the Government decreed that these debts should be considered as ordinary obligations, and that payment should be exacted in the usual legal manner; then prices fell suddenly, as low as fifty florins for the *Semper Augustus*, and the scandalous traffic ceased. Now the culture of flowers is no longer a mania, but is carried on for love of them, and Haarlem is the principal temple. She still provides a great part of Europe and South America with flowers. The city is encircled by gardens, which, towards the end of April and the beginning of May, are covered with myriads of tulips, hyacinths, carnations, auriculas, anemones, ranunculus, camelias, primroses, and other flowers, forming an immense wreath about Haarlem, from which travellers from all parts of the world gather a bouquet in passing. Of late years the hyacinth has risen into great honour; but the tulip is still king of the gardens, and Holland's supreme affection. I should have to change my pen for the brush of Von Huysem or Menendez, if I were to attempt to describe the pomp of their gorgeous, luxuriant, dazzling colors, which, if the sensation given to the eye may be likened to that of the ear, might be said to resemble a shout of joyous laughter or a cry of love in the green silence of the garden; affecting one like the loud music of a festival. There are to be seen the Duke of Toll tulip, the tulips called "simple precocious" in more than six hundred varieties; the "double precocious"; the late tulips, divided into unicolored, fine, superfine, and rectified; the fine, subdivided into violet, rose, and striped; then the monsters or parrots, the hybrids, the thieves; classified into a thousand orders of nobility and elegance; tinted with all the shades of color conceivable to the human mind; spotted, speckled, striped, edged, variegated, with leaves fringed, waved, festooned; decorated with gold and silver medals; distinguished by names of generals, painters, birds, rivers, poets, cities, queens, and a thousand loving and bold adjectives, which recall their metamorphoses, their adventures, and their triumphs, and leave a sweet confusion in the mind of beautiful images and pleasant thoughts.

After this, I thought I might leave for Amsterdam, whither I was impelled by an irresistible curiosity; and already I had my foot upon the step of the railway-carriage, and my eye upon a snug corner, near the door, when I felt myself seized by the skirt of my coat, and turned to behold the spectre of my courteous critic of Italy, who said, in a reproachful tone: "But, the commerce, the trade, the establishments of Haarlem, where have you left them?" "Ah, true," I replied, "you are one of those who desire description, guide, dictionary, treatise, railway indicator, and statistics, all in one book? Well, I will try and content you. Know, then, that there is in Haarlem a very rich museum of chemical, physical, optical, and hydraulic instruments, bequeathed to the city by one Peter Taylor van der Hulst, with a sum of money destined to serve every year for a scientific competition; that there is also a famous type-foundry of Greek and Hebrew characters; that there are several fine cotton factories founded under the patronage of King William II.; that there are washing establishments famous throughout Holland." At this moment I heard the whistle of the train. "One minute!" cried the critic, trying to keep me back. "How large are the electric machines in the Taylor museum? How much do the cotton factories produce yearly? What kind of soap is used in the washing establishments?" "Eh! leave me in peace," I answered, shutting the door as the train began to move; "don't you know the proverb, that you cannot bear the cross and sing?"

And now for thee, Amsterdam of the ninety islands, Venice of the north, queen of the Zuyder Zee!

AMSTERDAM.

Two travellers, one a poet and the other an engineer, were going together for the first time, from Haarlem to Amsterdam, when an unusual thing happened; the engineer felt himself something of a poet, and the poet experienced a desire to be in the engineer's shoes. Such is this strange country, where the writer, to rouse his imagination, and excite enthusiasm, has only to enumerate kilometres, cubic metres of water, and years of labor; whence a poem upon Holland would be a poor affair without an appendix full of numbers, and a complete relation from an engineer would need only verse and rhyme to make it a splendid poem.

Immediately upon leaving Haarlem, the train passes over a handsome iron bridge of six arches which spans the Spaarne; which bridge, after the passage of the train, parts in the middle as if by enchantment, and leaves the way open to vessels. Two men only moving a machine at a signal from the bridge-keeper remove in two minutes two arches, and in the same time replace them for the passage of another train. A short time after having crossed the bridge the waters of the Y became visible upon the horizon.

Here one feels more than ever a certain sentiment of anxiety which often disturbs those who travel for the first time in Holland. The road runs along a strip of land which separates the bottom of the antique lake of Haarlem from the waters of the Y, a prolongation, called thus from its form, of the gulf of Zuyder Zee, which projects into the land between Amsterdam and North Holland, as far as the downs of the North Sea. In order to construct this railway, which was opened in 1839, before the draining of Haarlem lake, it was necessary to pile fascine upon fascine, to add pile to pile, stone to stone, sand to sand; to make, in a word, the land upon which the road was to pass, a sort of artificial isthmus across the marshes; and it was a most difficult and costly work, which demands perpetual care and continual expenditure. This tongue of land grows more and more slender until it reaches Halfweg, which is the only station between Haarlem and Amsterdam. Here the waters of the Y, and the bottom of the drained lake are divided by colossal sluice-gates, to which the existence of the greater part of South Holland is confided. If these sluices were to open, the city of Amsterdam, hundreds of villages, the ancient lake, an extent of country comprising fifty kilometres would be invaded and devastated by the waters.

The draining of the lake has diminished the danger, but has not entirely removed it; and therefore, at Halfweg there is established a special agency of the so-called water administration, which keeps guard over this Dutch Thermopylæ, with its eye on the enemy, and its hand on the sword.

Passing the station at Halfweg, you see on the left, beyond the gulf of the Y, a confused movement as of thousands of masts of vessels beaten by the tempest, and rising and falling with the waves of the sea; they are the arms of about a hundred windmills half hidden by the dykes, which extend along the coast of North Holland, in the neighbourhood of the town of Zandam, opposite to Amsterdam. Shortly after these, Amsterdam appears. At the first aspect of the city, even after having seen all the other parts of Holland, you cannot restrain a gesture of astonishment. It is a forest of lofty windmills in the form of towers, steeples, pyramids, light-houses, truncated cones, and aerial houses, waving their enormous arms, and whirling above the roofs and domes like a cloud of monstrous birds beating their wings over the city. In the midst of these mills rise innumerable factory-chimneys, masts of ships, fantastic steeples, tops of strange-looking edifices, pinnacles, and points, and unknown objects; far off are seen more windmills, thick and intricate, looking like a great net suspended in the air; the entire city is black, the sky dark and troubled: a grand, confused, and strange spectacle, causing your entrance into Amsterdam to be effected with the accompaniment of a vivid curiosity.

The first impression produced by the sight of some of its streets is difficult to describe. It seems an immense

WINDMILLS AT ZAANDAM. (*Page* 246.)

and disorderly city—Venice, grown large and ugly; a Dutch city, certainly, but seen through a lens which makes it seem three times larger, the capital of an imaginary Holland of fifty millions of inhabitants; an antique metropolis, founded by giants upon the delta of a measureless river, to serve as a port for ten thousand ships, majestic, stern, almost gloomy, and exciting a feeling of astonishment, in which one finds cause for reflection.

The city, posted upon the shore of the Y, is built upon ninety islands, almost all of rectangular form, which are joined together by about three hundred and fifty bridges. Its figure is that of a perfect semicircle with canals in the form of concentric arches extending to the one which closes the city, and crossed by other canals converging to a centre like the threads of a spiders web. A broad watercourse called the Amstel (which, with the word *dam*, or dyke, forms the name Amsterdam) divides the city into two almost equal parts, and empties itself into the Y. Almost all the houses are built upon piles, and it is said that if Amsterdam should be turned bottom upwards, it would present the spectacle of a great forest of trees, without branches or leaves; almost all the canals are bordered by two wide streets and two rows of linden-trees.

This regularity of form, by which the eye can range on every side, gives to the city a grandiose aspect. At every turn of a street you see in a new direction three, four, or even six drawbridges, some rising, some falling, some closed, and some in motion, presenting a confused perspective of beams and chains, as if Amsterdam were composed of so many enemies' quarters, all fortified against each other.

Canals, as broad as rivers, form here and there spacious basins, around which you can go, by a succession of bridges joined one to the other. From every crossing can be seen distant perspectives of other bridges, canals, shipping, edifices, all veiled in a light mist which makes them look more distant.

The houses, almost all very high, in comparison to those of other Dutch cities, black, with doors and windows bordered with white, with pointed façades decorated with bas-reliefs representing urns, flowers, and animals, are almost all defended in front by columns, balustrades, posts and chains, or iron bars, and divided from each other by low walls and partitions; and within this species of advanced fortress, which encumbers a large part of the street, there are tables, benches with vases of flowers, chairs, buckets, wheelbarrows, baskets, and carcasses of old furniture; so that to look down a street, from one end of it to the other, it appears as if the inhabitants had carried out their household goods preparatory to a general remove. Many houses have a floor below the street, which is approached by a short flight of steps; and in the area between the street and the wall there are more pots of flowers, merchandise exposed for sale, people at work—a world warming under the feet of the passenger.

The principal streets present a spectacle unique in the world. The canals are covered with ships and barges; and in the streets that flank them are seen on one side heaps of casks, cases, bales and sacks; on the other a row of splendid shops. Here, a crowd of people, well-dressed ladies, maid-servants, pedlars, and shopmen; there, the rough and vagabond race of sailors and boatmen with their wives and children. To the right is heard the vivacious chatter of the citizens; to the left the long, shrill cry of the sea-going people. On one side the nostrils are saluted by the perfume of the flowers which adorn the windows, and the odour of cook-shops; on the other by the smell of tar and the fumes of the humble kitchen of the sailing vessels. Here a drawbridge rises to give passage to a ship; there, the people swarm upon one which has but just fallen into its place again; further on, a raft ferries over a group of persons from the other side of the canal; from the bottom of the street a steamboat is just setting off; at the opposite extremity a long file of laden barges are just coming in; here opens a sluice-gate; there glides a *trekschuit*; not far off whirls a windmill; and down there they are planting piles for a new house. The rattle of chains from the bridges mingles with the roll of carts; the whistle of steamers breaks into the chimes from the steeples; the cordage of the ships tangles itself among the branches of the trees; carriages pass side by side with boats; shops are reflected in the water, sails are reflected in shop windows; sea-life and land-life are intermingled, cross, and pass each other continually, and the result is new, and gay beyond description.

If you leave the principal streets and strike into the older quarters of the town, the scene changes completely. The narrowest streets of Toledo, the darkest lanes of

Genoa, the craziest houses in Rotterdam are nothing in comparison with the narrowness, the darkness, and the craziness of architecture that confront you here. The streets seem like cracks opened by an earthquake. The houses, tall and black, half hidden by the rags that are hung from every window, bend and lean in a frightful way. Some appear on the point of falling forward into the street; others almost touch each other with their roofs, leaving only a slim strip of sky visible; they look like scenes in a theatre in the act of being changed. Have they been built in this way on purpose, in order to let the water run off, or has the ground sunk beneath them? Both suppositions are probably correct. And even in those labyrinths, swarming with depressed and pallid creatures to whom a ray of sun-light comes as a benediction from heaven, there are pots of flowers, and little mirrors and curtains in the windows, revealing a poverty not unaccompanied by a love of home and family.

The most picturesque part of the city is that comprised in the curve of the Amstel around the square of the new market. There are to be seen dark streets crossed by deserted canals; solitary squares, surrounded by walls dripping with water; mouldy old tumble-down houses, bathed by stagnant filthy water; vast warehouses with all their doors and windows closed; boats and barges abandoned in canals without issue, which look as if they were waiting for sorcerers or conspirators; heaps of building material, basins covered with weeds and muddy scum, walls, water, bridges, all black and dismal, and alarming

AMSTERDAM. THE AMSTEL. (*Page* 250.)

the chance passenger with dread of some lurking danger or misadventure.

Who loves contrast has only to betake himself to that part of the city where lies the square called the *Dam*, where all the principal streets converge, and where he will find the Royal Palace, the Exchange, the New Church, and the monument called the Metal Cross, raised in commemoration of the war of 1830. There is a continual moving crowd of people on foot and in carriages, reminding one of Trafalgar Square in London, the Porta del Sol of Madrid, and the Place de la Madeleine in Paris. Standing there for an hour, you can enjoy the most varied spectacle that is to be found in Holland. There pass the rosy faces of the patrician merchants, bronzed visages from the colonies, foreigners of all shades of blonde, guides, organ-grinders, announcers of death with long black veils, maid-servants in their white caps, the many-colored waistcoats of the fishermen of the Zuyder Zee, the great ear-rings of the women of North Holland, the silver diadem of Friesland, the gilded helmet of Gröningen, the yellow shirt of the workman in the *torbière*, the petticoat, half black, half red, of the orphan from the asylum, the odd costume of the inhabitant of the islands, outrageous *chignons*, and impossible hats; broad shoulders, broad hips, great bellies, and the whole procession surrounded by the smoke of cigars and pipes, and accompanied by the sounds of German, Dutch, English, French, Flemish, and Danish words, until the spectator almost believes himself in the valley of Jehoshaphat or at the foot of the Tower of Babel.

From the piazza of the Dam you, in a few minutes, arrive at the port, which also offers a fine and strange spectacle. At first you cannot comprehend it. On every side you see dykes, bridges, locks, palisades, and basins, presenting the aspect of an immense fortress, so constructed as to baffle the curiosity of anyone who might seek to discover its form; and this, indeed, can only be done by help of a map, and after several hours' walk. From the centre of the city, at a distance of a thousand metres from each other, two great dykes on arches start in opposite directions, and embrace and defend from the sea the two extremities of Amsterdam which extend beyond the semicircle of her houses like the two horns of a half-moon. These two dykes, which have each a lock furnished with gigantic gates, close in two basins or harbors capable of containing a thousand ships of large tonnage, and several islets upon which are storehouses, arsenals, and workshops, where thousands of workmen are employed. From the two great dykes advance several smaller dykes, made of robust piles, and serving as landing-places for the steamboats. On all these dykes there are houses, sheds, barracks, among which swarms a throng of sailors, passengers, porters, women, boys, carriages, and carts, brought there by the arrivals and departures which go on from dawn until night. From the two extremities of these dykes the eye embraces the interior of the harbour; two forests of ships with flags of every color lying in the two basins; vessels arriving from the North Sea and entering the Zuyder Zee with folded canvas; boats and barks crossing and recrossing each other from all sides of

AMSTERDAM. THE LIME MARKET. (*Page 253.*)

the gulf; the green coast of North Holland; the hundred windmills of Zandam; the long file of the first houses of Amsterdam, with their thousand-peaked black roofs cut against the sky; the innumerable columns of sooty smoke rising from the city against the grey horizon; and, when the clouds are in motion, and constant, rapid, marvellous variation of color and aspect, which makes Holland sometimes the gayest, sometimes the gloomiest, country in the world.

Returning into the city and observing more particularly the buildings, the first to attract attention are the steeples. In Amsterdam there are temples for all religions: Jewish synagogues, churches for Reformed Calvinists, churches for Lutherans where the Augsburg Confession is strictly observed, and churches for Lutherans where the same is more broadly interpreted, churches for Remonstrants, for Mennonites, for Walloons, for English Episcopalians, for English Presbyterians, for Catholics, for Greek schismatics; and every one of these temples lifts to heaven a steeple that seems made to distance all the others in originality and oddity. What Victor Hugo says of the Flemish architects—who build steeples by putting an inverted salad-bowl upon a judges' cap, a sugar-bowl upon the salad-bowl, a bottle upon the sugar-bowl, and an *ostensorio* (or golden stand from which the Host is shown) upon the top of that—might be said of almost all the Amsterdam steeples.

Among the historical edifices, which are not numerous, there is the Royal Palace, the first of the palaces of Holland, built in 1648-55, upon thirteen thousand six hundred and fifty-nine piles—grandiose, heavy, and black—of which the finest ornament is a ball-room said to be the largest in Europe; and the greatest defect that of having no great entrance-door, from which it is generally called the house without a door.

The Exchange, on the contrary, which stands facing the palace, and has a porch sustained by seventeen columns, is known as the door without a house; a joke which every Dutchman makes a point of repeating to strangers, with the slightest possible smile curling his lip. Whoever arrives in Amsterdam in the first week of the Kermesse, which is the Dutch carnival, may behold a curious spectacle within this building. For seven days, at the hours when no business is done, the Exchange is open to all the boys and girls of the city, who rush into it with a deafening noise of drums and whistles and cries; a license which, if the tradition be true, was conceded by the municipality in honor of some boys, who, in the time of the war for independence, playing near the ancient Exchange, discovered some Spaniards who were preparing to blow up the building by means of a boat laden with powder, and ran to warn the citizens, thus bringing to nought the enemy's plan. Besides the Royal Palace and the Exchange, there is the Palace of Industry, made of glass and iron, and surmounted by a light dome, which gives it, at a distance when the sun strikes upon it, the look of a mosque; and as an historical monument, there are the ancient towers which stand on the shores of the harbour.

Among these towers there is one called the "Tower of the Corner of Lamentation," or "Tower of Tears," because there in ancient times Dutch sailors embarking for long voyages took leave of their families who came to see them off. Over the gate is a rusty bas-relief, bearing the date of 1569, and representing the port, with a ship about to sail, and a weeping woman. It was put up in memory of a sailor's wife who died of grief at the departure of her husband.

It has been observed that almost all strangers who go to see that tower, after having given a glance at the bas-relief, and at the guide-book which explains it, turn towards the sea and look thoughtfully out, as if in search of the departing vessel. What are they thinking of? Perhaps what I myself was thinking of. They follow that vessel into the Arctic seas, to the whale fishery, and in search of a new road to the Indies, and the tremendous epic of the Dutch navy in the midst of the horrors of the Pole presents itself to their imagination: seas encumbered with ice, cold which makes the flesh fall in fragments from the face and hands, white bears attacking the sailors and breaking their weapons in their teeth, walruses rushing to overturn the boats, icebergs beaten by wind and sea, and vast plains of moving ice which imprison and grind the fleet to powder; desert islands strewn with corpses of dead sailors, carcasses of ships, and leathern girdles gnawed in their agony by men dying of hunger; then the whales that come about the ships, the formidable contortions of the wounded monster in the blood-stained water, the boats overturned with a blow of his tail, the sailors struggling in the sea; shipwrecked men wandering half-naked amid darkness and cold, graves dug in the ice and covered in with ice to keep their contents from wild beasts, and the sleep that brings death. And still white and misty solitudes, where no sound is heard save the rattle of the oars in the rowlocks echoing from the caves, and the lamentable cry of seals; and other deserts where no trace of life exists, with mountains of incommensurate ice, immense unknown spaces, snows that have endured for centuries, eternal winter, the solemn sadness of the polar night, the infinite silence in which the soul is appalled; and the poor dying sailors, kneeling on the deck, stretch their joined hands towards the horizon all on fire with the aurora-borealis, and pray God to vouchsafe them once more to see their country and their friends. Men of science, merchants, poets, all bend before that humble vanguard who have traced with their bones upon the immaculate snows of the Pole the first path for living men.

Turning to the right from this tower, and walking along the edge of the harbour, you reach the Plantaadije, a vast space composed of two islands joined together by many bridges, in which are a park, a botanic garden, a zoological garden, and a public promenade, forming a large green oasis in the midst of the livid waters and the blockhouses. Here are given concerts of music, nocturnal festivals, and here comes the flower of the beauty of Amsterdam; a flower which, fortunately for travellers of sensitive fibre, gives out a sweet odor, which does *not* affect the head. And in any case, there is a refuge from danger in the zoological garden, the property of a company of fifteen thousand subscribers; the finest zoological garden in Holland, and one of the richest in Europe; in which it is easy to forget the pale faces and blue eyes of the lovely Calvinists, among the gigantic salamanders of Japan, the serpents of Java, and the *Bradypi didactyli* of Surinam.

From the Plantaadije, crossing sundry bridges and skirting numerous canals, one reaches the great square of the Boter Markt, where there is a gigantic statue of Rembrandt, and also the office of the Italian Consulate. From this square you go to the Jewish quarter, one of the wonders of Amsterdam.

I asked my way there of our Consul, who answered, "Go straight on until you find yourself in a quarter infinitely dirtier than any which you have heretofore considered the dirtiest in the world; that is the *ghetto*—you cannot mistake it." I went on, it may be imagined with what expectations; I passed a synagogue, stopped a moment in a piazza, took a narrow street, and in a few moments recognised the *ghetto*. My expectations were surpassed.

It was a labyrinth of narrow lanes, dark and filthy, flanked by ruined houses that look as if a kick would bring them down. From cords stretched from window to window, from nails planted in the doors, and from the window-sills, hung and waved in the wind, upon the damp walls, ragged shirts, patched gowns, and darned breeches. Before all the doors and upon the broken steps, old second-hand goods were exposed for sale. Refuse of furniture, fragments of weapons, devotional objects, rags of uniform, remains of instruments, old iron, fringes, rags; everything that is nameless in any human tongue, everything that is spoiled by moth, or rust, or fire, or ruin, or dissipation, or sickness, or misery, or death; everything that is despised by servants, rejected by pawnbrokers, thrown aside by beggars or overlooked by beasts; everything that encumbers, soils, stinks, and contaminates; it is all there, in piles and heaps, destined for a mysterious trade and incredible transformations. In the midst of this cemetery of things, this Babylon of filth, swarms a people so ragged, dirty, and wretched, that beside them the gipsies of the Albaicin of Granada are sweet and clean and perfumed. As in all countries, they have borrowed from the people among whom they live the color of the skin and the face; but they have preserved the hooked noses, the sharp chins, the curling hair, and all the features of the Semitic race. There are no words to describe these people. Locks which have never seen a comb, eyes which make you shudder, leanness like that of corpses, pitiful ugliness, old men who retain scarcely a semblance of humanity, wrapped in garments which no longer betray by color or form to what sex they belong, from which protrude long skeleton claws, like those of some noxious insect. And everything is done in the middle of the street. Women are frying fish on little stoves; girls are rocking babies; men are looking over their stores of old duds; half-naked boys are rolling on the stones, which are covered with rotten vegetables and entrails of fish; decrepit old women, seated on the ground, scratch their filthy bodies, uncovering as they do so, limbs from which the eye turns away in horror. Walking on the points of my toes, stopping my nose, and turning away my eyes from things which they could not endure, I

AMSTERDAM. IN THE POOR DISTRICTS (*Page* 258.)

reached at last a clean and open place on the edge of a broad canal, where I breathed with delight the air impregnated with salt and tar, and felt as if I had entered a terrestrial paradise.

In Amsterdam, as in all the other Dutch cities, there are many private societies, some of which have the importance of great national institutions; foremost among them is the Society of Public Utility, founded in 1784, which is almost a second government for Holland. Its scope is popular education, for which it provides by the publication of elementary books, public readings, libraries for working people, schools for primary instruction, professional schools, singing schools, asylums, savings banks, prizes for good conduct, and rewards for acts of courage and unselfishness. The society, directed by a council composed of ten directors and a secretary-general, is composed of more than fifteen thousand members, divided into three hundred groups, which form as many independent societies, scattered among the towns and villages. Every member pays about ten francs a year. With the sum (modest in relation to the vastness of the institution) which this tax produces, the society exercises, as Alphonso Esquiroz says, a sort of anonymous magistracy over public manners; binds together with impartial beneficence all religious sects; distributes with liberal hand about the country instruction, aid, and comfort; and as it was born independent, so it works and proceeds faithful to the principle of the Dutch people, that the tree of beneficence must grow without graft or puncture. Other societies, like that of *Arti et Amicitiæ*, *Felix Meritis*, and *Doc-*

trina et Amicitiæ, have in view the growth of arts and sciences, the promotion of public works, readings, and meetings, and are at the same time delightful places of meeting, furnished with fine libraries, and almost all the great European journals.

Upon the charitable institutions of Amsterdam a book might be written. The words of Louis XIV. when he was preparing to invade Holland, to Charles II. of England, are noteworthy:—" Have no fear for Amsterdam; I have the firm hope that Providence will save her, if it were only in consideration of her charity towards the poor." All human misfortunes find an asylum and work there. Admirable above all is the Asylum for Orphans of Amsterdam Citizens, which had the honor of sheltering that immortal Van Speyk, who, in 1831, upon the waters of the Scheldt, saved the honor of the Dutch flag by the sacrifice of his own life. These orphans wear a very curious costume, half black and half red, so that, seen in profile, on one side they seemed dressed for a carnival, and on the other for a funeral; and this odd device was chosen so that they might be recognised by the tavern-keepers, who are forbidden to allow them to enter, and by the officials of the railways, who may not permit them to travel without express permission from the directors; which results, it may be remarked in passing, could have been obtained with a less ridiculous costume. These bi-colored orphans are seen everywhere, clean, fresh, and courteous, and refreshing to the heart. In all public festivals they occupy the first place; their song is heard on all occasions of solemn ceremony; the first stone of national monuments is placed by their hands; and the people love and honor them.

To have done with the institutions, we should take note of the particular industries of Amsterdam, such as the refining of borax and camphor and the manufacture of enamel; but these are things for the travelling encyclopedists of the future. Diamond-polishing, however, merits special mention, being the chief of the industries of Amsterdam, and a secret between the Jews of Antwerp and Amsterdam, by whom it is entirely exercised. This trade amounts to one hundred millions of francs yearly, and supports more than ten thousand persons. One of the finest workrooms is that in the Quanenburger Straat, where the workmen themselves explain in French the three operations of cutting, and first and final polishing, done under the eyes of the visitor, with admirable dexterity and courtesy. It is astonishing to see those humble little stones, resembling fragments of dirty gum-arabic fit to be thrown out of window in company with cigar ends, in a few seconds transformed, glowing and animated with a flashing and festive life, as if they understood the destiny that had drawn them from the bowels of the earth to make them serve the pomps of the world. In how many strange events will this little stone, now held in the workman's iron glove, be actor, or witness, or cause? It may glow upon the forehead of a queen, who will some night leave it in its casket while she escapes from the crowd besieging the gates of her palace. Fallen into the hands of a Communist, it may gleam upon the table of a court of justice, side by side with a blood-stained dagger.

It may pass through many scenes of nuptial feasts and banquets and dances, and flying through the door of the pawnbroker's shop, or out of the window of a carriage assailed by robbers, go from hand to hand, and from country to country, until it sparkles on the hand of some princess in her box at the opera at St. Petersburg. From thence it may go to add a point of light to the sabre-hilt of a pasha in Asia Minor, and then to tempt the virtue of a youthful milliner in the Saint Antoine quarter of Paris; and at last—who knows?—to ornament the watch of a descendant of him who first presented it to worldly honors, since among these workmen there are some who put by a little capital for their children. Among others there was, a few years ago, in the Quanenburger Straat, the old Israelite who cut the famous gem called the Koh-i-noor, which, besides the grand medal of honor at the Paris Exposition, brought him a reward of ten thousand florins, and a present from the Queen of England.

At Amsterdam there is the finest picture gallery in Holland.

The stranger who enters it prepared to admire the two greatest works of Dutch painters, has no need to inquire where they are. He has scarcely crossed the threshold, when he sees a small room filled with silent, motionless people, and entering, finds himself in the most sacred *penetralia* of the temple. On the right is Rembrandt's "Night Patrol"; on the left, Van der Helst's "Banquet of the Civic Guard."

After having seen these two pictures over and over again, I often amused myself by watching the people who came there for the first time. Almost all, upon their entrance, stopped, looked in astonishment first at one and then at the other, and then, smiling, turned to the right. Rembrandt was the victor.

The " Night Patrol," or, as it is sometimes called, " The Arquebusiers," and also "The Company of Banning Cock," the largest of Rembrandt's canvases, is more than a picture, it is a spectacle, and an amazing one. All the French critics, to express the effect which it produces, make use of the same phrase, " *C'est écrasant!* " (" It is overpowering! ") A great crowd of human figures, a great light, a great darkness—at the first glance this is what strikes you, and for a moment you know not where to fix your eyes in order to comprehend that grand and splendid confusion.

There are officers, halberdiers, boys running, arquebusiers loading and firing, youths beating drums, people bowing, talking, calling out, gesticulating—all dressed in different costumes, with round hats, pointed hats, plumes, casques, morions, iron gorgets, linen collars, doublets embroidered with gold, great boots, stockings of all colors, arms of every form ; and all this tumultuous and glittering throng start out from the dark background of the picture and advance towards the spectator. The two first personages are Franz Banning Cock, lord of Furmerland and Ilpendam, captain of the company, and his lieutenant Willem van Ruijtenberg, lord of Vlaardingen, the two marching side by side. The only figures that are in full light are this lieutenant, dressed in a doublet of buffalo - hide, with gold ornaments, scarf gorget, and white plume, with high boots ; and a girl who com behind, with blonde hair ornamented with pearls, and a yellow satin dress; all the other figures are in deep shadow, excepting the heads, which are illuminated. By what light? Here is the enigma. Is it the light of the sun? or of the moon? or of the torches? There are gleams of gold and silver, moonlight-colored reflections, fiery lights; personages which, like the girl with blonde tresses, seem to shine by a light of their own; faces that seem lighted by the fire of a conflagration; dazzling scintillations, shadows, twilight, and deep darkness, all are there, harmonised and contrasted with marvellous boldness and insuperable art. Are there discordances of light? gratuitous shadows? accessories too much brought out to the detriment of the figures? vague and grotesque figures? unjustifiable oddities and defects? All this has been said about the picture. There have been arguments of blind enthusiasm and of spiteful censure. It has been raised to the skies as a wonder of the world, and pronounced unworthy of Rembrandt, discussed, interpreted, explained in a thousand ways and senses. But, in spite of censure, defects, conflicting judgments, it has been there for two centuries triumphant and glorious; and the more you look at it, the more it is alive and glowing; and even seen only at a glance, it remains for ever in the memory, with all its mystery and splendor, like a stupendous vision.

The picture by Van der Helst (a painter of whom nothing is known beyond the fact that he was born in Amsterdam at the beginning of the seventeenth century and passed the greater part of his life there) represents a

AMSTERDAM.

banquet given by the Civic Guard of Amsterdam, to commemorate the peace of Munster, on the 18th of June 1648. The picture contains twenty-five figures of lifesize, all faithful portraits of noted personages, whose names have been preserved. There are officers, sergeants, banner-bearers, and guards, grouped about a table, holding each others' hands, speaking, and drinking toasts; some eating, some carving, some peeling oranges, and some pouring out wine. Rembrandt's picture is a fantastic apparition; Van der Helst's, a mirror reflecting a real scene. There is neither unity, nor contrast, nor mystery; everything is represented with the same care and the same relief. Heads and hands, figures near or distant, steel armour and lace fringes, plumed hats and silken standards, silver horns and gilded goblets, vases, spoons and knives, plates and dishes, food, wines, weapons, ornaments, all stand out, splendidly real and fascinating the eye. The heads, considered one by one, are portraits wonderfully rendered, from which a physician might securely judge of the owner's temperament and prescribe for the health of all. With regard to the hands, it has been argued, and with reason, that if taken from the figures and mixed together, they could be recognised and replaced without danger of mistake, so fine, distinct, and individual are they. The variety and splendor of color, the openness and freshness of the countenances, the splendid costumes, the thousand glittering objects, all together give to this great picture an air of joyous festivity, which causes the vulgarity of the subject to be forgotten, and excites in the beholders a sentiment of friendly sympathy and admiration, which reveals itself in a pleased smile upon the faces of the most ill-disposed visitors.

There is also in this gallery Rembrandt's great picture called "The Syndics of the Cloth Merchants," painted nineteen years after the "Night Patrol," with less of youthful fire and eccentricity of fancy, but with all the vigor of mature genius, and not less wonderful than the other for effects of *chiaroscuro*, expression of the figures, strength of color, and exuberance of life, preferred by some critics to the "Patrol." There is another picture by Van der Helst, "The Syndics of the Confraternity of St. Sebastian at Amsterdam," in which all the great qualities of the master are still resplendent, though somewhat less than in the "Banquet."

Steen has eight pictures, among them his own portrait, which represents him as young and handsome, with long hair, and a quiet meditative air, which seems to say: „No, stranger, I was not a dissipated man, nor a drunkard, nor a bad husband; I was calumniated; respect my memory." The subjects of the other pictures are, a maid-servant cleaning a pot, a peasant family returning home in a boat, a baker making bread, a family scene, a village wedding, a children's festival, a mountebank in the square; all with the usual drunken figures, the usual laughter, the usual grotesque personages, admirably colored and lighted up. In the picture of the "Mountebank," above all, his mania for the grotesque reaches its climax. The heads are deformed, the faces grimace, the noses are beaks, the backs are humps, the hands are claws, the attitudes are contortions, the smiles grins—

figures, in a word, whose like can only be found in an anatomical museum, or in the grotesque animalisms of Grandville. It is impossible not to laugh, but it is with the feeling of those who looked at "Gymplaine," saying in their hearts, " What a pity he is a monster."

There was, however, an artist who brought this kind of painting even lower than Steen: Adrian Brouwer, one of the most famous of his school in Holland. He was a disciple of Francis Hals, and got drunk with him regularly once a day, until, persecuted by his creditors, he fled to Antwerp, where he was arrested as a spy and thrown into prison. Rubens procured his release and received him into his own house; but Rubens led a respectable life, and Brouwer, who detested restraint, left him. He went to Paris, where he rushed into all sorts of excesses until, reduced to a mere shadow, he came back to Antwerp and died miserably in the hospital in his thirty-second year. As he cared only for the tavern and its frequenters, so he painted only coarse and disgusting scenes of drunken men and women, the merit of which lies in their vivid and harmonious color and marked originality. The gallery at Amsterdam has two of his pictures, one representing "Peasants Fighting," and the other "A Village Orgy." The last is completely Brouwer. It represents a room in a tavern, where a company of tipsy men and women are drinking and smoking. One woman is stretched on the floor dead drunk, with her baby crying beside her.

Gerard Douw has here his famous picture of the "Night School," or, the *picture of the four candles*, worthy of a place beside his " Dropsical Woman" in the Louvre, and among the most exquisite of the gems of Dutch art. It is a small picture, which represents in the foreground a schoolmaster with two boy scholars and a girl seated around a table; another girl is intent upon a small scholar who is writing on a slate; and in the background there are other pupils at their studies. But the originality of the picture consists in this, that the figures are the accessories, and the principal part, the protagonists—the subject of the picture, in a word—are the four candles: one burning in a lantern left on the floor; one which lights the group of the master and his scholars; a third held by the girl and illuminating the slate; and a fourth upon a table behind, among the boys who are studying. It is easy to imagine what a variety of lights and shadows, tremulous rays, and shafts of light an artist like Douw knew how to draw from his four flames; what infinite difficulties were created by them, what infinite care was necessary to conquer them, and with what wonderful power he has accomplished it. The picture, painted, as a critic has said, "with the eye-lash of a new-born baby," and covered with glass, like a relic, was sold in 1766 for eight thousand francs, and in 1808 for thirty-five thousand; and certainly a cipher added to the last sum would not be sufficient to buy it now.

There would never be an end of description if I were to attempt to mention only the principal pictures in this gallery. The sublime and melancholy Ruysdael has a winter scene and a forest, *full of his own soul,* as it is customary to say of his landscapes. Zerburg has his celebrated "Paternal Counsel"; Wouvermanns, ten admirable pictures of game, battles, and horses; Potter, Karel du Jardin, Van Blade, Cuyp, Metzu, Van der Verde, Everdingen, are represented by some of the best of their works, of which it would be labor lost to attempt to give written descriptions. And this is not the only gallery of paintings in Amsterdam. There is another, which was bequeathed to the city by one Van der Hoop, formerly a deputy to the States Parliament, and which contains about two hundred pictures by the first Dutch and Flemish artists; and there are besides several very rich private collections.

* * * * * *

Napoleon the Great was bored in Amsterdam, but I firmly believe that it was his own fault. I was very well amused. All those canals, bridges, basins, and islands, form so various and picturesque a prospect that one is never tired of gazing at them. There are a hundred ways of passing time agreeably. You go to see the arrival of milk-boats from Utrecht; you follow the barges that are transporting various kinds of cargo to their destinations, with white-capped maid-servants standing on the prow; you pass half an hour on the tower of the Royal Palace, from whence can be seen at one glance the gulf of the Y, the ancient lake of Haarlem, the towers of Utrecht, the red roofs of Zandam, and all that fantastic forest of masts of vessels, steeples, and mills; you look on at the dredging of the canals, at the mending of bridges and locks, at the thousand necessities of this singular city, obliged to spend four hundred thousand florins a year in the governing of its waters; and when everything else fails, there is always the spectacle of the servants of both sexes, who with pumps and pipes are for ever washing the streets before the houses, the first-floor windows, and the clothes of the passers-by. In the evening, there is the street called Kalver Straat, flanked by two rows of splendid shops, and cafés half lighted up and half plunged in darkness, where until late at night there swarms a dense and slow-moving crowd of people, full of beer and money, mingled with certain fac-similes of *cocottes* parading in eccentric toilettes, three or four together, silent and smileless, and looking as if they were meditating some aggression. From the lighted and crowded streets you, in a few moments, reach the borders of dark canals, among motionless vessels, and the profoundest silence. Crossing a bridge, you come to a quarter where the lights from subterranean cellars twinkle and the music of sailors' balls is heard; and so every moment the scene changes—no offence to Napoleon I.

Such is this famous city, whose history is not less strange than its form and aspect. The poor fisherman's village whose name in the eleventh century was still unknown, in the sixteenth had become the grain emporium for the whole of southern Europe; it depopulated the flourishing cities of the Zuyder Zee, gathered into its hands the commerce of Venice, Seville, Lisbon, Antwerp, and Bruges, attracted merchants from all countries, received the victims of religious persecutions, rose again from beneath terrible inundations, defended itself against the Anabaptists, defeated the Earl of Leicester's plots, gave laws to William II., repulsed the invasion of Louis XIV., and finally, like all things here below, began to decline, and shone once more with ephemeral glory as the third city of the French empire, an honorary distinction very similar to those crosses which are given to discontented placemen to compensate them for ruinous changes. It is still a rich commercial city; but slow, circumspect, wedded to traditions, and more fond of playing on the Exchange than of undertaking bold enterprises, and a grumbling but inactive rival of the more youthful and hopeful cities of Hamburg and Rotterdam. Nevertheless, she still lays claim to her ancient dignity of conqueror of the seas, is still the fairest gem of the United Provinces; and the stranger leaving her, carries away with him an impression of grandeur and power which no other European city cancels.

UTRECHT.

From Amsterdam it is usual to go to that famous city of Utrecht, whose name we have so often pronounced when as boys we tried to fix in our minds the date of 1713 in our history lessons. One goes to Utrecht, which in itself offers nothing extraordinary after having seen other Dutch cities—not so much out of curiosity as to be able, in future, to refer to the spots when recalling the famous events which took place within its walls. You go to breathe the air of that place where was completed the most solemn act in the history of Holland, the alliance of the Netherland provinces against Philip II.; where the treaty was signed which gave restored peace to Europe after the formidable wars of the Spanish Succession; where the innocent head of the aged Van Dieman fell under the Duke of Alva's axe; where memories of Saint Boniface are still alive and speaking, and also those of Adrian IV., Charles V., and Louis XIV.; and where still boils and bubbles the combative rage of the ancient

UTRECHT. THE OLD CANAL. (*Page 273.*)

bishops, transfused into the blood of orthodox Calvinists, and ultramontane Catholics.

The road, leaving Amsterdam, passes beside the Dimmermeer, the *polder* (the drained lands are called *polder*) which is the deepest in Holland, and runs along the branch of the Rhine called Vecht, then winding among villas and kitchen-gardens, reaches Utrecht, which is seated in the midst of a most fertile country watered by the Rhine, crossed by canals, and sprinkled with houses and gardens.

Utrecht, like Leyden, has the solemn, sad aspect of a great city fallen into decadence: great deserted squares, broad silent streets, and wide canals, in which are mirrored houses of antique form and gloomy colors. But there is one thing new to the stranger. The canals are, like the Arno at Florence and the Seine at Paris, deeply sunken between the streets that flank them; and below the streets there are shops, and workshops and stores, and habitations with their doors opening on the water, and the street-pavement for a roof. The town is encircled by beautiful shaded alleys, and has a famous promenade which Louis XIV. generously preserved from the vandalism of his soldiers—a street half a French league in length, shaded by eight rows of beautiful lindens.

The history of Utrecht is closely entwined with that of its cathedral, which is, perhaps, of all the churches in Holland, the one that has seen the strangest vicissitudes. It was founded, towards 720, by a bishop of Utrecht; rebuilt from floor to roof towards the middle of the thirteenth century by another bishop; in 1674, on the 1st of August, a hurricane carried off completely one great nave which has never been rebuilt; the iconoclasts of the sixteenth century devastated it; it was restored to Catholic worship by the French in the following century; the Protestant faith was re established in it by the Dutch after the invasion of Louis XIV.; and finally, its statues, its altars, and its crosses have been carried off and replaced, raised and ruined, venerated and abused, by every change of the wind of opinion. It was certainly at one time one of the largest and finest of the Dutch churches; now it is bare and mutilated, and encumbered in great part with benches, which give it the look of a chamber of deputies. The hurricane of 1674, which destroyed a nave, separated the church from its very lofty tower, from which can be seen, with a telescope, almost all the provinces of Holland, a part of Gueldres and Brabant, Rotterdam, Amsterdam, Bois-le-Duc, the Leck, the gulf of Zuyder Zee, whilst a clock furnished with forty-two bells shakes out into the air, as it strikes the hours, the amorous strains of Count Almaviva's romance, and the prayer of *I Lombardi alla prima Croceata.*

Near the church is the celebrated university, founded in 1636, which still gives life to the city, although declined, like that of Leyden, from its primitive importance. The University of Leyden has a literary and scientific character; that of Utrecht a religious character, which it both receives from and communicates to the city, the seat of Protestant orthodoxy. For this reason it is said that you see in the streets of Utrecht the pallid and attenuated Puritan visage which has disappeared elsewhere, and which seems a shade evoked from older times.

The people are graver of aspect than in the other cities, ladies affect a nun-like demeanor, and even among the students there is a certain air of penitence and reserve, which, however, does not exclude beer, or banquets, or scandal, or evil practices. Besides being the seat of orthodoxy, Utrecht is also one of the strongest citadels of Catholicism, professed by twenty-two thousand of its inhabitants; and no one can have forgotten the tempest which broke out in Holland when the Pope wished to re-establish the bishopric of that city—a tempest which roused the hidden rancor of Protestants and Catholics, and overthrew the ministry of Zorbecke, the little Cavour of the United Provinces.

But in the matter of religion, Utrecht possesses a precious rarity, a curious archæological relic, worthy of a museum, the principal seat of the Jansenist sect, which is no more found in the condition of a constituted church, except in the Low Countries, where it counts still thirty communities and some thousands of believers. The church, decorated with the simple inscription *Deo*, rises in the midst of a group of small houses disposed in the form of a cloister, and joined together by small alleys shaded by fruit-trees; and in this silent and sad retreat, to which, not many years ago, there was but one entrance, which was closed at night and barred like the gate of a fortress, the decrepit doctrine of Jansen languishes, and his last devotees doze. To this day at each new nomination of a bishop it is regularly announced to the Sovereign Pontiff, who responds as regularly with a bull of excommunication, which is read from the pulpit and then buried and forgotten. Thus this little Port-Royal, which already feels the silence and solitude of the tomb, still continues to prolong its last resistance against death.

Of notable public institutions Utrecht has none but the mint and a college for military surgeons for the kingdom and colonies. The antique factories, for the making of that beautiful velvet once famous in Europe, have disappeared. Except the cathedral there are no public monuments. The City Hall, which preserves some ancient keys and some old standards, together with the table on which the peace of Utrecht was signed, was built in 1830. The Royal Palace, which I did not see, must be one of the most modest of palaces, for the guides, who are not apt to overlook anything, did not point it out to me.

This palace, however, if tradition does not lie, was the scene of a comic adventure that befell Napoleon the Great. During his very brief sojourn at Utrecht he occupied the bedroom of his brother Louis, which was contiguous to the bath-room. It is known that, wherever he went, he took with him one servant whose exclusive duty it was to have a bath in readiness for him at any hour of the day or night. On the evening of his arrival at Utrecht, in a bad humor, as was usual with him in Holland, he went to bed early, and, whether by inadvertence or design the story does not tell, left the door of his chamber open. The bath-servant, who was a good-natured Breton, after having prepared the bath, went to bed also in a small room not far from the imperial chamber. Towards midnight, awakened by sudden pain, and obliged to leave his bed in a hurry, half asleep and in his shirt, he began feeling about for the door of his room. He found it, but, for his evil fortune, instead of going where he wished, he found the door of the Emperor's room and went in, overturning a chair in the darkness. A terrible voice—that voice!—called out, "Who's there?" The poor fellow, frozen with fear, tried to answer, but the words died in his throat; he attempted to get out by the way he had come, but the door was not to be found; bewildered and terrified he sought it on the other side. "Who's there?" thundered the Emperor, jumping out of bed. The servant, now completely out of his wits, tumbled over chairs and tables, and vainly tried to escape. Then Napoleon, no longer doubting that treason was at work, seized his large silver watch, threw it at the head of the intruder, and seizing him by the throat, and shouting with what voice he had left, pounded the man's head with formidable blows. Then came running the valets, the chamberlains, the aides-de-camp, the prefect of the palace, with weapons and lights, and saw——the great Napoleon and the poor serving-man, both in their shirts, in the midst of the most infernal disorder, and looking in each other's faces, the one in profound amazement, the other in humble supplication, as in a pantomime. The news of the event ran all over Europe; as is usual, it grew as it spread; there was talk of an attempt on the Emperor's life, a conspiracy, an assassination accomplished, Napoleon in his grave, the universe convulsed—and all this to-do was caused by a poor servant's bad supper.

But the prince who has left the most memories in Utrecht is Louis XIV. The French say, you must go to Utrecht to see the reverse of the medal of the great king; and this reverse of the medal is the war of 1670, during which he made a long sojourn in that city.

On the reverse side of the medal of Louis XIV. is written one of the most glorious and pathetic pages of the history of Holland.

France and England entered into an alliance for the conquest of Holland. For what reason? There was no reason. To the States-General demanding the wherefor, the ministers of the King of France replied alleging impertinences in the gazettes, and a medal struck in Holland with an inscription wanting in reverence towards Louis XIV. The King of England, on his side, adduced as pretexts a picture in which English vessels were represented as captured and burned, and the failure of the Dutch fleet to salute an English ship. They spent fifty millions of francs in getting ready for the war. France sent out thirty vessels loaded with cannon, and England added a fleet of one hundred sail. To the French army, one hundred thousand strong, men disciplined and accustomed to war, and accompanied by a formidable artillery, were joined the army of the Bishop of Munster and the Elector of Cologne, numbering twenty thousand swords. The generals were Condé, Turenne, Vauban, and Luxembourg; Minister Louvois presided over the staff; the historian Pélisson followed with the task of writing down the actions; Louis XIV., the greatest king of the century, surrounded by a splendid court, escorted, like an Asiatic monarch, by a phalanx of gentlemen, cadets of noble houses, and plumed and gilded Swiss, accompanied the army. All this force and this greatness, enough to crush an empire, threatened a little country abandoned to itself, defended only by twenty-five thousand soldiers and by a Prince only twenty-two years of age, unprovided with munitions of war, torn by factions, infested by spies and traitors. War is declared; the splendid army of the great king begins its triumphal march; Europe looks on. Louis XIV., at the head of thirty thousand soldiers commanded by Turenne, scatters gold and favors all along the way, like a god. Four cities fall at once into his hands. All the fortresses of the Rhine and the Yssel fall also. At the approach of the pompous royal vanguard, the enemy melts away before it. The invading army crosses the Rhine almost without encountering resistance, and the passage is celebrated as a marvellous event, with the army, at Paris, and all over France. Doesburg, Zutphen, Arnhem, Nosemburg, Nimegnen, Shenk, Bommel fall. Utrecht sends the keys of her gates to the victorious king. Every hour of the day and night brings news of a victory. The provinces of Gueldres and Over-Yssel submit. Narden, near Amsterdam, is taken. Four French cavaliers advance even to the gates of Muiden, which is only two miles from the capital. The country is a prey to despair, Amsterdam is preparing to open her gates to the invaders, the States-General sends four deputies to implore the clemency of the king. To such a pass is reduced the country that was once the arbitrator of monarchs! The deputies arriving at the enemy's camp, the king will not admit them to his presence, and Louvois receives them with derision.

Finally, the conditions of peace are intimated to them. Holland is to cede all the provinces beyond the Rhine, and all roads by land or sea by which the enemy can penetrate into her heart; to pay twenty millions of francs; to embrace the Catholic religion; to send every year to the King of France a gold medal, upon which it shall be inscribed that Holland owes her liberty to Louis XIV.; and to accept conditions imposed by the King of England and the Princes of Munster and Cologne. The announcement of these outrageous and insupportable pretensions produces in Amsterdam an outburst of despair and fury. The States-General, the nobles, and the people, resolve to defend themselves to the very last. The dykes of Muiden, which restrain the sea, are cut, and the sea, breaking in upon the land, is received with shouts of joy, as an ally and a saviour; the country around Amsterdam, the innumerable villas and flourishing villages, Delft, Leyden, and all the neighbouring cities, are inundated; everything is changed; Amsterdam is a fortress encircled by the sea and defended by a bulwark of ships; Holland is no longer a State, it is a fleet, which, when every other hope of safety shall have perished, will carry the wealth, the magistrates, and the honor of the country to the remote ports of the colonies. Admiral de Ruyter scatters the French and English fleets, makes secure the coasts of Holland, and introduces the Indian mercantile fleet into the port of the island of Texel. The Prince of Orange gives up his property to the State, inundates more lands, startles Spain; moves the Governor of Flanders, who sends him some regiments; wins the heart of the Emperor of Germany, who sends to his help Montecuccoli at the head of twenty thousand men; gets aid from the Elector of Brandenburg, and persuades England to peace. Thus he holds front against the French until the winter, which covers Holland with ice and snow, and checks the invading army. But at the approach of spring the fight begins once more on sea and land. Sometimes fortune smiles on the French arms; but neither the care of the great king, nor the genius of his famous generals, nor the efforts of his powerful army avail to wrest victory from the Republic. Condé in vain attempts to penetrate into the heart of the submerged country; Turenne cannot prevent the Prince of Orange from making a junction with the army of Montecuccoli; the Dutch take Bonn and invest the Bishop of Munster; the King of England withdraws from the league; the French army is constrained to retire from the enterprise. The invasion had been a triumphal march: the retreat was a precipitous flight. The triumphal arches which were being built at Paris to celebrate the victory were not yet completed when the vanguard of the discomfited army arrived there; and Louis XIV., upon whom Europe smiled at the beginning of the war, found himself opposed by all. Such a triumph did little Holland carry off over the *Grande Monarque;* love of country over the rage for conquest, despair over arrogance, justice over force.

A few miles from Utrecht, near a beautiful wood, is the village of Zeist, which is approached by a road bordered with the parks and country houses of the rich merchants of Rotterdam. In this village there is a colony of those renowned brothers of Bohemia, or Moravian brothers, a religious sect derived from those founded by Valdus and John Huss, which turned Europe upside down. I had a desire to see the direct descendants of those Waldensians and Hussites " who were burned on all the piles, hanged on all the gallows, nailed on all the crosses, broken on all the wheels, torn in pieces by all the horses," and I made an excursion to Zeist. This Moravian house was founded towards the middle of the last century, and contains about two hundred and fifty men, women, and children. The aspect of the place is as austere as the lives of its inhabitants. There are two spacious courtyards, separated by a wide street, each one of which is enclosed on three sides by a great building as bare as a barrack. In one of these buildings are the married couples and unmarried men, and the schools; in the other, the widows and girls, the church, the pastor, and the head of the community. The ground-floor is occupied by shops, containing merchandise, partly the work of the Moravians, such as gloves, soap, candles, &c., partly purchased to be sold again at fixed and very moderate prices. The church is nothing but a great hall, with two tribunes for strangers, and some rough benches for the brothers. The interior of the two buildings is like that of a convent, with long corridors bordered by small cells in which each brother lives in profound meditation, working and praying. Their lives are of the strictest. They profess, at least ostensibly, the Augsburg Confession. They admit original sin, but in the faith that the death of Jesus Christ has absolutely purified humanity. They believe that the unity of the Church consists more in the charity which should unite all the disciples of Christ in one single mind and one single heart, than in uniformity of faith. They practise, in a certain sense, community of goods, and bring voluntary offerings to the common fund. All necessary professions are exercised among themselves: doctors, nurses, teachers, &c. The Superior can punish by a reproof, by excommunication, or by expulsion from the community. The occupations of the day are regulated as in a college: prayer, private meeting, reading, work, religious exercises, at certain fixed hours, and among the brethren of the classes named. To give an idea of the order which reigns among them, I may point out, among many other peculiar customs, that the different conditions of the women are indicated by differently colored ribbons worn upon the head. Girls wear a bright rose-colored ribbon until the age of ten, a red ribbon until eighteen, and a pale red one until their marriage; married women wear a blue ribbon, and widows a white one. Thus in that society everything is classed, established, measured; life goes on with the regularity of a machine; man moves like an automaton; rules take the place of will, and the clock governs thought. When I entered the building I saw no one but two servants standing at the threshold, and one girl with a red ribbon at a window. The courtyards were deserted, no sign of life was there, not even a fly buzzed. I looked here and there, as one looks at a cemetery through the bars of a gate, and went thoughtfully back to Utrecht.

BROEK.

From the moment that I began writing the first pages of this book I have been in the habit of encouraging myself to proceed by thinking of the pleasure I should experience upon my first arrival at the village of Broek. I had my days of discouragement and fatigue, when I was ready to throw the whole manuscript into the fire; but the thought of Broek was always enough to revive me from that prostration of soul. The image of Broek was my polar star. "How long before we arrive at Broek?" asked my friends at home, smiling. And I answered, with a sigh, "Two months more; twenty days; a week." Here I am at last at the day so much desired. I am happy and impatient; I should like to express myself at once with pen, pencil, and voice. I have a hundred things to tell, and I do not know where to begin; and I laugh at myself, as my readers will doubtless laugh at me.

In the different cities where I had been, from Rotterdam to Amsterdam, I had heard more than once of the village of Brock, but always in a way to tickle my curiosity rather than to satisfy it. The name of Brock pronounced among a group of people always raised a laugh. When I asked why they laughed, I got the dry answer, "Because it is ridiculous." One person, at the Hague, had said to me, half pleasantly and half annoyed, "Oh, when will strangers have done with that blessed Brock? Is there nothing else for them to quiz us about?" At Amsterdam, the landlord of my hotel, tracing out for me on the map the way to Brock, laughed in his beard with an air as if he were saying, "How childish!" I had asked for information from various people, and they had one and all refused to give it, shaking their heads, and saying, "You will see." Only from a few words dropped here and there had I been able to gather that Brock was a very queer place, famous for its oddity since the last century, described, illustrated, derided, and made by foreigners a pretext for an infinite number of jokes and stories against the Hollanders.

My curiosity may be imagined. Enough to say that I dreamed of Brock every night, and that the description of all the fantastic, wonderful, and impossible villages which I saw in my dreams would fill a volume. It was with an effort that I gave precedence to Utrecht, and had no sooner returned to Amsterdam than I started for the mysterious village.

Brock is in North Holland, about halfway between Edam and Amsterdam, and not far from the shore of the Zuyder Zee. I had then to cross the gulf of the Y, and go through a portion of the Northern canal. I embarked early in one of the small steamboats which leave every hour of the day for Alkmaar and Helder, and in a few minutes reached the Grand canal.

This is the largest canal in Holland, and one of the most wonderful works of the nineteenth century in Europe. Everyone knows in what way and with what purpose it was opened. Formerly to reach the port of Amsterdam, large vessels had to cross the gulf of Zuyder Zee, which is obstructed by sand-banks and agitated by storms. The crossing, long and full of peril, was especially difficult at the point where the gulf of Zuyder Zee joins that of the Y, by reason of a great sand-bank called Pampus, which large vessels could not get over except by unshipping a part of their cargo, and being towed, with great loss of time and at great expense. To open an easier way to the port of Amsterdam, there was constructed this great canal which runs from the gulf of the Y into the North sea, crossing the whole of North Holland, almost eighty kilometres in length, forty wide, six deep. It was begun in 1819, finished in 1825, and cost thirty millions of francs. Thanks to this canal, in favorable weather the largest ships can go in four-and-twenty hours from the North Sea to the port of Amsterdam. Nevertheless, the city is still, in comparison to other maritime cities, in a position of disadvantage with regard to commerce, since the entrance to the Northern canal, near the island of Texel, is exceedingly difficult; ships have to be towed even in the canal itself, so that transit, up as well as down, costs about a thousand francs; and in severe winters the water freezes, navigation is impeded and delayed, and sometimes as much as thirty thousand florins is spent in opening a passage. But the courage of the Hollanders is not arrested even in the face of such difficulties, and it has opened a new road to commerce. Another canal, which is now in course of construction, will cross the gulf of the Y in the direction of its greatest length, cross the downs, and come out into the sea near the village of Wyk-aan-zee, separating North Holland from the continent. This canal will be twenty-five kilometres in length and as wide as the Suez canal; by it ships can reach Amsterdam from the sea in two hours and a half; a large part of the gulf of the Y, filled up with the material taken from the canal, will be converted into ground capable of cultivation; and thus the way will be for ever closed against inundations by the sea, by which Amsterdam is constantly threatened. The works, begun in 1866, are almost finished; and already on the 25th of September 1872, a vessel belonging to the society that carries on the enterprise passed triumphantly through the new canal, joyfully saluted by the city as the herald of prosperity and fortune.

Hardly had the steamboat passed beyond the monumental gates of the Northern canal, when the gulf, the port, Amsterdam itself, all vanished from my gaze; for at this point the waters of the canal are almost three metres lower than the level of the sea; and I could see only a myriad of topmasts, points of steeples, and the ends of the wings of windmills, rising above the lofty dykes between which we were gliding. From time to time we passed through a narrow lock, shut in between high walls, not even the horizon visible; we seemed to be steaming through the intricacies of some submerged fortress. After half an hour of this furtive navigation, we reached a village, a real enigma of a village, made up of a few small colored houses ranged along a dyke, and almost entirely concealed by a row of trees cut in the form of fans and planted in front of the houses as if to defend them from the indiscreet gaze of curious passengers. The steamboat was passed through another lock and came out into the open country, where an entirely new spectacle presented itself. The waters of the canal, being much more elevated than the surrounding country, the boat was on a level with the tops of the trees and the roof-ridges of the houses which bordered the dykes; and the people walking in the roads turned their faces upwards to look at us, as we had raised ours a little while before to look at persons walking on the dykes. We met vessels towed by horses, barges towed by the entire family, ranged in a line by order of age, from the grandfather down to the youngest child, and the dog; steamboats coming from Alkmaar and Helder, full of peasant women wearing the gold circlet on their heads; and everywhere over the fields we could see the sails of boats gliding about in the hidden canals, and looking as if they were sailing on the grass.

Arrived at my destination I landed and waited to see the steamboat go on before I took the road alone to Brock, flanked on the left by a canal, and on the right by a hedge. I had an hour's walk before me. The country was green, striped by many canals, sprinkled with groups of trees and windmills, and as silent as a steppe. Beautiful black and white cows wandered at will, untended by anyone, or reposed upon the banks of the canals; flocks of ducks and white geese swam about the basins; and here and there a boat, rowed by a peasant, darted through a canal between the meadows. That vast plain, animated by a life so mute and tranquil, inspired me with a feeling of such sweet peace, that the softest music would have disturbed me there like an importunate noise.

After half an hour's walk, although no sign of Broek appeared beyond the top of a tall steeple, I began to see here and there something which announced the neighbourhood of a village. The road ran along a dyke, and upon the side of it there were a few houses. One of these, a wooden hutch whose roof scarcely reached to the level of the road—a rough, disjointed, tumble-down place, more like a kennel than a house—had a little window with a smart white curtain tied up with a bow of blue ribbon, and showing through the panes a little table covered with cups, glasses, flowers, and shining trifles. A little further on I saw two posts planted in the ground and supporting a hedge, which were painted in blue and white stripes like the banner-poles which are erected for public festivals; and still beyond, I came upon another peasant's house, before which were displayed small buckets, benches, rakes, shovels, and picks—all painted red, blue, white, yellow, and striped and bordered with contrasting colors, like the utensils of a mountebank. As I went on I saw other rustic houses with their windows ornamented with net curtains and ribbons, with little movable mirrors, and toys hung up; their doors and window-frames painted in bright colors. The brightness and variety of tints, the cleanliness and shining neatness of everything increased as I advanced. I saw embroidered white curtains with rose-colored bows in the windows of a mill; the nails and metal bands of the carts and agricultural implements shone like silver; the wooden houses were painted red and white; the windows were bordered with stripes of two or three colors; and finally, strangest of all, trees with their trunks colored bright blue from the root to the first branches.

Laughing to myself at this last oddity, I arrived at a large basin of the canal surrounded by thick and leafy trees, beyond which, on the other side, arose a steeple. I looked about and discovered a boy lying on the grass. "Broek?" inquired I. "Brock," he responded, laughing. Then I looked, and beheld amid the green of the trees such a show of harlequin colors, that I could only cry out in astonishment. Skirting the basin and crossing a small bridge of wood as white as snow, I entered a narrow road. I looked. Broek! Broek! I knew it, there was no mistake; it could not be any other than Brock.

Imagine a *presepio** made of pasteboard by a boy of eight years old, a city made for the show-window of a Nuremburg toy-shop, a village constructed by a ballet-master after the drawing on a Chinese fan, a collection of barracks of wealthy mountebanks, a group of houses

---

* *Presepio:* a representation of the manger where Christ was born; seen in the churches at Christmas.

made for the scenes of a puppet-theatre, the fancy of an Oriental drunk with opium, something which makes you think of Japan, India, Tartary, and Switzerland all at once, with a touch of Pompadour *rococo*, and something of the constructions in sugar that one sees in a confectioner's window; a mixture of the barbaric, the pretty, the presumptuous, the ingenious, and the silly, which, while it offends good taste, provokes at the same time a good-natured laugh; imagine, in short, the most childish extravagance to which the name of village can be given, and you will have a faint idea of Broek.

All the houses are surrounded by small gardens, separated from the street by a sky-blue paling, in the form of a balustrade, with wooden apples and oranges on the top of the pales. The streets bordered by these palings are very narrow, and paved with tiny bricks of various colors, set edge-wise and combined in different designs, so that, at a distance, the street seems to be carpeted with Cashmere shawls. The houses, for the most part built of wood, and all of one storey only, and very small, are rose-colored, black, grey, purple, blue, and grass-green; their roofs are covered with painted tiles disposed in squares of different colors; the eaves ornamented with a kind of wooden festoon, carved in open work; the façades pointed, with a little flag at the top, or a small lance, or something resembling a bunch of flowers; the windows with red and blue glass, and having curtains decorated with embroidery, ribbons, fringes, and a display of cups, and vases, and toys within; the doors painted and gilded, and surmounted with all sorts of bas-reliefs representing flowers, figures, and trophies, in the midst of which can be read the name and profession of the proprietor. Almost all the houses have two doors, one front and one back—the latter for every-day use, the other for solemn occasions, such as a birth, a death, or a marriage.

The gardens are not less odd than the houses. They seem made for dwarfs. The paths are scarcely wide enough for the feet, the arbors can contain two very small persons standing close together, the box borders would not reach the knee of a child of four years old. Between the arbors and the tiny flower-beds there are little canals, apparently made for toy-boats, which are spanned here and there by superfluous bridges with little painted railings and columns; basins about as large as an ordinary sitz-bath contain a liliputian boat tied by a red cord to a sky-blue post; tiny steps, paths, gates, and lattices abound, each of which can be measured with the hand, or knocked down with a blow of the fist, or jumped over with ease. Around houses and gardens stand trees cut in the shape of fans, plumes, discs, &c., with their trunks painted white and blue, and here and there appears a little wooden house for a domestic animal, painted, gilded, and carved like a house in a puppet-show.

After a glance at the first houses and gardens, I advanced into the village. There was not a living soul in the streets, or at the windows. All doors were closed, all curtains drawn, all canals deserted, all boats motionless. The village is so constructed that from no point can more than four or five houses be seen at a time; consequently, at every step a new scene is discovered, a new combination of bright colors, a new caprice, a new absurdity. One expects every moment to see the doors fly open and a population of automatons come forth with cymbals and tambourines in their hands, like the figures on hand-organs. Fifty paces carry you around a house, over a bridge, through a garden, and back to your starting point. A child looks like a man, and a man appears a giant. Everything is tiny, compressed, smooth, colored, childish, and unnatural. At first you laugh; then comes the thought that the inhabitants of this village believe you find it beautiful. The caricature seems odious to you; the owners of the houses are all idiots; you would like to tell them that their famous Broek is an insult to art and nature, and that there is in it neither good taste nor good sense. But when you have relieved your mind a little in this way, the laugh returns and prevails.

After having walked about for a while without meeting anyone, I began to wish to see the inside of one of these houses. Whilst I looked about in search of some hospitable soul, I heard someone call "Monsieur!" and turning, saw a woman in a door-way, who asked me, timidly, "Would you wish to see a private house?" I accepted, and the woman, leaving her wooden-shoes outside, as is the custom in this country, led me in. She was a poor widow, she told me, and had only one room; but what a room! The floor was covered with clean matting; the furniture shone like ebony, all the little points of metal here and there looked like silver. The chimney was a real temple, lined with colored tiles, and as clean and polished as if it had never seen a fire. Not seeing any bed, I asked the good woman where she slept. She immediately opened a folding door in the wall which was concealed by the paper. The bed (in this case as in all others) was shut in a kind of closet in the thickness of the wall, and consisted of a mattress or two laid upon the lower part of the same wall, without any bedstead—a convenient bed in winter, but suffocating, one would think, in summer. She showed me the utensils for cleaning the room— enough to set up a shop; brooms, brushes, toothbrushes, cloths, scrapers, dustpans, pokers, shovels, feather brushes, aquafortis, Spanish white for the window-panes, Venetian red for the knives, coal-dust for the copper vessels, emery for polishing the iron things, brick for rubbing the pavements, and sticks for poking out the microscopic straws that get into the cracks of the floors.

She gave me some curious information about the fury of cleanliness for which the village of Broek is famous throughout Holland. It is not long since an inscription to the following effect could be seen at the entrance to the village: "Before and after sunrise, it is forbidden to smoke in the village of Broek except with a cover to the pipe-bowl (*so as not to scatter the ashes*); and, in crossing the village with a horse, it is forbidden to remain in the saddle: the horse must be led."

It was also forbidden to go through the village in a carriage, or with sheep or cows, or any other animal that might soil the street; and although this prohibition no longer exists, carts and animals still go round the village, from old custom. Before every house there was once (and some may still be seen) a stone spittoon, into which smokers spat from the windows. The custom of being without shoes within doors is still in vigor, and before every door there is a heap of shoes and boots and wooden pattens.

That which has been told about popular risings in Brock in consequence of strangers having scattered some cherry-stones in the street, is a fable; but it is quite true that every citizen who sees from his window a leaf or straw fall upon the pavement, comes out and throws it into the canal. That they go five hundred paces outside the village to dust their shoes, that boys are paid to blow the dust out of the cracks of the pavements four times an hour, and that, in certain cases, guests are carried in the arms lest they should soil the floors, are things which are told, said this good woman, but which probably have never happened. Before letting me go, however, she related to me an anecdote which almost made these extravagances seem possible. "In former times," she said, "the mania for cleanliness arrived at such a pass, that the women of Brock neglected their religious duties for it. The pastor of the village, after having tried all means of persuasion to cause the cessation of the scandal, took another way. He preached a sermon in which he said that every Dutch woman who should have faithfully fulfilled her duties towards God in this earthly life, would find in the other world a house full of furniture, utensils, and trifles various and precious, in which undisturbed by other occupation, she could sweep, wash, and polish for all eternity, without ever coming to an end. The image of this sublime recompense, the thought of this immense felicity, infused such ardor and piety into the women of Broek, that from that moment they were assiduous at religious exercises, and never had need of further admonition."

And yet, neither in this rage for cleanliness, nor in its oddities of architecture, lies the reason for the semi-serious celebrity of the village of Broek. This celebrity arises from an extravagance of forms and customs, beside which those which now exist are nowhere. The Broek of to-day is only the pale shade of the Broek of former times. To know this it is only necessary to visit a house placed at the entrance of the village, and open to strangers, which is a perfect model of the ancient houses, and has been preserved by the proprietor as an historical monument of past folly. The exterior of the house is not different from the others. The wonders are in the chambers and in the garden. The rooms, very small, are so many bazaars, each one of which would require a volume of description. The Dutch mania for piling object upon object and seeking elegance and beauty in the excess of the utmost disparity of ornament, is here seen pushed to the superlative of the ridiculous. There are porcelain figures on the shelves, Chinese cups and sugar-bowls on and under all the tables, plates suspended on the walls from ceiling to floor, clocks, ostrich eggs, boats, ships, vases, saucers, goblets, stuck in every space and hidden in every corner; pictures which present different figures according to the point from which they are viewed, closets full of thousands of toys and trifles; nameless ornaments, senseless decorations, a confusion and dissonance of color, bad taste so innocently displayed that it is pitiful to see.

But the absurdity is still greater in the garden. Here are bridges a palm long, grottoes and cascades of miniature proportions, small rustic chapels, Greek temples, Chinese kiosks, Indian pagodas, painted statues; tiny figures with gilded feet and hands, which bounce out of flower-baskets; automata of life size that smoke and spin; doors which open with a spring and display a company of puppets seated at a table; little basins with swans and geese in zinc; paths paved with a mosaic of shells, with a fine porcelain vase in the middle; trees cut into a representation of the human figure, bushes of box carved into the shapes of bell-towers, chapels, ships, chimeras, peacocks with spread tails, and children with arms stretched out; paths, arbors, hedges, flowers, plants, all contorted, tormented, twisted, and bastardised. And such in former times were all the houses and gardens of Broek.

But now, not only the aspect of the village but the population is much changed. Broek was formerly called a village of millionaires, because almost all its inhabitants were very wealthy merchants, who went there for the love of peace and quietness. Little by little the annoyance, the ridicule which was excited by their houses and themselves, the importunity of travellers, the desire for more agreeable surroundings, drove away almost all the rich families from Broek, and those who remained allowed the old order of things to vanish. Now Broek has about a thousand inhabitants, the greater part of whom make cheeses, and the rest are shopkeepers, manufacturers and artificers, living on their incomes.

In spite of its decadence, Broek is still visited by almost all strangers who go to Holland. In one of the rooms of the house I have described there is a large book containing several thousand visiting cards and autographs of people of every country. The greater part are Americans and English; Italians are fewest, and of these, almost all nobles from the southern provinces. Amongst the many illustrious names, I saw those of Victor Hugo, Walter Scott, Gambetta, and Emile Augier the dramatic writer. Among other things there is a paper signed by the Emperor and Empress of Russia, and given to a citizen of Broek in gratitude for hospitality shown by him to the Grand Duke Nicolas Alexandrovitch in 1864.

Apropos of illustrious visitors, the Emperor Alexander of Russia and Napoleon the Great were both at Broek. The local tradition says that each of them having wished to see the interior of a house, they were obliged before entering to draw on a pair of coarse woollen stockings presented to them by the maid-servant, so that they should not soil the floors with their boots.

The Emperor Joseph II. also made a visit to Broek; but, as it is related, not having brought any letters of introduction, he was not permitted to enter any house. An aide-de-camp having insisted that His Majesty should be admitted, the owner answered, " I do not know your Emperor, and if he were the Burgomaster of Amsterdam in person, I would not receive him if I did not know him."

When I had visited the house and garden above described, I went to a small café, where a girl without shoes, understanding my signs, brought me half of an excellent Edam cheese, with some eggs and butter and bread, each thing in a covered dish, protected by a wire netting, and hidden under the whitest of fringed napkins; and then I went with a boy, who conversed with me by gestures, to see a dairy-farm. Many people among us who wear tall hats and gold watches, have not so pretty and clean an apartment as that in which the cows of Brock reside Before entering, you are requested to wipe your feet on a mat laid there for that purpose. The pavement of the stalls is of various colored bricks, so clean that the hand could be passed over it; the walls are covered with pine-wood; the windows decorated with muslin curtains and pots of flowers; the mangers are painted; the animals themselves are scraped, combed, washed, and, that they may not soil their coats, their tails are held up by a cord which is attached to a nail in the ceiling; a clear stream of water running through between the stalls, carries off all impurities; except under the animals' feet there is not a straw or a stain to be seen; and the air is so pure that if you close your eyes you may imagine yourself in a drawing-room. The rooms where the peasants live, the cheese-rooms, the courts and corners, are all clean and sweet. Before returning to Amsterdam I took one more turn about the village, taking care to hide my cigar when I saw a woman with a gold circlet on her head looking at me from a window. I crossed two or three white bridges, touched a few boats with my foot, lingered a moment before the gayest of the painted houses; and then, seeing no living soul in the street or in the gardens, I resumed my solitary way on the horse of St. Francis,* with that feeling of weary sadness which accompanies in general curiosity satisfied.

---

* The horse of St. Francis; *Anglicè*, Shank's mare.

ZAANDAM.

Most strangers, after having visited Broek and the town of Zandaam, go to Friesland and return to the Hague under the impression that they have seen Holland. I, on the contrary, wished to push on to the extremity of North Holland, believing that in that out-of-the-way province, where no foreigners reside and few travellers go, I should find manners, customs, and ancient usages more distinctly marked than in the others. The dangers of not being able to make myself understood, of putting up at bad inns, of being alone, perhaps ill and sad, in some small place scarce mentioned in the guide-books, and which the most patient travellers pass through without stopping— nothing turned me from my purpose. One fine morning in August, the travelling devil, the most potent of all devils who invade the human soul, transported me and my valise into a steamboat that was leaving for Zaandam, embarked me on the same day for Alkmaar, the metropolis of cheeses, and on the same evening gave me a second-class ticket for Helder, the Gibraltar of the North.

Zaandam, seen from the gulf of the Y, presents the aspect of a fortress crowned with innumerable towers, from the summits of which the citizens are calling for succour with frantic gestures to a distant army. There are hundreds of tall windmills, which rise among the houses, upon the dykes, along the shore, over the whole country about the town, some of which are busy in draining the lands, some in making colza oil, which is one of the most important commercial products of Zaandam; others are crushing into powder a species of volcanic tufa rock brought from the Rhine, and which is used in the composition of a particular cement for hydraulic works; others saw wood, grind colors, clean barley, make paper, mustard, rope, starch, and paste. The town becomes visible only a few minutes before entering the port.

It looked like a scene in a pastoral ballet. The city is along the two banks of a river called the Zaan, which empties itself into the Y, and around it is a small basin formed by the Y itself, which serves it as a port. The two portions of the city are connected by a drawbridge. There are but few streets or houses near the port, the principal part of Zaandam extending along the banks of the Zaan.

Zaandam is a larger Broek, handsomer and less puerile than little Broek.

The houses are built of wood, with one storey, and pointed façades, and are almost all painted green. There are whole streets where no other color is seen, looking as if they were make of box and myrtle. The whole place has an air of cheerfulness and freshness that is very attractive; and although it is a rich and populous city, it seems a village. It has all the peculiar features of a Dutch town, but with them there is something new and exotic that distinguishes it from the others.

It being a holiday, the streets were full of people going to, or coming from, church. The first thing that struck me was the head-dress of the women. Under a hat covered with flowers, they wear a sort of lace cap which falls down upon the shoulders, and from beneath which protrude upon the forehead two bunches of hair, curled like clusters of grapes. The gold or silver band which encircles the head and gleams through the lace of the cap, terminates on each temple by a square bit of the same metal, turned towards the spectator, and with a rosette in the middle. Another little plate, gilded and carved, a sort of metallic ribbon, attached in some way to the band upon the head, crosses the forehead obliquely and comes down almost to the opposite temple, or to the eye-brow, looking rather like a piece of the band, broken off and hanging. Two large pins stuck vertically into the two extremities of the band rise like two horns above the two bunches of curls. Long ear-rings hang from the ears, the neck is ornamented with several rows of necklaces, and on the breast there are enough brooches, clasps, and chains to furnish out a jeweller's window. All the women, with slight differences, are decorated in this way; and as they are all fair and rosy, and dressed with the same bad taste, it is difficult for a stranger to distinguish a lady from a peasant. It cannot be said, exactly, that the head-dress and the superabundance of ornament are elegant or beautiful; but yet the fair complexions under all that gold and lace and flowers, that mixture of the princely and the rustic, the opulent and the coarse, the pompous and the ingenuous, has a grace of its own which agrees, as one may say, with the air of the place, and ends by pleasing you. Even the children have their lace and their diadem; the men being generally dressed in black. And all, old and young, have an air of contentment, a primitive, virginal, and youthful look, that makes them seem unlike Europeans of our time, and imparts a feeling of another continent and another civilization, a country where riches grow without labor, life flows on passionless, society moves without shock or attrition, and where no one desires any other good than peace. And if, while these thoughts pass through the mind, the clock of a neighbouring steeple chimes out in silvery notes some old national air, the illusion is complete, and you would like to bring your family and friends to Zaandam, and end your tranquil days in one of those green houses.

But if all this beatitude is but an illusion, it is still a fact that Zaandam is one of the wealthiest of the Dutch cities, that in many of those little green houses live shipbuilders who are millionaires, and that there is no family without bread, and no children without instruction.

Zaandam possesses, besides, what Napoleon called "the finest monument in Holland"—that is, the cabin of Peter the Great, in honor of whom the city was at one time called Czardam or Sardam. A whole squadron of cicerone whisper the name of this cabin into the ears of all strangers arriving in Zaandam, and it may be said to be the main object of all those who visit the city.

When and why the great Emperor lived in this cabin are known to all. After having conquered the Tartars and the Turks, and made his triumphal entrance into Moscow, the young Czar wished to make a journey through the principal European states to study their arts and industries. Accompanied by three ambassadors, four secretaries, twelve gentlemen, fifty guards, and one dwarf, he left his own states in April of 1697, crossed Livonia, passed through Prussian Brandenburg, by Pomerania, Berlin, and Westphalia, and arrived at Amsterdam fifteen days before his suite. In that city, unknown to all, he passed some time in the arsenals of the Admiralty; and then, in order to learn with his own eyes and hands the art of shipbuilding, in which Holland was at that time superior, he dressed himself as a sailor, and went to Zaandam, where the most famous arsenals were situated. Here, under the name of Peter Michaelhoff, he entered the ship-yard of a certain Mynheer Calf, was inscribed among the other workmen, worked in wood, iron, and cordage, and during the whole time of his stay, dressed and ate and slept exactly as his companions in labor did, living in the wooden cabin which is still shown. How long he remained in the city is not exactly known. Some say that he was there several months, but others, with more probability, believe that, annoyed by the curiosity of the inhabitants, he stayed only one week. Certain it is that, returning to Amsterdam after a short time, he finished with his own hands, in the arsenal of the East India Company, a vessel of sixty guns; that he studied mathematics, physics, geography, anatomy, and painting, and that he left Amsterdam in January 1698 to go to London.

The famous cabin is to be found at one end of Zaandam in sight of the open country; and is encased, as it were, in a little edifice of mason work, which the Queen of Holland, Anna Paulovna, who was Russian by birth, caused to be built for its preservation. It is a simple fisherman's hut, of wood, with two little rooms, and in such a tumbledown condition that, if it were not upheld in the manner described, the first high wind would level it to the ground. In one room there are three rough stools, a large table, a bed, and a large chimney of the antique Flemish pattern. In the second, there are two portraits; one of Peter the Great in his workman's dress, and the other of the Empress Catherine. The Dutch and Russian flags are spread out on the ceiling. The furniture, walls, doors, and beams are all covered with names and inscriptions in all the languages of the world. There is a slab of marble upon which is written: "Petro magno Alexander," placed there by order of the Emperor Alexander in commemoration of his visit in 1814. Another stone records the visit made by the present Czar, when hereditary prince, in 1839, and under it there is a verse by a Russian poet to this effect: "Over this humble abode, the holy angels watch. Czarevitch! bow down! Here is the cradle of thy Empire; here was born the greatness of Russia." Other stones record the visits of

ZAANDAM. INTERIOR OF PETER THE GREAT'S HOUSE. (*Page* 306.)

kings and princes, and there are many verses and inscriptions, generally in Russian, expressing the joy and enthusiasm of those who have reached the goal of their sacred pilgrimage. One of the inscriptions sets forth that from this cabin the carpenter Peter Michaeloff directed the movements of the Muscovite army, when fighting against the Turks in the Ukraine.

As I came out, I thought that if the most glorious day in the life of Peter the Great was that in which he lay down to rest in that hut, after having for the first time labored with his own hands, the happiest must ha e been that one in which he came back, after eighteen years had passed, in the height of his power and glory, and showed Catherine the place where, while working as a day-laborer, he had learned to be an emperor. The inhabitants of Zaandam remember that day with pride, and speak of it as of an event which they had witnessed. The Czarina had stopped at Wesel for her confinement; the Czar arrived alone at Zaandam. The joy and pride may be imagined with which he was received by those merchants, sailors, and carpenters who had known him eighteen years before. For the world at large, he was the conqueror of Pultowa, the founder of St. Petersburg, the civilizer of Russia, but for them he was *Peterbas*, Master Peter, as he was familiarly called when he worked among them; he was a son of Zaandam, who had become an emperor; he was an old friend come back to them. Ten days after arrived the Czarina and also visited the cabin. Emperor and Empress without pomp or attendance went to dine at the house of Mynheer Calf, the shipbuilder who had received the young crowned workman at his arsenal; the people accompanied him, shouting: "Long live Master Peter!" and Master Peter, the exterminator of boyards, the condemner of his own son, the formidable despot, wept.

To go to Alkmaar I took a steamboat, which went up the Zaan as far as the Northern canal, and thus saw East and West Zaandam, or those parts of the city which stretch for almost three miles along the two banks of the river.

It is a spectacle which vindicates Brock twenty times over.

Everyone remembers those landscapes painted when a boy, after Papa, or some kind uncle, had made a present of a box of colors. The general wish is to depict a delicious spot, such as is dreamt of at school when dozing over the last Latin lessons just before vacation. In order to render the place truly delightful, the boy crowds into a small space a villa, a garden, a lake, a wood, a field, a river, a bridge, a grotto, a cascade, all close together and well wedged in; and that nothing may escape the eye, every object is painted with the most vivid colors that the box can furnish; and when it is finished, struck with the idea that he has not really profited by every inch of space, he puts in a little house here, and a tree there, and a cottage in the corner, until, it being clearly impossible to insert another blade of grass, or stone, or flower, he lays down his brush delighted with his own work, and runs to show it to the maid-servant, who exclaims in admiration over that true terrestrial paradise. Well, Zaandam seen from the river, is precisely like one of these landscapes.

The houses are all green, with bright red roofs, upon which are little green kiosks, surmounted by gay flags, or wooden balls of different colors stuck upon iron rods; there are little towers crowned with railings and striped awnings, edifices in the form of little temples; sheds and barracks of unknown structure, capriciously crowded one upon the other, as if for lack of space; an architecture of expediency, full of show and vanity. In the midst of these buildings are streets, through which no one ever passes, squares about as big as ordinary rooms, courtyards but little larger than a table, canals scarce wide enough for a duck to swim; and in front, between the houses and the river-bank, childish little gardens, full of summer-houses, boxes for the chickens, arbors, toy windmills and weeping willows; and in front of these gardens, on the river-banks, little ports full of little green boats, tied to still greener posts. In the midst of this medley of gardens and barracks, tall windmills rise on every side, green edged with white, or white edged with green, with their wings painted like flagstaffs, and the centre gilded and ornamented with many-colored weathercocks; steeples green and varnished from top to bottom, chapels that look like booths at a fair, painted in squares like a chess-board and bordered with all the colors of the rainbow. But what is still more curious, the buildings, small enough at the beginning, go on growing smaller as you proceed down the river, as if the population were distributed in the order of stature, so that towards the end there are none but sentry-boxes—places to hide in—looking as if they protruded from a buried town; a tiny architecture that is there, under your feet, but seems to be far away; a human beehive, where the children look colossal, and the cats jump from the streets to the roofs.

ALKMAAR.

The vessel, passing beyond Zaandam, went on for a long time between two rows of windmills, touched at various villages, turned into the Marker-Vaart canal, crossed the lake of Alkmaar, and finally entered the Northern canal. I cannot describe the feeling of solitude, and of distance, that came over me in the midst of that crowd of peasant women, bediademed like queens, and motionless as images, on the steamboat as it glided along with the placidity of a gondola across a boundless and uniform expanse, under a melancholy sky. I found myself at certain moments wondering how I came there, and where I was going to, and when I should come back; I felt home-sick for Amsterdam and the Hague, as if the country through which I was passing were as far from South Holland as the latter was from Italy; I made a mental resolution never to travel again alone, and felt as if I should never see home again.

At that point I found myself in the very heart of

North Holland, at that little peninsula bathed by the North Sea, and the gulf of Zuyder Zee, which is almost all lower than the waters that surround it, and is defended on one side by the downs, and on the other by immense dykes, and intersected by an infinitude of canals, lakes, and ponds, which give it the aspect of a half-submerged territory destined some day to vanish under the waters. Over the entire space that can be embraced by the eye there are to be seen only a few groups of trees, some sails of vessels, and windmills.

That part of the Northern canal which the steamboat was going through runs along the Beemster, the largest extent of land that was drained in the seventeenth century, one of the forty-three lakes that anciently covered the province of Alkmaar, and which were transformed into beautiful meadows. This Beemster, which embraces an area of seven thousand hectares, and is administered, like all the other *polders*, by a committee elected by the proprietors—the expenses being covered by a tax divided at so much per hectare—is laid out in a large number of squares, surrounded by paved roads and canals, so that the country looks like a gigantic chess-board. The surface being almost three metres and a half lower than that of Amsterdam, the rain-water has to be constantly drawn off by means of windmills, which drain it into the canals, and they carry it to the sea. There are in the whole *polder* almost three hundred farms, possessing about six thousand beef cattle and more than four hundred horses. The only trees to be seen are poplars, elms, and willows, grouped about the houses as a defence against the wind. It is all meadow-land, and all the other *polders* are like the Beemster. The only salient objects upon those verdant plains are the posts which support the storks' nests, and here and there some enormous bone of a whale, the antique trophy of Dutch fishermen, planted upright in the earth, and serving for the cows to scratch themselves against. All transportation of produce from farm to farm is done by boat; the houses are entered by a drawbridge which is raised at night, like the bridge of a fortress; the herds pasture without any herdsmen; ducks and swans swim freely in the long canals; all things breathe security, plenty, and peace. These are, in fact, the provinces where flourish, in all its beauty, that famous race of cattle to which Holland, in great part, owes her riches; those large, pacific cows, which give as much as thirty quarts of milk a day, descendants of those glorious animals which, in the middle ages, were sent to ennoble the race in France, Belgium, Germany, Sweden, and Russia; one head of which, if tradition may be believed, crossed the continent as far as Odessa, going back, step by step, over the road which had been followed by the great Germanic invasions. With the milk of these animals is made that exquisite cheese called Edam, after the town of that name in North Holland. On market days, all the towns in this province are overflowing with these handsome reddish forms piled up like cannon-balls in the streets and piazzas, and pointed out to the stranger with a sentiment of national pride. Alkmaar sells more than four millions of kilogrammes per year, Horn three millions, Purmerende two, Medenblick and

Enkhuysen from seven to eight hundred thousand, the whole of North Holland more than fifteen millions of francs worth.

As the steamboat drew near to the city, I went on as usual, exciting my curiosity by recalling to my memory everything that I knew about Alkmaar; far from foreseeing, poor soul, the disagreeable circumstances in which I was to find myself within its walls. I imagined it destroyed by John of Avesnes, Count of Holland, in punishment for rebellion. I followed the courageous carpenter, who crossed the camp of the Spaniards, carrying to the governor of the province the order of the Prince of Orange to cut the dykes, and who afterwards lost the governor's answer; which, being found and read by Frederic, the Duke of Alva's son, caused him to raise the siege in the fear of being drowned. I saw a troop of schoolboys amusing themselves by looking at the snowy landscape through bits of ice applied to the tubes of their ink-stands, and the good Mezio coming amongst them to find in their play the first idea of the spy-glass. I met at the corner of a street the painter Schornel, his head all scarred with the sticks and fisticuffs which he had got in the taverns at Utrecht, where he had been drinking with that good fellow John of Manburg, his master in painting and debauchery. And, last of all, I imagined the lovely women of Alkmaar, who, with their modest and innocent air, had the power to indemnify Napoleon for the ennui of Amsterdam and the boredom of Broek. Meantime, the steamboat arrived at Alkmaar; where a porter who knew three French words, *Monsieur, hôtel,* and *pourboir,* took my valise and conveyed me to my inn.

To those who have seen other cities of Holland, Alkmaar offers nothing remarkable. It is a town of regular form, with broad canals and streets, and the usual red houses with the usual pointed façades. Some of the larger squares are entirely paved with small red and yellow bricks, disposed in symmetrical designs, and looking at a distance like a carpet; and the streets have two sidewalks, one of bricks for passengers, and one above it of stone, projecting from the walls of the houses, upon which no one must place his foot if he wishes to avoid the angry looks of the inhabitants who may observe him from the windows. Many of the houses are whitewashed, no one can tell why, halfway up; some are painted black as if in mourning, and some are varnished like coaches from top to bottom. The windows being very low, one can see, through the beautiful tulips and hyacinths that adorn them, the parlors glittering with mirrors and porcelain, and the family gathered about a small table covered with beer-glasses, liquor-stands, cakes, and cigar-boxes. For long distances in the streets you meet no one; and, what is unusual in a town of more than ten thousand inhabitants, the few people, men, women, and children who pass, or stand in the door-ways, all salute the stranger courteously. A company of collegians, accompanied by a tutor, passed me; at a sign from the latter, they all raised their caps; and my dress was certainly not that of a person of distinction. The city has no noticeable monuments, beyond the city hall, an edifice of the seventeenth century, partly Gothic and partly of no style at all, resembling in miniature the one at Brussels; and the large church of St. Lawrence, of the same date, in which is the tomb of Count Florentius V of Holland, and, hanging over the choir, like a lamp, a model of the flag-ship of de Ruyter. To the east of the city lies a thick grove of trees which serves as a public garden, and which is used occasionally for certain grand festivals called *harddraverij*, or trotting matches, for the thoroughly Dutch prize of a silver coffee-pot. But notwithstanding its fine grove, its church, its city hall, and its eleven thousand inhabitants, Alkmaar looks like a big village, and so profound a silence reigns in her streets that the music of the steeples, wilder even than in the other cities, is heard all over as distinctly as in the quiet of the night.

Passing through some solitary streets towards the centre of the city, I began to see more people, principally women, who, as it was a holiday, were dressed in all their bravery, particularly the peasants. Truly, I cannot imagine what ailed Napoleon's eyes when he arrived at Alkmaar. There are certainly some pretty nun-like faces which express the utmost simplicity and innocence, and in especial some cheeks of the softest rose that was ever diffused by modesty over a virgin visage; but the effect of these simple graces is quite destroyed by the abominable head-dress and the still more abominable fashion of the garments. Besides the tufts of curled hair, the earrings like a horse's blinders, the gold band across the forehead, and the white cap concealing the ears and the nape of the neck, they wear upon their heads a great straw hat of an almost cylindrical form, with a broad brim lined with green or yellow silk, turned up in front, and having a large gap between the forehead and the brim, reminding one of the open mouths of those monsters which Chinese soldiers used to wear to strike terror into their enemies. Their hips are absurdly high, either made so by the fashion of the petticoat or by nature, and the bust, which is very large at the girdle, grows smaller as it rises, contrary to our women, who make their chests broad and their waists small. And as if this were not sufficient, they compress (as I suppose, because I cannot believe that nature has treated them so badly) the bosom in such a way that not the slightest curve is visible, as if that, which in other women is the perfection of beauty, in them were a ridiculous defect or something to be ashamed of. Even the prettiest of them scarce look like women in such a costume, and the appearance of those less favoured by nature, who are the most numerous in Alkmaar as elsewhere, can be imagined.

Thus passing the fair sex in review, I reached a large square full of booths and people, and became aware that I had arrived in Alkmaar on a *kermesse* day.

This is one of the strangest and most characteristic points of Dutch life.

The *kermesse* is the carnival of Holland; with this difference from the carnival of our own country, that it lasts only eight days, and that each town and village celebrates it at a different time. It is difficult to say in what this festival consists. At the time of *kermesse* there rises within a Dutch city another city, composed of cafés, theatres, shops, tents, and kiosks, which vanish at the end of the festival, break up like an encampment, and are piled in boats and carried off to some other place. The inhabitants of this vagabond city are traders, musicians, actors, jugglers, giants, colossal women, monstrous children, deformed animals, wax figures, wooden horses, automata, monkeys, trained dogs, and wild beasts. In the midst of the innumerable sheds under which this strange population shelters itself, there are hundreds of little painted and gilded houses, each composed of one large and four small rooms, in which some young girls in the Friesian costume, with the gold helmet and lace cap, serve all comers with that peculiar sweet cake called *broedertijes*, which is the emblematic delicacy of this festival, as the *panetone* at Christmas and the *focaccia* at Twelfth-day are with us. Beside the booths of the mountebanks, and the cafés, there are bazaars, circuses, theatres for musical performances, and every sort of entertainment to suit the taste of the people. Such is the place for the occasion provided for the *kermesse;* but the festival itself, properly speaking, is quite another thing. In those cafés and booths, in the streets and squares, day and night, throughout the time of the *kermesse,* servants and laborers, peasant men and women, all classes and both sexes of the lower order of the people, get drunk, dance, jump, sing, yell, and make love, with a fury and license beside which the disorders of our carnival are innocent and childish diversions. In those days the Dutch people change their character so as to be no longer recognisable. Habitually serious, economically modest, and domestic, in the time of the *kermesse* they become boisterous, laughing at decency, and passing the whole night away from home, while they spend, in one day, the fruit of a whole month's labor.

The servant-women, to whom extraordinary liberty is conceded at that time, and who would take it if it were not given, are the principal performers in the festival. Each one is accompanied by her betrothed husband, or her lover, or by some young fellow hired for the occasion, the price varying according as he wears a hat or a cap, or if he be handsome or ugly, a clown or a smart fellow. The peasants come into the town or village, to enjoy the *kermesse*, on some fixed day, which is called the peasants' day. The culmination of the uproar is on the Saturday night. It is then no longer a festival, but an orgie, a saturnalia, which has not its parallel in all Europe. I refused for some time to believe some Dutch friends, who painted the *kermesse* to me in the most horrible colors, and thought that they were too rigorous in their judgments. But when I heard the same things confirmed by unprejudiced persons, native as well as foreign, I was obliged to accept the judgment of the Hollanders themselves, who call the *kermesse* a national disgrace. It must be said, however, that for some time the custom has been losing ground. Public opinion is divided upon the point. There are some who favor it, because it amuses them both as actors and spectators; and these deny or excuse the disorders, and insist that a prohibition of the *kermesse* would cause a revolution.

There are others who wish to see it suppressed, and desire the substitution of honest and decent public entertainments, the want of which, in their opinion, is the principal reason for the excesses to which the people abandon themselves on the occasion of the *kermesse*. This latter opinion is growing stronger day by day. In some towns measures have been taken to restrain license; in others an hour is fixed, after which all shops and booths are closed; in others the booths are erected away from the centre of the city. The authorities of Amsterdam have fixed a certain number of years, after which no preparations will be allowed for the festival. It may therefore be affirmed that the time is not far distant when the famous *kermesse* will be reduced to a cheerful and temperate carnival, with great advantage to public morality and national dignity.

These festivals, however, are not everywhere noisy and scandalous in the same degree. At the Hague, for instance, they are much less so than at Amsterdam or Rotterdam; and I fancy (perhaps because I was not there at night) that at Alkmaar they are still less objectionable than at the Hague; which, however, by no means indicates that they are models of decency.

The piazza when I reached it was full of booths, painted in different colors, at whose doors mountebanks in pink tights, and female rope-dancers, attitudenised and chattered to attract an audience. Before each one stood a crowd of lookers-on, from which two or three peasants would every now and then emerge and enter the booth to see the spectacle. I never have seen gentler or simpler mannered people, or more easy to amuse. Between one tune and another, a boy of ten years old, dressed as a pantaloon or clown, and parading upon a platform in front of the booth, sufficed to entertain and keep in good humour a crowd of two hundred persons. And this he did, not by telling funny stories, and making puns like the mountebanks of Paris, nor by jumping and grimacing, but simply by every now and then making and throwing among the crowd, with a smile, a little paper arrow. This was enough to make them all laugh in the best possible humour.

As I wandered about among the shops and shows, I met a few peasant women slightly overcome with liquor, a little shaky on their legs, and singing in cracked voices; saw a few couples exchanging amorous glances, and met some groups of women who were preluding the nocturnal exercises by giving shoves with hip and shoulder strong enough to throw each other down; but nothing worse than this. The whole thing seemed to be a confusion of people who did not know what to do with themselves. But as I foresaw that with the evening would commence a much more dramatic spectacle, and did not care to find myself alone in an unknown city under such exceptionable circumstances, I decided to leave at once for Helder, and returned to my inn by the shortest way.

Upon my arrival there in the morning I had spoken with no one, because the porter who accompanied me had arranged about my room and had taken my valise to it. However, I imagined that the landlord or some one of the waiters would be sure to understand French. When I returned, landlord and waiters were probably drinking at some booth; for at the inn there was no one but an old woman, who showed me into a room on the ground-floor, and giving me to understand that she did not comprehend me, went about her business. In the room there was a company of fat citizens of Alkmaar, who were seated round a table where they appeared to have been solemnly consuming quantities of food and drink, and were now chattering and giggling with extraordinary vivacity and in a cloud of smoke. Beholding me mute and solitary in my corner, they turned upon me from time to time compassionate glances, and whispered in each other's ears words which I imagined to express the same sentiment as the glances. There is nothing more disconcerting to a stranger than to find himself the object of commiseration to a company of cheerful natives. The figure which I made at the moment may, therefore, be imagined. After a few minutes, one of the stout citizens rose and took his hat to go out; but before doing so, he stopped opposite me, and said, with a smile of polite commiseration, while he pronounced every syllable with emphasis, " Alkmaar pas de plaisir, Paris toujours plaisir." He took me for a Frenchman. This said, he put on his hat, and, believing that he had administered sufficient consolation, went gravely out of the house. He was the only one of the party who knew three words of French. After about fifteen minutes, during which I had fallen back into my miserable state, a waiter came in. I breathed again, ran to meet him, and told him that I wished to leave. Oh delusion! he did not understand a word. I took him by the arm, led him to my room, pointed to my valise, and made signs that I wished to go. To go! it is easily said, but how? by boat? by rail? by *trekschuyt?* He assumed that he did not understand. I tried to intimate that I wanted a carriage. He caught the idea, but said or signed that there were no carriages. I thought that I would try and find the railway station myself, and made signs that I wanted a porter. He answered that there were no porters. With my watch in my hand, I asked at what hour the landlord would be back. He answered that the landlord was not coming back. I signed to him to take up my valise and carry it. He answered that he could not. I demanded, with a gesture of despair, what I was to do. He made no reply and stood looking at me in silence. On such occasions I have an alarming facility in losing my patience, my courage, and my head. I began to rave in a dialect composed of German, French, and Italian, opening and shutting my guide-book, tracing and effacing lines in my note-book which were intended to represent ships and locomotives, and rushing up and down the room like a madman, until the poor waiter, either frightened or bored, I know not which, slipped out at the door, and left me in the lurch. Then I seized my valise in my hand, and went downstairs. The citizens below, warned by the waiter of my eccentric behaviour, had come out of the dining-room, and were standing in the hall as I came down, looking at me as if I were some patient escaped from a madhouse. I grew red as fire, at which they were still more astonished;

and dropping my heavy valise, stood with my eyes fixed on the floor. Everybody looked at me, and no one spoke. I was more humiliated than I had ever been in my life before. Why? I cannot tell. I only know that I had a mist before my eyes; that I would have given a year of my life to have been able to vanish like a flash of lightning; that I cursed travelling, Alkmaar, the Dutch language, my own stupidity; and that I thought of my own home like one abandoned of God and man. All at once a boy emerged from I know not where, seized my valise, signed to me to follow, and made off with speed. I followed without questioning, crossed a street, went through a large gate, crossed a court, and reached another gate that opened on another street, where the boy threw down my valise, got his pay, and making no answer to my questions, vanished as he had come. Where had he brought me? What had I to do there? How long should I stay there? What was going to happen next? All was mystery.

It began to grow dark. Troops of peasant men and women went by arm in arm, boys singing, lovers whispering in each other's ears; everybody gay and happy, and everybody looking at me as I stood there forlorn, with a glance of astonishment and pity. Just as I, in a rage, was about to seize my valise and go back to the inn, where my revenge should be swift and sure—behold! a diligence. It stopped, and the conductor signed to me to come. I inquired anxiously, "To the railway station?" "Oui, Monsieur," he answered readily, "to leave for Helder." "Ah! may heaven bless you, conductor of my soul!" I exclaimed, as I jumped in and put a florin in his hand; "you have brought me back to life!"

The diligence took me to the station, and in a few minutes I was on my way to Helder.

HELDER.

THE definition that has been given of Holland, as a "sort of transition from land to sea," refers to no part of the country more appropriately than to the space which lies between Alkmaar and Helder. You travel, to be sure, in going from one city to the other, on land; but on land so broken, threatened, and undermined by the sea, that, looking at it from the railway carriage, you could easily fancy yourself on board ship. Not far from Alkmaar, between the two villages of Kamp and Petten, in the direction of the North Sea, and over a long tract where one of the mouths of the Rhine anciently existed, the chain of downs is interrupted, and the coast is furiously beaten by the sea, which, in spite of the strong defensive works which oppose it, continually gnaws into the bosom of the land. A little further on there is a large inundated *polder*, across which the great Northern canal passes. Beyond this *polder*, and around the village of Zand, extends a great desert plain, sprinkled with brushwood and stagnant pools, and with a few peasants' huts with pyramidal roofs that, at a distance, look like gravestones. Beyond the village of Zand there is a vast *polder* (called Anna Paolovna, in honor of the wife of William II. of Orange, a Russian Grand Duchess) which was drained between 1847 and 1850. Then came vast plains, brushwood, and pools, to the extreme point of North Holland, where stands, veiled in fogs and beaten by wind and wave, the youthful and solitary city of Helder, the dead sentinel of the Low Countries.

Helder has this peculiarity, that when you are in it, you look for the city and fail to find it. It may be described as one single very long street, bordered by two rows of little red houses, and protected by a gigantic dyke, forming a sort of artificial beach on the North Sea. This dyke, which is one of the most wonderful works of modern times, extends a length of almost ten kilometres from the Nieuwediep, (where is situate the entrance to the great Northern canal,) as far as the fort of the Hereditary Prince (which is at the opposite extremity of the city); and it is constructed entirely of granite from Norway and Belgian limestone. It has a fine carriage-road on the top, and descends towards the sea with an inclination of forty degrees, and is sixty metres in depth. At various points it is reinforced by smaller dykes, composed of beams, fascines, and earth, which advance two hundred metres into the sea. The highest tides do not wet its top, and the indefatigable wave spends itself in vain upon the monstrous bulwark that rises against it, in an attitude of defiance rather than defence.

The Nieuwediep, which opens at one of the extremities of Helder, is an artificial port which protects, with its great moles and robust dykes, the ships which enter the Northern canal. The gates of the basin, called fan-gates, the largest in Holland, close of themselves under the pressure of the water. In this harbor a great number of vessels are lying at anchor, many of which are English and Swedish; and there is also a large part of the Dutch war fleet, composed of frigates and smaller vessels, cleaner than the cleanest of the houses at Broek.

On the left-hand shore of the Nieuwediep there is a large naval arsenal, with a Vice-Admiral in residence.

At the end of the last century none of these things existed. Helder was nothing but a fishing village, and its name was scarcely mentioned on the maps. The opening of the great Northern canal, and a brief passage made by Napoleon in a fisherman's boat from Helder to the island of Texel, which is seen distinctly from the top of the dyke, transformed the village into a city. Observing the tract of sea comprised between that island and the shore of Holland, Napoleon conceived the idea of making out of Helder a "Gibraltar of the North," and began by commanding the construction of two forts, one called at that time Lasalle, and now Hereditary Prince, and the other King of Rome, now Admiral Dirk. Events prevented the carrying into effect of his grand design; but the work begun by him was slowly carried on by the Hollanders, and Helder is, at this day, the first strong city of the State, capable of holding thirty thousand defenders, and of preventing the entrance of a fleet into the

Northern canal or the gulf of Zuyder Zee; and besides being defended at a great distance by a bulwark of rocks and sand-banks, it is so fortified as to be able, in case of need, to inundate the whole province that lies at its back.

But leaving aside its strategical importance Helder is a city worth seeing for its amphibious character, which leaves it always dubious whether one is on a continent or a group of rocks and islands a thousand miles distant from the European coast. In whatever direction you turn your steps you always come out in view of the sea. The town is crossed and surrounded by canals as broad as rivers, which the inhabitants cross on rafts. Behind the great dyke lies a mass of apparently stagnant water which rises and falls with the tide, as if it had subterranean communication with the sea. On every side there is water, imprisoned, indeed, between two banks, but high and threatening, and looking as if it watched for the moment when it might reconquer its dreadful liberty. The land all about the town is bare and desolate, and the sky, almost always cloudy, is crossed by great flocks of aquatic birds. The town itself, with its one row of houses, looks as if it were conscious of its dangerous situation, and expected hourly some catastrophe. When the wind howls and the sea roars, it seems as if every good citizen of Helder could only shut himself up in his house, say his prayers, cover his head with the bed-clothes and wait for God's decree.

The population, eighteen thousand in number, is as singular in its way as the town. It is a mixture of merchants, government clerks, naval officers, soldiers, fishermen, people arriving from India, people about to leave, and relations coming and going, who come there to give the first embrace or the last farewell; because this is the extreme angle of Dutch territory which the sailor salutes at parting, and the first which he greets on his return. But the town being so long and narrow, few people are visible at a time; and no sound is heard but the lamentable chant of the sailors, oppressing the spirits like the cry of shipwrecked men afar off.

Although so young, Helder is as rich in grand historical records as other Dutch cities. She saw the Grand Pensionary De Witt cross for the first time, in a small boat, the straits of Texel, sounding with his own hands the depth of the water, and demonstrating, to the pilots and captains who would not venture it, the possibility of the passage for the fleet sent to fight England. In those days Admirals de Ruyter and Van Tromp held front against the united French and English fleets. Not far from thence, in the *polder* called the Zyp, in the year 1799, the English general Abercrombie repulsed the assault of the French and Batavian army commanded by Brome. And lastly, since it seems that by some natural law every Dutch city must have some strange and incredible experience, Helder witnessed a sort of amphibious combat between land and sea, a name for which is wanting in military language; it saw in 1795 the cavalry and light artillery of General Pichegru gallop across the frozen gulf of Zuyder Zee to attack the Dutch fleet which was imprisoned in the ice near the island of Texel, and surrounding it as if it were a fortress, call upon it to surrender, which it did.

This island of Texel, which, as has been said, can be distinctly seen from the top of the dykes of Helder, is the first of a chain of islets which extends in the form of a bow across the opening of the Zuyder Zee as far as the province of Gröningen; and which, before the existence of the great gulf, is believed to have formed a continuous coast, which served as a bulwark to the Low Countries.

This island of Texel, which has only six thousand inhabitants scattered about in a few villages, has a harbor where ships of war and Indiamen can lie at anchor. It was from here that, at the end of the sixteenth century, the vessels of Heemskerk and Barendz set sail for that memorable voyage which furnished to the poet Tollenz the subject of his fine poem, "The Winter of the Hollanders in Nova Zembla."

And here, briefly, is the sad and solemn story, as it is told by Van Kampfen, and sung by Tollenz.

At the end of the sixteenth century, the Dutch, not being able to struggle front to front with the Spaniards and Portuguese for the mastery of the East Indian trade, bethought themselves of finding a new road through the Arctic seas, by which they might reach in less time the ports of China and Eastern Asia. A company of Dutch merchants confided the enterprise to an expert sailor named Barendz, who sailed with two ships from the island of Texel, on the 6th of June 1594, towards the pole. The vessel commanded by him reached the northern point of Nova Zembla, and returned to Holland. The other ship took the better-known way of the straits of Waigatz, pushed its way through the ice of the gulf of Kara, and arrived in an open blue sea, from which the Russian coast turned towards the north-east was visible. The direction of this coast made them believe that the vessel had passed beyond Cape Tabis, designated by Pliny (an authority at that time uncontested) as the northern extremity of Asia, and that, therefore, they could from there, by a short voyage, reach the eastern and southern ports of the continent. It was not known that, after the gulf of the Obi, Asia still extended for one hundred and twenty degrees in an easterly direction within the polar circle. The news of the supposed discovery caused great joy in Holland. Six large ships were immediately loaded with merchandise for the people of India, a smaller vessel was sent to accompany the squadron until it had sailed beyond the supposititious Cape Tabis, when it was to return with the news to Holland; and the fleet sailed. But this time the voyage did not answer to their hopes. The Dutch vessels found the straits of Waigatz all encumbered with ice, and after having in vain tried to open a passage, returned to Holland.

After this failure, the States General, while promising a reward of twenty-five thousand florins to whoever should succeed in the enterprise, refused to share in the expenses of a new voyage; but the citizens were not to be discouraged. Amsterdam hired two ships, selected the bravest of her sailors, bachelors, so that the remembrance of their families might not weaken their courage in time of peril, and gave the command of the expedition to the valiant Heemskerk. The two vessels sailed on the 18th of May 1596. Barendz was master-pilot on board of one, and Van de Ryp, captain of the other. At first they could not agree as to the direction to be taken; but finally Barendz was persuaded by Van de Ryp to steer towards the north instead of the north-east. They arrived at the 74° of north latitude, near a small island, to which they gave the name of Bear Island in memory of a combat of several hours which they sustained against a troop of those animals. Around them there was nothing to be seen but high and broken rocks which seemed to close in the sea on all sides. They continued to steer towards the north. On the 19th of June they discovered a country which they called Spitzbergen because of its sharp-pointed rocks, and which they believed to be a part of Greenland; and there they saw great white bears, deer, reindeer, wild ducks, enormous whales, and foxes of all colors. From here, having arrived between the seventy-sixth and eightieth degrees of north latitude, they were to turn southwards and come to anchor once more near Bear Island. Barendz, however, would not follow any more the northern course pointed out by Van de Ryp, and turned towards the south-east; Ryp made sail towards the north, and thus they were separated.

Barendz arrived on the 17th of July near Nova Zembla, followed the northern coast of that island, and continued to sail southwards. Then their adversities began. As they went on, the enormous masses of floating ice, becoming thicker, were joined together in vast strata, and piled up into steep and lofty mountains, so that in a short time the ship found herself in the midst of an icy continent, whose white peaks rose on the horizon all about her. Seeing that it was impossible to reach the eastern shore of Asia, they thought to turn back; but it was now the 25th of August, and in those regions the summer was already at an end. They were not long in finding out that to go back was impossible. They were imprisoned in the ice, lost in a frightful solitude, surrounded by dense fog, aimless and hopeless, and every moment exposed to the danger of being crushed under the mountains of floating ice that groaned and thundered about the ship. One only chance of safety remained to them, or rather a means of delaying death: they were near the coast of Nova Zembla, they could abandon the ship, and attempt to pass the winter in that desolate island. It was a desperate resolution, requiring not less courage than to remain on board; but at least they would have action, struggle, a new form of danger. After some hesitation, they left the ship and landed on the island.

It was uninhabited; none of the northern races had ever put foot upon it; it was a desert of snow and ice, beaten by wind and sea, upon which the sun but rarely let fall a fugitive ray, without warmth or cheer. Nevertheless the poor shipwrecked men sent up a shout of joy when their feet touched the land, and knelt down in the snow to give thanks to Providence. They set to work at once to build a shelter. There was not a tree on the island; but by good fortune they found a quantity of floating wood brought by the sea from the continent. They went to work, returned to the ship, and brought away planks and beams, nails, pitch, boxes, and casks; planted the beams in the ice, made a roof of what had been the deck, hung up their hammocks, lined the walls with sails, stopped up the holes with pitch. But as their work went on they suffered in unheard-of ways, and were in constant danger. The cold was so great that when they put nails in their mouths, they froze there, and could only be taken out by tearing the flesh and filling the mouth with blood. White bears, wild with hunger, assailed them furiously among the ice, around their cabin, even in the interior of the ship; and obliged them to leave their labor in order to defend their lives. The earth was frozen so hard that it had to be broken with the pick like stone. Around the vessel the water was frozen to a depth of three and a half fathoms. The beer was solid in its casks, and had lost all flavor; and the cold increased daily. At last they succeeded in rendering their cabin habitable, and were sheltered from the snow and wind. They lighted a fire and were able to sleep a few hours at a time when not wakened by the howls of the wild beasts that lingered about the cabin. They fed their lamps with the fat of the bears which they killed through the cracks of the walls, they warmed their hands in the bleeding bowels, they made coverings of the skins, and they ate foxes, and herrings, and biscuits from the ship's stores. Meantime the cold increased so that the bears did not leave their holes. Food and drink was frozen hard even when placed close to the fire. The poor sailors burned their hands and feet without feeling any heat. One night when from fear of the cold they had hermetically closed the cabin, they were within an ace of dying of suffocation, and were forced to brave once more that awful cold.

To all these calamities one more was added. On the 4th of November they awaited sunrise in vain; the sun appeared no more; the polar night had begun. Then these iron men felt their courage fail them, and Barendz, concealing his own anguish as he could, had to spend all the eloquence that he possessed in persuading them not to give way to despair. Food and fuel began to grow scarcer; the wood found upon the shore was thrown upon the fire with regret; the lamp hardly gave light enough to pierce the thick darkness. Notwithstanding all this, in the evening when they gathered about the fire, they still had some moments of cheerfulness. On the King's birthday they made a little feast with wine, and flour paste fried in whale-oil, and drew lots as to which of them should wear the crown of Nova Zembla. At other times they played cards, told old stories, gave toasts to the glory of Maurice of Orange, and talked about their families. Every day they sang psalms together, kneeling on the ice, their faces lifted to the stars. Sometimes the aurora borealis broke the great darkness which surrounded them; and then they came forth from their cabin, running along the shore, and greeting with tender gratitude the fugitive light as a promise of salvation.

According to their computation, the sun should reappear on the 9th of February 1597. They were wrong. On the morning of the 24th of January, exactly at a moment when they had reached the depths of sadness and discouragement, one of them, on awaking, saw an extraordinary light, gave a shout, sprang to his feet, woke his companions, and all went out of the cabin. There in the east the sky was illuminated by a clear radiance; the moon was pale, the air limpid, the summits of the rocks and mountains tinged with rose; the dawn at last, the sun, life, the benediction of God, and the hope of once more seeing their country after three months of darkness and anguish. For a few minutes they stood silent and motionless, overcome by emotion; then they broke into cries and tears, embraced each other, waved their ragged caps, and made those horrid solitudes resound with accents of prayer and joyful shouts. But their joy was brief. They looked in each other's faces, and were filled with terror and pity the one for the other. Cold, sleeplessness, hunger, and anguish of spirit had so consumed and changed them that they were unrecognisable. And their sufferings were not yet over. In that same month the snow fell in such abundance that the cabin was almost completely buried, and they were obliged to go in and out by the opening of the chimney. As the cold diminished the bears reappeared, and the danger, the sleepless nights, the fierce combats began again. Their strength declined, and their hearts, a little lifted, fell once more.

They had still, however, one slight thread of hope. It being hopeless to think of getting their vessel out of the ice, they had brought ashore a boat and a shallop, and little by little, always defending their lives against the bears, who attacked them even on the threshold of their hut, they had succeeded in repairing them. With these two small boats they intended to try and reach one of the small Russian ports, by running along the northern coast of Nova Zembla and Siberia, and crossing the White Sea; to make, in short, a voyage of at least four hundred German miles. During the whole month of March the variable weather kept them between hope and despair. More than ten times had they seen the sea cleared of ice up to the shore, and had made ready to depart; and as many times a great increase of cold had again piled up the ice and shut them in. April and May passed in this way. At last, in June, they were able to make ready to depart. After having drawn up a minute relation of all their adventures, a copy of which they left in the cabin, on the morning of the 14th of June, with beautiful weather, and the open sea on every side, after nine months' sojourn in that fearful place, they set sail towards the continent. In two open boats, exhausted by protracted sufferings, they went to brave the furious winds, the long rains, the mortal cold, the whirling ice-fields of that immense and terrible sea where it seemed a desperate enterprise to venture with a fleet. For a long time during the voyage they had to repulse the attacks of the white bears; they suffered from hunger, feeding on birds which they killed with stones, and eggs found upon the desolate shore; they hoped and despaired, they were cheerful or they wept, sometimes bewailing themselves that they had abandoned Nova Zembla, sometimes invoking the tempest and praying for death. Often they had to drag their boats over fields of ice, to tie them down lest they should be carried away by the wind, to gather themselves together in a close group in the midst of the snow in order to resist the cold, to call to each other through the dense fog, and hold together in the fear of being scattered and lost, and to gather courage from each other's touch. All did not resist such tremendous trials of their strength. Barendz himself, who was not well when he embarked, felt, after a few days, his end approaching, and told his companions. He never ceased, however, to direct their course, and to make every effort to shorten for those unfortunate men the tremendous voyage, the end of which he knew he could not live to see. Life left him as he was examining a map; his arm fell stiffly in the act of pointing out the distant land, and his last words were those of encouragement and counsel. In the bay of Saint Lawrence they met, it may be imagined with what joy, a Russian bark, which gave them some provisions, some wine, and lime-juice, a remedy against the scurvy, from which several of the sailors were suffering, and which speedily cured them. They coasted along Siberia, and met other Russian vessels more and more frequently, from them receiving fresh provisions and thus gradually restoring their strength. At the entrance of the White Sea a dense fog separated the two boats, which, however, both weathered Cape Caudnoes, and, favored by the wind, made one hundred and twenty miles in thirty hours, after which they met again with shouts of joy. But a still greater joy awaited them at Kilduin. They found there a letter from Von de Ryp, captain of the other ship which had sailed with them from Texel, announcing his safe arrival. In a short time the two boats rejoined the ship at Kola. It was the first time that the shipwrecked men from Nova Zembla had seen the flag of their country since their departure from Bear Island, and they greeted it in a perfect delirium of oy. The crew of Von de Ryp and the companions of poor Barendz embraced each other with tears, relating their adventures, lamenting their dead comrades, and forgetting their past sufferings in the joy of meeting. All set sail for Holland, where they arrived safe and sound on the 29th of October 1597, three months after their departure from the hut at Nova Zembla. Thus ended the last attempt of the Dutch to open a new road for the East Indian trade across the Polar seas. Almost three centuries later, in 1870, the captain of a Swedish vessel, thrown by a tempest on the coast of Nova Zembla, found there the carcass of a ship and a hut. In the last were two copper kettles, a pendulum, a gun-barrel, a sword, a hatchet, a flute, a Bible, and some boxes full of tools and rotten fragments of clothing. These objects, recognised by the Hollanders as having belonged to the crews of Barendz and Heemskerke, were carried in triumph to the Hague, and are exhibited as sacred relics in the naval museum.

With all these images in my mind, in the evening, on the dyke at Helder, by the light of the moon that now abruptly hid herself behind a cloud, and now showed herself in all her glory, I could not tire of looking at the sandy shore of that island of Texel, and that great North Sea, which on that side has no boundary but the Polar ice; the sea which the ancients believed to be the end of the universe—"*illum usque tantum natura,*" as Tacitus says; the sea on which, in days of tempest, the gigantic forms of the German divinities appeared; and as my eyes wandered over the immense and sinister waste, I could only express to myself my mysterious dread by exclaiming in an undertone, " Barendz! Barendz!" and listening to the sound of that name as if brought by the wind from an immense distance.

THE ZUYDER ZEE.

I HAD yet to see ancient Frisia, Rome's indomitable rebel, the land of handsome women, big horses, and invisible skaters, the most poetic of the Netherland provinces; and in going there I was to satisfy another lively wish of mine, that of crossing the Zuyder Zee, the latest-born of seas.

This great basin of the North Sea, which bathes five provinces, and has an extent of more than seven hundred square kilometres, six hundred years ago was not in existence. North Holland touched Friesland, and where the gulf now extends there was a vast region sprinkled with fresh-water lakes, the largest of which, the Flevo, mentioned by Tacitus, was separated from the sea by a fertile and populous isthmus. Whether the sea by its own force broke through the natural dykes of the region, or whether the sinking of the land left it free to invasion, is not certainly known. The great transformation was completed during the course of the thirteenth century.

In 1205 the island of Wieringen, posted at the extremity of North Holland, still made part of the continent; in 1251 it was already separated from it. In its later invasions, the sea submerged various parts of the isthmus which separated its waters from those of the lake of Flevo, until in 1282, opening for itself a breach in that shattered bulwark, it broke into the lakes, invaded the land, and enlarging as it proceeded, formed the vast gulf now known as the Zuyder Zee, or Southern Sea, which sends an arm, the Y, as far as Beverwijk and Haarlem. About the formation of this gulf there has collected a varied and confused history of cities destroyed and people drowned, to which has been added in later times another history, of new cities rising on new shores, becoming powerful and famous, and being in their turn reduced to poor and mean villages, with streets overgrown with grass, and sand-choked ports. Records of great calamities, wonderful traditions, fantastic horrors, strange usages and customs, are found upon the waters and about the shores of this peculiar sea, born but yesterday, and already encircled with ruins and condemned to disappear; and a month's voyage would not suffice to gather up the chief of them; but the thought alone of beholding from a distance those decrepit cities, those mysterious islands, those fatal sand-banks, irresistibly excited my imagination.

I left Amsterdam towards the end of February, in beautiful weather, on board one of the steamboats that go to Harlingen. I knew that it was the last time I should see the capital of Holland. Leaning over the railing at the prow as the vessel left the port, I contemplated for the last time the great city, trying to impress indelibly on my memory its fantastic aspect. In a few minutes I saw nothing but the black irregular outline of its houses, above which rose the dome of the palace and a forest of shining steeples. Then the city sank; the steeples vanished one after another; the highest point of the cathedral, visible for a moment above the rest, sank in its turn into the sea; and Amsterdam was nothing but a memory.

The steamboat passed between the gigantic dykes that shut in the gulf of the Y, rapidly crossed the "Pampus," the great sand-bank that nearly ruined the trade of Amsterdam, and entered the Zuyder Zee.

The shores of this gulf are all meadows, gardens, and villages, which, in the summer, present an enchanting aspect; but seen from the steamboat, and in February, show only as a faint streak of dull green separating the sea and sky. The shore of North Holland is the finest, and along this our vessel steamed.

After crossing the Pampus, we turned to the left and passed at a short distance the island of Marken.

Marken is as famous among the islands of the Zuyder Zee as Broek is among the villages of Holland; but with all its fame, and although distant but one hour by boat from the coast, few are the strangers, and still fewer the natives who visit it. So said the captain as he pointed out the light-house of the little island, and added that in his opinion the reason was, that when a stranger arrived at Marken, even if he were a Dutchman, he was followed by a crowd of boys, watched, and commented upon as if he were a man fallen from the moon. This unusual curiosity is explained by a description of the island. It is a bit of land about three thousand metres in length and one thousand in width, which was detached from the continent in the thirteenth century, and remains to this day, in the manners and customs of its inhabitants, exactly as it was six centuries ago. The surface of the island is but little higher than the sea, and it is surrounded by a small dyke which does not suffice to protect it from inundation. The houses are built upon eight small artificial elevations, and form as many boroughs, one of which—the one which has the church—is the capital, and another the cemetery. When the sea rises above the dyke, the spaces between the little hills are changed into canals, and the inhabitants go about in boats. The houses are built of wood, some painted, some only pitched; one only is of stone, that of the pastor, who also has a small garden shaded by four large trees, the only ones on the island. Next to this house are the church, the school, and the municipal offices. The population is about one thousand in number, and lives by fishing. With the exceptions of the doctor, the pastor, and the schoolmaster, all are native to the island; no islander marries on the continent; no one from the mainland comes to live on the island. They all profess the reformed religion, and all know how to read and write. In the schools more than two hundred boys and girls are taught history, geography, and arithmetic. The fashion of dress, which has not been changed for centuries, is the same for all, and extremely curious. The men look like soldiers. They wear a dark grey cloth jacket ornamented with two rows of buttons which are in general medals, or ancient coins, handed down from father to son. This jacket is tucked into the waistband of a pair of breeches of the same color, very wide about the hips and tight around the leg, fastening below the knee; a felt hat or a fur cap, according to the season; a red cravat, black stockings, white wooden shoes, or a sort of slipper, complete the costume. That of the women is still more peculiar. They wear on their heads an enormous white cap in the form of a mitre, all ornamented with lace and needlework, and tied under the chin like a helmet. From under the cap, which completely covers the ears, fall two long braided tresses, which hang over the bosom, and a sort of visor of hair comes down upon the forehead, cut square just above the eyebrows. The dress is composed of a waist without sleeves, and a petticoat of two colors. The waist is deep red, embroidered in colors and costing years of labor to make, for which reason it descends from mother to daughter, from generation to generation. The upper part of the petticoat is grey or blue striped with black, and the lower part dark brown. The arms are covered almost to the elbow with the sleeves of a white chemise, striped with red. The children are dressed in almost the same way, though there is some slight difference between girls and women, and on holidays the costume is more richly ornamented.

Such is the costume—a mixture of the oriental, the warlike, and the sacred; and the customs and manner of life of the inhabitants are quite as strange. The men are

WOMAN AND CHILD OF MARKEN. (*Page* 346.)

extraordinarily sober, and live to a great age. They leave the island every Sunday night with their boats, pass the week fishing in the Zuyder Zee, and return on the Saturday. The women educate the children, cultivate the ground, and make the clothing for the family. Like all the other Dutch women, they love cleanliness and ornament, and in their cabins also are to be seen the inevitable white curtains, glass cups, embroidered bed-covers, looking-glasses, and flowers. The greater part of them never see any other land than that of their little island. They are poor; but knowing nothing of any better condition, and having no wants or desires that cannot be satisfied, they are unconscious of their own poverty. Among them there is neither change of fortune nor distinction of class. Everybody works, nobody serves. The only events which vary the monotony of their lives are births, marriages, deaths, an abundant catch of fish, the arrival of a stranger, the passage of a vessel, a tempest on the sea. They pray they love, they fish. Such is their life; and so generation succeeds to generation, preserving unaltered, like a sacred heirloom, the innocence of their manners, and their ignorance of the world.

Passing beyond the island of Marken we see on the North Holland side a steeple, a group of red houses, and some sails. It is Monnickendam, a village of three thousand inhabitants, formerly a flourishing city, which, in conjunction with Hoorn and Enckhuysen, conquered and took prisoner the Spanish Admiral Bossu, and took from him, as a trophy, the collar of the Golden Fleece; the other two cities had his sword and his drinking-cup.

After Monnickendam is seen the village of Volendam, and after Volendam the small city of Edam, from which the famous cheese with the red rind takes its name, *fama super etera notus.*

A curious legend, represented in an old bas-relief over one of the doors, belongs to this place. Some hundreds of years ago some young girls of Edam, who were walking on the beach, saw a strange-looking woman swimming in the sea, and stopping every now and then to look curiously at them. They called to her, and she drew near; they made signs to her to come out of the water, and she stepped out upon the beach. She was a beautiful woman, naked as she was born, except for the mud, and the seaweed that grew upon her skin as moss grows on the bark of trees. Some think that she had a fish's tail, but a grave chronicler, who had heard the fact related by an eye-witness, declares that her legs were like those of other women. They questioned her, and she did not understand, but answered in a sweet voice and a language unknown to them. They took her home, scraped the sea-weed from her skin, dressed her like a Dutch woman, and taught her to spin. It is not known how long she remained in her new condition, but the legend goes on to say that, however scraped and clothed, she felt herself drawn towards the sea by a potent instinct, and that after having tried several times in vain to return to her native element, and although watched by a hundred eyes, she one day succeeded in getting away, and was never heard of again. Whence came she? Whither went she? Who knows? The fact is that on the shores of the

Zuyder Zee everybody knows about the marine woman of Edam, and talks of her to this day, and that to dare to say, as some do, in a group of peasants, that the woman must have been a seal, is to be treated as an impertinent person; and I think that the peasants are right, for who can pronounce upon a fact which they did not see? Edam, which in the old time was a flourishing city of more than twenty-five thousand inhabitants, has had the same fate as the other cities of the Zuyder Zee, and is now no more than a village.

From Edam to Hoorn the coast is scarcely visible, and so I turned my attention to the sea. In the gulf of Zuyder Zee may be seen reflected, as in a mirror, the marvellous mobility of the skies of Holland. It is the youngest of the seas of Europe, and it presents in its aspect all the caprice, the restlessness, and the inexplicable and unexpected changes of youth. On that day, as almost always, the sky was covered with clouds that dissolved and gathered again perpetually, so that in one hour there succeeded one another every variation of light which in our country is scarcely seen in the course of a day. At one moment the sea was black as pitch, with a distant edge of shining white, like a border of quicksilver. All at once the black was gone, and the gulf became covered with great green tracts, like patches of vegetation, the vessels leaving long blue wakes behind them, reminding one of the meadows and canals of the continent. Then all the vivid green died out, and was replaced by a muddy yellow giving to the sea the look of a vast and filthy bog, in which deformed and hideous animals might wallow. For an instant the steeples and windmills on the shore showed through the fog like distant and almost invisible phantoms, and it seemed that at that point it was dark and raining. A moment more, and mills, steeples, and houses appeared close at hand, and gleaming golden in the sun. Beside the vessel, along the shore, in the midst of the gulf, light and shadow, color, black darkness and noonday light, smiling sunshine and threatening tempest, continually followed each other, until it seemed as if it all had some mysterious meaning, some signification beyond human understanding, which invisible spectators above alone could explain. Here and there glided a boat with black sails, looking like a floating bier for the transportation of the dead.

The vessel passed within sight of Hoorn, the ancient capital of North Holland, where in 1416 the first great herring-net was made, and where that intrepid Schonten was born who was the first to go round the extreme southern point of America; and then we turned towards Enckhuysen. On that part of the coast that lies between the two cities there extends a chain of villages composed of little wooden and brick houses, with varnished roofs and carved doors, before which stand trees with painted trunks. From the steamboat nothing of these villages can be seen except the roofs, looking as if they emerged from the water or were floating upon it. The red color of these roofs, a few steeples, the wings of windmills, are the only colors and forms which vary here and there the long thin line of coast, like the profile of a very slender isthmus. A little before reaching Enckhuysen is seen the little island of Urk, which is believed to have once been a part of that of Schokland, placed at a short distance from the mouth of the Yssel. Urk is still inhabited; Schokland was deserted a few years ago, its inhabitants finding it impossible to contend against the sea.

The vessel stopped at Enckhuysen.

Enckhuysen is the most dead of all the dead cities of the Zuyder Zee. In the sixteenth century it contained forty thousand inhabitants, sent one hundred and forty boats to the herring fishery, had a fine harbor, twenty ships of war, a large arsenal, and sumptuous edifices. Now the harbor is choked with sand, the population reduced to five thousand souls; one of its ancient gates is at a quarter of an hour's distance from the first houses in the town, its streets are grass-grown, its houses ruined and abandoned, its people poor and scattered. The one sole glory that remains to it is that of having been the birthplace of Paul Potter. The steamboat stopped a few minutes before this shade of a dead city. On the landing-pier there were but one or two sailors; of the city nothing could be seen save a few houses half hidden by the dykes, and one tall steeple, which at that moment was ringing slowly out, like the tolling of a death-bell, the air from "William Tell," *O Matilde, t' amo, e vero.* The shore was deserted, the port silent, the houses closed, and a great black cloud hanging over the town seemed like a pall slowly descending to cover it up for ever. It was a spectacle to excite both compassion and dread.

Leaving Enckhuysen, the steamboat reached in a few

minutes the entrance to the Zuyder Zee, between the town of Stavoren, the most advanced point on this coast of Friesland, and Medemblijk, another decayed city of North Holland, which was the capital of the province before the foundation of Hoorn and Enckhuysen. At that point the gulf is about half as wide as the straits of Calais. When the gigantic undertaking for the draining of the Zuyder Zee shall be carried into effect, it is at this point that the enormous dyke will be placed which is to keep out the North Sea. The dyke will extend from Stavoren to Medemblijk, leaving in the middle a wide canal for the movement of the tides, and the flowing off of the waters of the Yssel and the Vecht; and behind it, the great gulf will be gradually transformed into a fertile plain, North Holland will be joined to Friesland, all the dead cities of the coast will be revived and animated with new life, islands destroyed, manners and customs changed, dialects commingled, a province, a people, a world created. This great work will cost, according to the calculations made, one hundred and twenty-five millions of francs; the studies for it have been going on for many years, and perhaps it will soon be commenced; but alas! before it is completed, we who were born towards the middle of the nineteenth century will be lying with folded hands, and the violets growing over us.

Just after passing Medemblijk, the steeples of Stavoren on the opposite side of the gulf came into view, the most ancient of the Frisian cities, its name, as the etymologists tell us, derived from the god Stavo, adored by the ancient Frisians. The city, which is now no more than a small village of melancholy appearance, surrounded by great bastions and marshes, was, in the times when Amsterdam did not exist, a great, beautiful, and populous city, the residence of the King of Frisia, and into it flowed the merchandise of the East and the West, so that it had gained the glorious title of the Nineveh of the Zuyder Zee. A strange legend—which is, however, founded upon a fact, the choking of the port with sand—gives the first explanation of its miserable decadence. The inhabitants, having grown immensely rich by commerce, had become vain, proud, and dissipated, and had pushed their foolish ostentation so far as even to gild the railings, the doors, the locks, and the humblest utensils of their houses. This was displeasing to God, who deliberated as to how He should best inflict a solemn castigation on the insolent city, and soon found the occasion to do so. A rich female merchant of Stavoren hired a vessel and sent it to Dantzic for a cargo of I know not what precious goods. The captain of the vessel arrived at Dantzic, but did not succeed in finding the merchandise which the female merchant desired, and not wishing to return without a cargo, loaded his ship with grain. When he came to Stavoren the female merchant, who was waiting for him at the port, asked what he had brought. The captain humbly answered that he had brought nothing but grain. "Grain!" cried the haughty woman, in an accent of anger and contempt. "Throw it at once into the sea!" The captain obeyed, and the anger of God burst forth. At the very point where the grain fell into the sea, there was formed before the port a great sand-bank, which gradually extinguished the commerce of the city. The sand-bank is there to this day, and is called Vrouwensand, or the Woman's Sand-bank, and is such an impediment that the smallest trading-vessels have to steer with great caution, in order not to run upon it; nor did a great mole, which was constructed to remedy this evil, in any way change the fate of the condemned city.

The sun was setting when the steamboat left Stavoren, but, in spite of the hour and the season, the weather was so mild that I was able to dine on deck, and, inspired by the grand idea of the draining of the Zuyder Zee, drain to its last drop a bottle of old Bordeaux wine, without having to blow upon the ends of my fingers. The passengers were all below, the sea perfectly calm, the sky all golden, the wine exquisite, and my soul at peace. Meantime, before me lay spread out the coast of Friesland, defended by two rows of piles, sustained by enormous blocks of German and Norwegian granite and basalt, giving to the country the look of a vast entrenched camp. We passed near Hindelopen, another decayed city, which has about a thousand inhabitants who still wear the absurd costume of centuries ago; we skirted a series of small hidden villages which gave token of their presence by raising above their dykes the iron finger of their steeples, and arrived at last at Harlingen—the second capital of Friesland—still illuminated by the last rays of the setting sun.

FRIESLAND.

As the boat approached the pier, I remembered what had happened to me at Alkmaar, and was troubled at the thought that I had brought no letters of introduction for Harlingen. I had reason to be troubled, since the Frisian language, which is a mixture of Dutch, Danish, and old Saxon, is almost incomprehensible to the Hollanders themselves; and, as for me, I did not know the first word of it. I was also aware that French was scarcely spoken at all in Friesland. I prepared myself, therefore, with melancholy resignation, to gesticulate, to set people laughing, and to be led about like a child, and I began to look about among the crowd of boys and porters on the pier for some face more humane than the others, to which I might confide my luggage and my life.

Before I had found the face the boat had stopped, and I landed. Whilst I stood hesitating between two sturdy Frieslanders who wished to take possession of my person and effects, I heard whispered in my ear a word that made my heart jump—my own name! I turned as if summoned by a voice from the other world, and saw a young gentleman, who, smiling at my astonishment, repeated in French, "Are you Monsieur So-and-so?" "I am," I answered, "or, at least, I think I am, for, to speak truth, I am so amazed at being recognised by you that I almost doubt my own identity. What prodigy is this?" The prodigy was very simple. A friend at Amsterdam who had accompanied me on board in the morning, had sent a despatch, immediately after the boat left, to an acquaintance of his at Harlingen, asking him to go down to the evening boat and meet a tall, dark stranger in coffee-colored overcoat, who would be in great need of an interpreter and companion. All my travelling companions being blonde, the friend of my friend had recognised me at once, and had come to my rescue.

If I had had in my pocket the collar of the order of the Annunziata, I should have at once bestowed it upon him. Not having it, I expressed my gratitude in a flood of words, at which he was much astonished, and we went into the town, where I purposed to remain only a few hours.

Great canals full of vessels, broad streets bordered by rows of small, neat, many-colored houses, very few people out of doors, a profound silence, and a nameless air of melancholy tranquillity—such is Harlingen, a city of about ten thousand inhabitants, founded near the site of a village which was destroyed by the sea in 1134. Having taken a turn about the town, my companion took me to see the dykes, without which the place must have been a hundred times submerged, since the whole of that portion of the coast is exposed to the waves and currents of the open sea. The dykes are formed of two rows of immense piles, joined together by transverse beams of great size, and the whole set with monstrous flat-headed nails as a defence against the small marine insects which destroy the wood. Between these piles there are stout planks, or, rather, great beams sawed in two and set deep in the sand, one beside the other; behind these a wall of Cyclopean masses of red granite brought from the province of the Drenta, and behind this wall another row of stout piles, which alone would suffice to restrain the waters of a furious torrent. Upon this dyke extends a shady avenue of trees which serves as a public promenade, from which the sea can be seen, and a few houses with masts of vessels rising from among them. When we were there the horizon was still golden in the west, and very dark in the opposite quarter; there was no boat on the sea, and no movement in the port; some boys passed us, arm in arm, chattering and laughing; one turned back to look at us, and then disappeared; the moon came out of a cloud; a cold wind blew, and we walked on in silence.

"Are you in low spirits?" asked my companion. "Precisely," I replied. And I was so. Why, I cannot tell. The place and the moment remain impressed on my memory. I have only to shut my eyes, and I see it, and smell the salt odor of the sea.

My companion took me to a club, where we occupied ourselves in finding out at what hour the train left for

Leuwarde, the capital of Friesland. He was the first Frieslander to whom I had had the honor of speaking, and I studied him. He was blonde, erect, grave, like almost all Dutchmen; but he had a singularly animated expression in his eyes; he spoke little, but what he did say was delivered with a rapidity and emphasis which indicated a more vivacious disposition than that of his fellow-citizens on the opposite side of the Zuyder Zee. Our conversation fell upon ancient Frisia and Rome, and was most agreeable, for he spoke of the events of antique times with extraordinary seriousness, as of things that had happened the other day, and I following his lead, we talked as if he had been a Frisian of the days of Oleunius, and I a Roman of the time of Tiberius, each advocating his own country. I reproached him with the Roman soldiers crucified, and he answered placidly that we had been the provokers, since as long as we were content with the tribute imposed by Drusus, consisting as it did of raw hides only, it had not been refused; and that if they rebelled later it was because we were no longer satisfied with hides, but wanted cattle, fields, boys, and women; and that was destruction for them. "*Pacem,*" says Tacitus, "*esuere, nostra magis avaritia quam obsequii impatientes,*" and adds that Drusus had imposed a small tribute because they were poor, "*pro angustia rerum.*" And if we were to take cattle and lands from the poor, what would we take from the rich? When I heard him quote Tacitus from memory, I beat a retreat, and asked him amicably if he felt any rancor towards me because of the power of my forefathers. "Oh, Sir!" he answered, giving me his hand, as if I had spoken seriously, "not a shadow." "Either I am much mistaken," thought I, "or in my own country I could not find a vestige of such ingenuousness." And I could not but look at him in wonder, of so different a stamp did he seem from the men I was accustomed to meet.

We remained together until night, when he accompanied me to the railway station, and was then going to a concert. In that little town of sailors, butter-merchants, and fishermen, there was a concert given by four artists, two Italians and two Germans, who had come from the Hague expressly to play for two hours for the sum of two hundred and fifty florins! Where this concert was to take place, in a town like Harlingen, composed of lilliputian houses, I could not make out, unless the musicians were to play in a house and the audience to assemble in the street.

Friesland is one plain; a mixed soil of sand, clay, and peat; low everywhere, especially towards the west, where at the end of autumn it is not rare for the sea to rise and cover large tracts. There are many lakes, which form a chain across the province from Stavoren to Dokkum. The country is covered with immense meadows, and traversed in all directions by broad canals, along which for nine months in the year pasture immense herds of cattle, unguarded by herdsman or dog. Along the shore of the North Sea there are found little mounds of earth called *terpen*, raised by the ancient inhabitants as refuges for themselves and their herds against the rising tides, and on some of these mounds there are villages.

Other villages and towns are built upon piles, on land gradually conquered from the sea. The province has two hundred and seventy-two thousand inhabitants, who gain not only their living, but wealth, from the trade in butter, cheese, fish, and peat, and communication is made easy by the canals and lakes. A few trees which hide the farm-houses and villages; some sails of vessels; flocks of lapwings, crows, and rooks; and the beautiful herds of cattle dotting the green fields with black and white, are the only objects which attract the eye upon that vast plain, whose confines are perpetually concealed by a white vaporish veil. Man, who in that country has done all, appears nowhere, and water alone seems the active living principle, while the land is possessed by the animals.

I reached Leuwarde late in the night, and was fortunate enough to find an inn where French was spoken. Very early in the morning—I do not think there were a hundred persons a-foot in the town—I was out wandering about the deserted streets, under a slow cold rain that wetted me to the bone.

Leuwarde looks like a big village. The streets are spacious, with the usual canals and small many-colored houses. The interior canals join those of the exterior, which extend along the bastions of the city and in their turn join other canals leading to other towns and villages. Leuwarde has an air of antiquity, a primitive look, as if it were founded by a people of fishermen and herdsmen, and gradually restored, refined, and beautified. But notwithstanding its fine bridges, rich shops, and ornamente windows, its general aspect is strange and foreign, and it seems strange to see the inhabitants wearing overcoats and cylindrical hats like other people. The streets were deserted, every door closed; I felt as if I were wandering in an unknown or abandoned place which I had myself discovered. I looked at the queer little houses, and thought with amazement that within them there were doubtless well-dressed ladies, pianos, books that I had read, maps of Italy, and photographs of Rome and Florence. As I went from street to street, I passed the ancient castle of the Governors of Friesland, of the house of Nassau Diez, the ancestors of the reigning family of Orange. I discovered a very curious prison, a white and pink palace, surmounted by a lofty roof, and decorated with columns and statues, giving it the aspect of some princely villa; and I finally came out into a great square, where I saw an old brick tower, which is now ten miles from the coast, but which, five hundred years ago, bathed its base in the waters of the sea. From here, passing through streets as clean as drawing-rooms, and sheltered by my umbrella from the droppings of the eaves, I returned to the centre of the city.

In all my walk I had seen no women beyond skinny old hag looking out of window at the weather; and it may be imagined how curious I was to see others, not so much for their celebrated beauty as because of the strange covering which they wear on their heads, and of which I had read descriptions and seen pictures in every town of Holland. The evening before, on my arrival, I had caught one glimpse, at a corner, of a group of women's heads strangely shining and glittering, but it was for a moment only, and in the dark. It must be quite another thing to see all the fair sex of the capital of Friesland in full daylight and as long as I pleased. But how to gratify this curiosity? The skies promised rain for the entire day, the women would probably remain shut up in their houses, and I should be devoured with impatience. Fortunately there came into my head one of those luminous ideas which are sometimes vouchsafed to the dullest brain. Seeing a musician of the Civic Guard pass by, with plumed hat, and trombone under his arm, I remembered that it was the birthday of the King of Holland, and that this band of music would probably march through the city, when, if I were to accompany it on its rounds, I might see the ladies come to their windows as it passed. "Bravo!" said I to myself, and humming Figaro's air, "*Che invenzione prelibata,*" I followed the musician to the great square, where the Civic Guard were intrepidly gathering under a heavy rain and in presence of about a hundred lookers-on. In a few minutes the battalion was formed, the major gave a loud shout, the band burst into music, the column moved out of the square, and I marched beside the drum-major, delighted.

The windows of the first houses were opened, and a few women appeared at them, with heads glittering as if with helmets; and they did in fact wear two broad plates of silver, concealing the hair and a part of the forehead, and looking like the casque of an ancient warrior. As we went on, others appeared, some with silver, some with golden helmets. The battalion turned into one of the

FRIELSAND AND ZEALAND. TYPES AND COSTUMES. (*Page* 363.)

principal streets, and then at every door and window,
in the corners, in the shops, and leaning over the garden
gates, appeared casques of gold and silver, great and
small, with veils or without, bright and glittering; mammas
with their little girls about them, all in helmets; tottering
old women, servant-maids with saucepan in hand, young
ladies, all in the same warlike head-gear: Leuwarde seemed
a great barrack full of beardless cuirassiers, a metropolis
of dethroned queens, a place where the entire population
had turned out for a mediæval masquerade. I cannot
describe my astonishment and pleasure at the sight. The
shining helmets threw gold and silver reflections on the
window-panes and on the varnished doors, shone dimly in
the darkness of the ground-floor rooms, and darted lightning rays through the transparent curtains and flowers
in the windows. As we passed I could see reflected in
the casques of the girls upon the side-walks the trees,
the shop-windows, the sky, the Civic Guard, my own
figure with its ugly and dark attire. At every step I
saw something odd. A boy, to teaze a little girl, breathes
upon her helmet, and the latter angrily scolds at him, and
repolishes it with her sleeve, like a soldier whose accou-
trements have been soiled by a companion just before a
review. A young man at a window touches with the end
of a stick the casque of a young lady at the next window,
making it resound, and people turn to look, while the
lady blushes and retires. Within a doorway a servant-
maid arranges her own casque, using that of a friend,
who bends prettily before her, as a looking-glass. In
the vestibule of a house that must be a school, about fifty

little girls, all in casques, range themselves silently two and two, like a regiment of small warriors making ready for a sortie.

From the beginning I had been so absorbed in the contemplation of the helmets, that I had paid no attention to the faces of the lovely Frieslanders, who have the reputation of being the handsomest women in the Low Countries, descending in a direct line from the sirens of the North Sea. It is also said that they disturbed the equanimity of the Grand Chancellor of the German Empire, who is not very excitable by nature. Recovered from my first amazement at the casques, I considered the persons of the ladies themselves, and am constrained to say that I saw, as is the case in other countries, but very few who were really beautiful, and those few worthy of their fame. They are in general of tall stature, with broad shoulders; fair, white, straight as palms, and grave as antique priestesses; some with very small hands and feet; and despite their gravity, they have a soft, smiling expression, that seems a distant reflection from their fallen ancestresses. The silver helmet, which, concealing the hair, deprives them of one of beauty's best ornaments, in part makes up for this defect by displaying the noble form of the head, and gives to the face certain white and azure gleams of indescribable delicacy. To all appearance they have not a shadow of coquetry.

I was very curious to have a close view of these helmeted heads, and to know how the casque was made, and how put on. For this end I had brought a letter to a family in Leuwarde, which I proceeded to deliver, and was courteously received in a pretty little house on the border of the canal. We had hardly exchanged the first compliments when I asked to see a casque, at which my hosts began to laugh, and declared that it was the first demand made by all strangers arriving there. Then the lady of the house rang a bell, and there appeared a servant-maid wearing a lilac gown and a golden helmet, who at a sign from her mistress came forward. She was as tall as a grenadier, robust as an athlete, white as an angel, haughty as a princess. Planting herself before me, she stood with head erect and eyes cast down. Her mistress told me that her name was Sophia, that she was eighteen years old, and was engaged to be married, her casque being a present from her betrothed.

I asked what metal it was made of.

"Of gold," the lady answered, with a slight expression of surprise at the question.

"Of gold!" I exclaimed. "Excuse me; but will you have the goodness to ask her how much it cost?"

The lady questioned the maid, and then turning to me, said: "It cost, without the chain and pins, three hundred florins."

"Six hundred francs!" cried I. "Excuse me once more; what is the young man's profession?"

"He is a wood-sawyer," answered the lady.

"A wood-sawyer!" I repeated; and thought regretfully of the size of the book that I should have to write before I could rival the magnificence of this wood-sawyer.

"They do not all have them of gold, however," said

the lady; "the lover who has little money gives a silver casque. Poor women and girls wear casques of gilded copper, or very thin silver, which cost a few florins. But the great ambition is to have one of gold, and with this purpose in view, they work, and save, and sigh for years together. And as for jealousy, I, who have a maid with a gold casque, and a housemaid with a silver one, can tell something about that."

I asked if ladies also wore the casque. She answered that very few wore it now; but that all, even the first families, remembered having seen their mothers and grandmothers wearing them; and they were chased and set with diamonds, costing very large sums. In ancient times, however, the casque was not worn, but only a sort of diadem made of very thin silver, or iron, without ornament, which, little by little, was enlarged, and assumed its present form. At present, like all fashions that have become exaggerated, the casque is beginning to pass away. The women begin to think that they would like to show their beautiful fair hair. Also the casque produces baldness, and many women who are still young have bald places on their heads. The physicians, on their side, declare that the constant pressure upon the head arrests the development of the bosom; which is not difficult of belief, since, in fact, the Friesland women, robust and round in flesh as they are, are flat there, where there should be a bold curve. All these reasons have induced many ladies of the province of Gröningen, where the same fashion exists, to form a sort of league against the casque, and discontinue the use of it themselves. It will, however, be many years before it entirely disappears, the women of the lower and middle classes still clinging to it.

I wished to see Sophia's casque, but it was covered by the usual lace veil, and I did not like to ask her to remove it. I took hold of the edge of the veil, however, and explaining my words by gesture, asked if I might raise it.

"Lift it, certainly," said her mistress.

I did so. Heavens! what whiteness! I compared the neck with the veil, and could not tell to which the palm should be given. Sophia's casque was quite different from the silver ones which I had seen in the streets; indeed, the name of casque or helmet is only applicable to the gold ones. The silver ones are made of two almost circular plates, joined by a flexible ring of metal which encircles the head, and is ornamented with two chased buttons that stand out at the temples. These two plates only cover the front part of the head. The gold casques, on the contrary, are one large circle enclosing the head, except at the crown, and leaving only a small part of the forehead visible. The lamina are fine and flexible as Bristol board, so that they can be easily adapted to any head. Under the casque they wear a black silk cap that covers the hair like a night-cap, and over it a sort of veil of lace that falls over the shoulders. Upon the top of this some of the women put an indescribable little hat ornamented with flowers and fruit. The veil and hat, however, are only assumed on full-dress occasions.

My hostess told me of some singular customs still in use among the peasants of Friesland. When a young man presents himself to ask the hand of a girl in marriage, she makes him understand at once whether or no he is accepted. If she accepts him she leaves the room, and returns immediately wearing her casque. If she does not do this, it is understood that he does not please her, and that she refuses to become his queen. Betrothed lovers present their brides with a pair of garters, on which sentences of love or good wishes are embroidered. Sometimes the lover presents his lady with a handkerchief knotted up with money or trinkets inside, and an inscription on the knot. If the lady unties the knot, it is a sign of acceptance; if she does not, the contrary is the case. The highest honor hoped for by a lover is to be permitted to fasten his lady's shoe or patten on her foot, when she rewards him with a kiss. For the rest, young men and maidens enjoy the most entire liberty. They walk together like husband and wife, and often remain for hours alone at night, when the parents have gone to bed. "And do they never have to repent at leisure what has been done in haste?" I inquired. "The fault," replied my informant, "is always repaired."

During the whole of this conversation the handsome maid had remained, grave and silent as a statue. Before she went away I, to thank her with a compliment, begged her mistress to tell her for me that she was one of the most beautiful of the warrior women of Friesland. She listened with a serious face, and blushed to the roots of her hair; then, as if she had thought better of it, she smiled slightly, and, with a half-curtsey, went out of the room, with the slow, majestic step of a tragedy queen.

Thanks to the kindness of my hosts, I was enabled to see a small "Museum of National Antiquities of Friesland," but lately formed, and already rich in many precious objects. With my small knowledge of such matters, I gave but a hasty glance at the coins and medals, and stayed long before the collection of ancient skates, rusty diadems from which the casque is derived, and certain strange-looking pipes found at a great depth under the ground, which appear to be anterior to the time of tobacco, and are believed to have been used in smoking hemp. But the oddest thing in the museum is a woman's hat, which was in use towards the end of the last century; such a ridiculous and utterly absurd hat, that if the antiquary who showed it to me had not assured me that he had seen, with his own eyes, one similar to it on the head of an old lady of Leuwarde, not many years ago, on the occasion of a festival for the arrival of the King of Holland, I could not have believed it possible that reasonable creatures could ever have crowned themselves with such things. It is not a hat, it is a tent, a canopy, a roof, under which an entire family could be sheltered from the rain and sun. It is composed of a circular piece of wood twice as large as an ordinary coffee-table, and a straw hat with a brim of the same dimensions, wanting on one side, so that it has a semicircular form. The circular piece of wood is ornamented with a deep fringe, and has a small opening in which the head is inserted, and is fastened in some way unknown to me. When this is done, the straw hat, which is separate, is put on, and stretched over it, like an awning over a booth, and the edifice is complete. When the wearer entered a church, she unroofed herself, so to speak, in order not to take up too much space, and put it on again on coming out, an operation which was thought very convenient and the hat itself extremely elegant. So true is the proverb that there is no accounting for tastes.

A courteous Friesland gentleman, to whom I had been recommended by a friend at the Hague, took me into the country to see the peasants' houses. We went from Leuwarde towards the town of Freck, crossing one of the most fertile parts of Friesland, by a fine road paved with bricks, and as clean as a Parisian boulevard. Arriving after a short walk in front of a house, my companion stopped and said with gravity, "Behold the *friesche hiem* of the Friesland peasant, the old farm-house of his ancestors." It was a brick house with green blinds and white curtains, surrounded by trees, and planted in the midst of a small garden, which was encircled by a deep trench full of water. Next the house stood a barn, made of immense beams of Norway pine, and covered by a roof woven of canes; and in the barn was the cow-house, shut in by a stout wooden partition. The cows, like those of North Holland, have no litter, and are tied in couples, with their tails fastened up to the beams above, so that they shall not soil themselves. Behind them runs a deep stream of water which carries off all impurities. The floors, the walls, the animals themselves are as clean as possible and have no unpleasant smell. Whilst I examined this animal drawing-room, my companion, who was a learned agriculturist, gave me much precious information with regard to the Friesland method of farming. A farm of thirty to thirty-five *hectares* (two and a half acres each), usually has one horse and seventy beef cattle. There is a milch cow for every *hectare*, and on almost all the farms eight or ten large sheep, with whose milk they make certain small cheeses which are esteemed as a great delicacy all over Friesland. The principal product, however, is not cheese; but butter. The room where the butter is made is the second chamber of all peasants' houses. We entered, and it was no small concession that we were allowed to do so, because the profane are usually stopped on the threshold. It was a room as clean as a temple and cool as a grotto, where we saw many rows of copper vessels filled to the brim with milk already covered with thick cream. The churn was put in motion by a horse, as is the custom almost everywhere in Friesland. A thermometer hung on the wall, the windows were adorned with curtains, and a pot of hyacinths bloomed on the sill of one. This Friesland butter is so exquisite, my companion told me, that in the markets of London it is sold in great quantities, and brings a large price. Every year in the different markets of the province from seven to eight millions of kilogrammes are collected. The butter is packed in little barrels made of Russian oak, and holding from twenty to forty kilogrammes each, which are transported to the municipal weighing-place of the different towns. Here an expert examines, tastes, weighs it, and stamps it with the city arms; after which it is carried to Harlingen, and put on board a steamer which takes it to London. "These are our riches," concluded the courteous Frieslander, " with which we console ourselves for the lack of the oranges and palms which you favorites of nature enjoy." He ended by telling me the anecdote of the Spanish general who one day showed an orange to a Friesland peasant, and said with pride, " This is a fruit which my country produces twice a year!" " And this," said the peasant, putting a pound of butter under his nose, " is a fruit which my country produces twice a day!"

The peasant who accompanied us allowed us to peep into a room where his wife and daughter were seated at work one on each side of a table, one wearing a gold casque and the other a silver one. It seemed a room expressly arranged for a stranger to see. There were great presses of antique form, mirrors in gilded frames, Chinese porcelain, carved flower-vases, and silver vessels standing on shelves. " And you see the smallest part of it," whispered my companion, observing my astonishment. " Those presses are full of linen, jewellery, and silk gowns, and there are some peasants who have cups, plates, and coffee-pots of silver; there are even some who have forks and spoons and tobacco-boxes of massive gold. They gain much, live very economically, and spend their savings in articles of luxury." This explained why in the smallest villages there are jewellers' shops such as are not to be found in some large cities. There are peasant women who purchase coral necklaces worth a thousand francs, and who have in their boxes more than ten thousand florins-worth of rings, pins, and trinkets. They live economically, it is true, the greater part of the year;

but on great holidays, marriage, or *kermesse,* when they go into the towns in search of entertainment, they instal themselves in the best inns, take the best boxes at the opera and theatres, and crack, in the intervals, many a bottle of choice champagne. A peasant who possesses a capital of one hundred thousand francs is not considered rich, because there are many with two or three hundred thousand, half a million, and much more.

The character of the Frieslander is, by universal and antique testimony, bold, open, and generous. "What a pity you are not a Frieslander!" they say to one whom they esteem. They are proud of the nobility of their race, which they believe to be the first of the great Germanic family, and they boast that they are the only people of that family that has preserved its name from the time of Tacitus. Many of them still believe that their country was called Frisia, after Frisio, the son of Alan, the brother of Mesa, the nephew of Shem, and are proud of this antique origin. The love of liberty is their dominant sentiment. "The Frisians," says their old codex, "shall be free as long as the wind shall blow in the clouds, and as long as the world shall endure." It is Friesland, indeed, that sends to parliament the most ardent deputies of the Liberal party. The population is almost entirely Protestant, and very jealous of its faith; as also of its language, which is illustrated by a great popular poet, and cultivated with great care. "The peasant in particular," says Laveleye, "cites with pride the names of the illustrious men who were born under the Frisian *hiem,* the two poets Gisbertus Japhis and Salverda, and the philologist Tiberius Hemsterhuys and his son Franz, that good and profound philosopher whom Madame de Stael calls the Dutch Plato."

On our way back to Leuwarde we met some peasants' carts, drawn by those famous Friesland horses which are esteemed the best trotters in the world. They are black with long necks, heads small and full of fire. The finest are those raised in the island of Ameland. They have wonderful endurance; are good both for draught and racehorses, and, what is curious in a country where all things are marked by placidity of movement, their phlegmatic masters keep them always at a rapid trot, in the hay-cart as well as when they are in haste to arrive. The races in which these horses run, called *harddraveryen*, are very characteristic relics of ancient Frisia. In all the small towns an arena is prepared, divided into two parallel straight roads, on which the horses run in couples and successively; after which the victors run, against each other, until one is victor over all and obtains the prize. The people go in crowds to these races, and accompany them with applause and cries of delight, as at the skating matches.

Upon reaching Leuwarde, I had the most unexpected pleasure in the sight of a nuptial procession of peasants. There were more than thirty carriages, all with shell-shaped bodies, covered with gilding and painted flowers, and drawn by robust black horses. In each carriage sat a peasant in his gala costume, and a rosy woman with her golden casque and lace veil. The horses went at a quick trot, the women clung each to her companion's arm, and

OFF FOR THE FAIR. (*Page* 375.)

threw sugar-plums to the crowd, the white veils fluttered, and the casks glittered in the light. The cortége passed by and disappeared like some fantastic cavalcade in the midst of festive shouts and laughter.

In the evening I amused myself by standing at the inn door, looking at the women and girls with their glittering head-gear, like a general inspector at the annual review when the soldiers pass before him, one by one, with arms and baggage. At a certain moment, however, observing that they were all moving in one direction, I followed and came out into a vast square, where a band of music was playing in the midst of a great crowd and in front of a building with illuminated windows, where the appearance, from time to time, of gentlemen in white cravats, seemed to indicate that an official dinner was in progress. Although a fine rain was falling, the people stood immovable, and the women being in the first row formed a circle of casques around the band, which, from a distance, and seen through the veil of mist, seemed a line of cuirassiers on foot keeping back the crowd. Whilst the band played, about twenty infantry soldiers, grouped in a corner of the square, accompanied it with their voices, and hopped, now on one leg, now on the other, waving their caps, and assuming the grotesque attitudes of the sots of Steen and Brouwer. The crowd looked on, and I fancy that the spectacle must have given them unmixed delight, for they shouted with laughter, got on tip-toe to see, exclaimed, and applauded noisily. For myself, I looked about for some handsome Frisian woman, and when I found her, she shot me a glance full of pride and defiance, after which I entered into conversation with a bookseller always an agreeable thing in Holland, where the booksellers are, in general, very courteous and very well informed.

That night, at the inn, I scarcely closed an eye in consequence of a rascally performer in some steeple, who, perhaps because he could not sleep himself, took a barbarous pleasure in giving samples of all Rossini's operas and various popular songs to the sleeping city. I have not yet spoken of the mechanism of these aerial organs, but this is how they are contrived. The clock of the steeple sets in motion a wheel and cylinder furnished with pins, similar to those of a hand-organ. To these pins, disposed in the order necessary for the melody, are attached wires, which move the clappers of the bells, and their respective hammers. When the hour strikes a certain air is played; but any air which is desired may be played upon the cylinder by means of springs moved by two key-boards, one of which is played by the hands, the other by the feet. The performance requires a considerable degree of strength and skill, some of the keys demanding a pressure equivalent to two pounds in weight; and yet such is the pleasure which the players take in their music—and, apparently, they ascribe the same to others—that they will play for hours together with a vigor and a passion worthy of a more harmonious result. I cannot say if the player of Leuwarde was a good performer; but I am quite sure that he must have possessed Herculean muscles and a terrible passion for Rossini. After having sent me to sleep with the "Barbiere," he woke me with the "Semiramide," sent me off again with the "Otello," roused me once more with the "Mosè in Egitto," and so on. We contended with each other, he firing off his notes and I retorting with maledictions. We ceased together at an advanced hour of the night, and I cannot tell which of us remained in debt to the other. In the morning I complained to the waiter, a phlegmatic Dutchman, the sweetness of whose repose had probably never been troubled by any sound from heaven or earth. "Do you know," I said to him, "that this steeple-music of yours is very annoying?" "How?" he answered innocently, "have you not remarked that there are all the octaves with tones and semi-tones?" "Really?" said I with clenched teeth. "That of course alters the case; excuse me."

Early in the following morning I left for Groningen, taking with me, in spite of the musical persecution, a pleasant remembrance of Leuwarde and the few persons I had known there, but embittered by a regret which I still cherish—that of not having seen the handsome, courageous, and severe daughters of the North skating and sliding on the ice, when they pass, according to Alphonso Esquiroz, wrapped in mists, and crowned with a nimbus of gold and lace, like the fantastic figures seen in a dream.

The plains of Holland, which, seen for the first time excite a vague and agreeable sensation of sadness, and present, in their uniformity, a hundred new and admirable effects which divert the fancy, end, however, by producing weariness and ennui even in those who are by nature inclined to understand and enjoy their peculiar form of beauty. There comes a day when the stranger travelling in Holland suddenly feels an irresistible longing for heights to which he may lift his eyes and his thoughts; for curves along which his gaze may glide and turn and fall; for forms which the imagination may animate with those lovely and wonderful resemblances to backs of lions and women's breasts, profiles and edifices which are presented by the mountains, cliffs, and rocks of his own land. The mind and the eye are satiated with space; and losing themselves in that boundless sea of verdure, they feel the need of peaks and abysses, of shadow, blue skies, and sunlight. Then one has seen enough of Holland, and thinks of home and country with impatient longing.

I felt this longing for the first time on my way from Leuwarde to Groningen, capital of the province of the same name. Tired of seeing through the fog, meadow after meadow, and canal after canal, I coiled myself up in a corner of the railway-carriage, and thought of the sunny slopes of Tuscany and the hilly borders of the Rhine, as Dante's *Maestro Adamo* thought of the little brooks of the Casentino. At a small station about midway between the two cities, a man came into the carriage who looked like, and was in fact, a peasant, fair and fat, of the color of rotten cheese, as Taine remarks of the Dutch peasantry, dressed very cleanly, with a broad woollen scarf around his neck, and a gold chain across his waistcoat. He gave me a good-humored glance and sat down opposite to me. As the train went on I continued to dream of hills and sunny slopes, and from time to time turned my head to look at the country, hoping for some change, but seeing ever the same endless plain, made unconsciously a gesture of weariness. The peasant looked for some time in silence, now at me, now at the landscape; then smiling, and pronouncing his words with great distinctness, he said in French:

"Tedious—isn't it?"

I answered hastily No, that I did not find it so; on the contrary, the landscape pleased me.

"Oh, no," he said, still smiling, "it is tiresome—all plains," and making a gesture with both hands, "no mountains."

After a moment, occupied in mentally translating his thoughts, he asked, pointing at me with his finger:

"From what country?"

"From Italy," I answered.

"Italy," he repeated. "Are there many mountains there?"

"So many," I replied, "that you might cover all Holland with them."

"I," he said, pointing at himself with his hand, "have never seen a mountain in my life; I do not know what they are like; not even the hills of Gueldres."

A peasant who spoke French was already an extraordinary thing in my eyes; but a man who had never seen a hill or mountain seemed a fabulous creature. So I questioned him and drew from him some curious information.

He had never been further than Amsterdam, and had never seen Gueldres, the only mountainous province in the Netherlands; he had no idea of a mountain, beyond what he had gathered from books and pictures. The greatest heights to which his eyes had ever been raised were the tops of the steeples and the sand-banks. Like thousands of his countrymen, he said "I should like to see a mountain," as we say "I should like to see the Pyramids of Egypt." He told me that, as soon as he could, he intended to go and see the Wiesselschebosch. I asked what that was. He answered that it was a mountain in Gueldres, near the village of Apeldoorn, one of the highest in the country.

"How high is it?" I asked.

"One hundred and four metres," he replied.

This worthy man was destined to surprise me still more. After a moment's silence, he asked again:

"Italy?"

"Italy," I repeated.

He was thoughtful for a moment, and then said:

"The law for obligatory instruction was rejected, was it not?"

"*Cospetto!*" thought I, "I shall presently learn that he is a subscriber to the 'Gazzetta Ufficiale.'" It was a fact that only a few days before the House had rejected the law for obligatory instruction. I told him what little I knew about it, and after a little he smiled, seemed to be composing a sentence, and then said:

"And Garibaldi, does he still continue"—here he made the gesture of digging with a spade—"in his island?"

"He does," I replied, looking at him with astonished eyes, and wondering whether he were really the peasant which he so plainly looked.

He was silent for a time; then pointing his finger at me, he said:

"You have lately lost a great poet?"

At this sally I almost jumped out of my seat.

"Yes; Alessandro Manzoni," I replied; "but how the deuce do you come to know all these things?" Now, I thought, he will certainly bring the question of the unity of tongues upon the carpet. "Tell me," I said, "do you happen to speak Italian also?"

"No, no, no," he answered, shaking his head and laughing; "not at all, not at all."

After this he sat smiling to himself, and apparently preparing more surprises for me, until the train glided into the station at Groningen, when he got up, took up his wraps, and, pointing each syllable with his forefinger, said in Italian, with a pronunciation impossible to express, and the air of one who is making a great revelation:

"*Nel mezzo!*"

"*Nel mezzo?*" I exclaimed in amazement. "In the midst of what?"

"*Nel mez-zo del cam-miu di nostra vita,*"* he shouted, and jumped out of the carriage.

"One moment!" I cried; "stop! one word! How in the world——" But he was gone.

Did ever anyone hear of a peasant like this Dutchman? And I can take my oath that I have added nothing to the picture.

---

* The first line of the "Purgatorio" of Dante.

GRONINGEN.

Groningen is, perhaps, of all the provinces of the Low Countries the one which the hand of man has most wonderfully transformed.

In the sixteenth century a great part of this province was still uninhabited. It was a country of sinister aspect, covered with brambles, stagnant pools, tempestuous lakes, and constantly inundated by the sea. In it there were packs of wolves and innumerable swarms of aquatic birds, and no voice was heard save that of frogs and deer. Three centuries of patient and courageous labor, often given up in despair and again renewed with obstinate determination, and carried on through every kind of difficulty and peril, have transformed that savage and dangerous region into a most fertile country, intersected by canals, dotted with towns and factories, where agriculture flourishes, commerce and labor go hand in hand, and a population of wealthy and well-instructed people swarms. Groningen, which in the last century was still a poor province, which paid to the State one-half less than Friesland and twelve times less than Holland properly so called, is now, taking into consideration its size, one of the richest provinces in the kingdom, and produces itself alone four-tenths of the oats, barley, and colza which are gathered in the Low Countries.

The most flourishing part of Groningen is in the north, and to such a degree does it flourish that it needs to be seen to be appreciated. Even I, who have been over it, cannot describe it better than by adding to my own observations and those which I gathered from the natives, the descriptions which are given by the French agriculturist, Count de Courcy, who, however, made but a hasty survey of the country, and the Belgian Delaveleye, the author of a fine work upon the rural economy of the Netherlands, which I have already had occasion to cite.

The houses of the peasants are extraordinarily large, and have in general two storeys and many windows ornamented with handsome curtains. Between the street and the house there is a garden planted with exotic trees and covered with flowering shrubs; and beside the garden an orchard full of fruit-trees and various sorts of vegetables. Behind the house rises an enormous edifice which covers under its lofty roof the stables, the cow-house, the hay-loft, and a great empty space which might contain the harvest of a hundred *hectares*.* In this great barn are to be found every kind of agricultural implement from Eng-

---

* A French measure containing two and a half English acres each.

land and America, many of them improved and perfec'ed by the peasants; long files of cows, great black horses, and a marvellous cleanliness everywhere. The interior of the houses might rival any gentleman's house. There is furniture of American woods, pictures, carpets, a pianoforte, a library, political journals, the monthly reviews, the most recent works on agriculture, and not unfrequently the last number of the "Revue des Deux Mondes." Although fond of ease and luxury, these peasants have preserved the simple manners of their forefathers. The greater part of them, possessors of half a million of francs, a little less, or a great deal more, do not disdain to put their hands to the plough and direct in person the labors of the field. Some of them send one of their sons to the university, no small sacrifice, when it is considered that each student costs his parents about four thousand francs a year; but the majority disdain, as inferior to their own condition, the professions of doctor, lawyer, or teacher, and prefer to keep their sons at home. There is no class of the population which ranks above the peasants. Among them are chosen almost all the members of the different elective bodies, even to the deputies to the States-General. The labors of agriculture do not prevent them from taking an active part in political life and in the administration of public affairs. Not only do they follow the progress of the art of agriculture, but also the movements of modern thought. At Haven, near the city of Groningen, they maintain at their own cost an excellent school of agriculture, presided over by an illustrious professor and having fifty students. Even the smaller villages have museums of natural history and botanic gardens, founded and kept up at the common cost of a few hundreds of peasants. Even the women on market days go to visit the museums of the University of Groningen, and stay a long time, asking and obtaining information. Some of the men occasionally make a journey into Belgium or to England. The greater part of them are much interested in theological questions, and many belong to the sect of Mennonites, the Quakers of Holland.

Delaveleye relates that having seen on the road which connects the two flourishing villages of Usquert and Uythuysen four large factories, he asked the innkeeper to whom they belonged, and was answered that they belonged to some Mennonites, adding, "They are well-to-do people; each of them must be worth six hundred francs apiece." "I have heard," went on Delaveleye, "that there are no poor among that sect. Is that true as regards this district?" "No," answered the host; "that is, to be just, yes; because the only poor man there was died a few days ago, and now there is none." The severity of manners, the love of labor, and reciprocal charity banish poverty from those small religious communities where all know, watch over, and help each other. Groningen, in fact, is like a species of republic governed by a class of educated peasants; a new and virgin country, where no patrician castle rears its head above the roofs of the tillers of the soil; a province where the produce of the land remains in the hands of the cultivators, where wealth and labor always go hand in hand, and idleness and opulence are for ever divided.

The description would not be complete if I failed to speak of a certain right peculiar to the Groningen peasantry and called *beklem-regt,* which is considered as the principal cause of the extraordinary prosperity of the province.

The *beklem-regt* is the right to occupy a farm with the payment of an annual rent, which the proprietor can never augment. This right passes to the heirs collateral as well as direct, and the holder may transmit it by will, may sell it, rent it, raise a mortgage upon it even, without the consent of the proprietor of the land. Every time, however, that this right passes from one hand to another, whether by inheritance or sale, the proprietor receives one or two years' rent. The farm-buildings belong, in general, to the possessor of the *beklem-regt,* who, when his right is in any way annulled, may exact the price of the materials. The possessor of the *beklem-regt* pays all taxes, cannot change the form of the property, nor in any way diminish its value. The *beklem-regt* is indivisible. One person only can possess it, and consequently one only of the heirs can inherit it. However, by paying the sum stipulated in case of the passage of the *beklem-regt* from one hand to another, the husband may inscribe his wife, or the wife her husband, and then the consort inherits a part of the right. When the possessor is ruined, or does not pay his annual rent, the *beklem-regt* is not at once annulled. The creditors can cause it to be sold, but the purchaser must first of all pay all outstanding debts to the proprietor.

The origin of this custom is obscure. It appears to

have begun in Groningen, in the middle ages, on the convent farms. The land at that time being of small value, the monks easily granted to the cultivators the possession of a certain portion of their lands, with the condition that a certain annual sum should be paid, and another sum at every decease. This contract assured to the convent a fixed rent, and exempted the monks from the charge of farms which in general produced nothing. The example of the convents was followed by the large landowners, and by the civil corporations. They reserved to themselves the right to dismiss the tenant at the end of every ten years; but they did not use their right, because if they did so, they would have had to pay the value of the buildings put up on their land, and they would not easily have found another tenant. During the troubles of the sixteenth century, the *beklem-regt* became, in fact, hereditary, or, at least, many authorities declared it to be such. Jurisprudence and custom decided the various points that were subjects for disagreement; a clearer formula was declared and generally accepted, and from that time the *beklem-regt* maintained its position by the side of the civil code, always respected, and gradually diffused over the whole of the province of Groningen.

The advantages derived by agriculture from this kind of contract are easily understood. By virtue of the *beklem-regt* the farmers have a continuous and very strong interest in making every possible effort to increase the produce of their land. Secure, as they are, of the sole enjoyment of all the ameliorations which they may introduce into the cultivation, of not having, like ordinary tenants, to pay a rent which grows higher and higher in proportion as they succeed in increasing the fertility of the land. They undertake the boldest enterprises, introduce innovations, and carry out the costliest experiments. The legitimate recompense of labor is the entire and certain profit that accrues from that labor. Therefore the *beklem-regt* is a powerful stimulus to work, study, and perfection.

Thus a strange custom, inherited from the middle ages, has created a class of farmers, who enjoy all the benefits of property, excepting that the net product is not all reserved for them, which would, indeed, divert them from their task. Instead of tenants continually in trepidation lest they should lose the land, adverse to any costly innovation, subject to a superior, and always interested in concealing the prosperity of their condition, there is in Groningen a population of free and self-respected citizens, simple in their habits, but eager for instruction, of which they comprehend all the advantages, and are interested in propagating it in every way; a class of peasants who practise agriculture, not blindly and as if it were to be contemned, but as a noble occupation which demands the exercise of the highest faculties of the intelligence, and procures for those who follow it fortune, social importance, and public respect; peasants who are economical in the present, prodigal for the future, disposed for any kind of sacrifice that will fertilize their land, enlarge their houses, buy them better tools and a better race of animals; a rural population, in short, who are content with their condition, because their fate depends only upon their own prudence and activity.

As long as the possessor of the *beklem-regt* cultivates the land himself, the hereditary tenancy produces only good effects. These good effects cease, however, from the moment when he, availing himself of his power to underlet, cedes to another his rights for a given sum, with which he continues to pay the proprietor or landlord. In this case all the inconveniences of the system at once make themselves felt, with the difference that here the farmer has to maintain two idlers instead of one. Subletting was formerly very rare, for the produce of cultivation was barely sufficient to maintain the family of the tenant when he farmed the land himself. But since the increase in prices of all kinds of food, and, above all, since the opening of trade with England, the profits are very considerable, because the possessor of the *beklem-regt* can find a second tenant disposed to pay him a higher rent than that which he pays to his landlord; and as the custom of subletting extends more and more, the consequences cannot fail to be injurious.

Meantime, when the future conditions of the human race are considered, it is generally desired that two things should be brought about: first, a growing increase in production; secondly, a division of property according to the principles of justice. Now one fact that justice demands is this: that the laborer should enjoy the fruits of his labor, and their progress. It is then consolatory to see upon the distant shores of the North Sea an antique custom which answers in some sort to this economic ideal, and which gives to a whole province an extraordinary and equally apportioned prosperity.

One capital objection, among others, has been made to these opinions of Delaveleye. It is questioned whether the extraordinary prosperity of Groningen is really due to the *beklem-regt*, or to the exceptional fertility of the soil. Delaveleye rejects this doubt, saying that the extraordinary prosperity and the perfection of cultivation exist in the stormy zone of Groningen, which is anything rather than fertile; but are not found in any other part, except in a very inferior degree in Friesland, where the soil is of the same quality. If, then, hereditary tenancy has not produced in other countries the same consequences as in Groningen, it is because it has been differently practised, as in some provinces of Italy, where the *condotto di livello*, which is very nearly a *beklem-regt*, hampers the liberty of the farmer with the obligation to pay every year to the landlord a certain quantity of produce of a kind settled upon beforehand.

All Dutch economists conclude and are agreed in recognising the excellent effects of this custom, affirming that to the *beklem-regt* Groningen owes all her wealth, and in the agricultural meetings which discuss the question the desire is expressed that the same kind of contract shall be adopted in the other provinces.

Pursuing my excursion across the country, I reached the shore of the North Sea, near the mouth of the Gulf of Dollart. This gulf was not in existence prior to the thirteenth century. The river Ems emptied itself directly into the sea, and Groningen was joined to Hanover.

The sea destroyed the wild region that extended between the two provinces, and formed the gulf which, since the sixteenth century, has been growing smaller by reason of the deposits of mud and slime which accumulate along its banks. Already numerous dykes, built one before the other, testify to the conquest of the land over the sea, and new ones are continually being constructed, gradually increasing the agricultural dominion of Groningen, and beautiful fields of barley and colza flourish where, a few years ago, the waves roared in their fury and destroyed the boats of the fishermen. It is a fine thing to see, from the tops of the dykes which defend those coasts, how the sea and the land meet, mingle, and are transformed. At the foot of the dykes extends a muddy marsh already in great part covered with grass and small green weeds; a little beyond this a small bit of peat rescued and turned into soil; still beyond, marshes and wet mud which gradually becomes thick and turbid water; and beyond again, sand-banks, some of which rise so as to form dunes and little islets. On one of these islets, called Rottum, there lived some years ago a family who lived by catching seals; and strange stories are told about the other islands, in which figure mysterious hermits, apparitions, and monsters. The pools of turbid water which lie at the foot of the dykes are called *wadden*, or *polders* in a state of formation, and are land covered with water at high tide and rising gradually higher and higher as the currents of the river Ems and the Zuyder Zee go on depositing new strata of clay. At low water the cattle ford them; at some points boats can pass; and immense flocks of sea-birds frequent them in search of the shell-fish left by the receding tide. In less than a hundred years birds, boats, pools and arms of the sea will have vanished; the islets will be dunes that defend the coasts, and agriculture will have called forth from the virgin soil a luxuriant and beneficent vegetation. Thus on that side Holland advances victoriously upon the sea, avenging old injuries with the iron of the plough and the blade of the scythe.

With all this, however, I should have formed no conception of the richness of the country, if I had not had the chance of seeing the market of Groningen.

But before speaking of the market, I must mention the city itself.

Groningen—so called, according to some, from Trojan Grunio, and founded, according to others, one hundred and fifty years before the Christian era, around a Roman fortress which Tacitus calls *Corbulonis monumentum* (all which assertions have been affirmed and denied for centuries and remain undecided to this day)—is the most considerable of the cities of North Holland for size and commerce, but perhaps the least curious to a stranger. It is situated on a river called Hunse, at the junction of three great canals which connect it with several other commercial towns; is surrounded by high bastions constructed in 1698 by Coehorn, the Dutch Vauban; and has a port, which although distant several miles from the mouth of the Ems, can receive the largest merchant ships.

The streets and squares are large, the canals as wide as those of Amsterdam, the houses taller than in almost any other Dutch city, the shops worthy of Paris, the cleanliness worthy of Broek; with nothing peculiar in form, color, or general aspect. Arriving there from Leuwarde you feel as if you were a hundred miles nearer home, and in the atmosphere of Germany or France. The sole peculiarity of Groningen are certain houses covered with a greyish tint all encrusted with small bits of glass, which, when the sun shines upon them, burn with a strange radiance, looking as if the walls were set with pearls and silver beads. There is a fine town hall, built during the French domination, a market-place which is said to be the largest in Holland, and a vast church, anciently dedicated to Saint Martin, which presents various noteworthy features of the different phases of the Gothic, and has a very tall steeple composed of five diminishing stories, so that it seems to be made up of five steeples, each one smaller than the lower one, and placed one atop of the other.

Groningen has a university, for which reason it is honored by its neighbor cities with the name of the Athens of the North. This university, established in a new and vast building, has but a small number of students, since the peasants, the only rich men in the province, seldom send their sons to it, and the wealthy gentlemen of Friesland are educated at Leyden. It is, however, a university well worthy of standing with the other two. There is a fine anatomical cabinet, and a museum of natural history, containing many precious objects. The programme of studies differs little from that of the other wo universities; there is a difference, however, in the direction, which, in consequence of the neighborhood of Hanover, is subject to the influences of German literature and science, and presents a religious character entirely its own. The theologians of Groningen, says Alphonso Esquiroz, in his "Studio sulle Università Ollandese," form, in the intellectual movement of the Low Countries, a school apart, which originated, towards 1833, in the very bosom of the most orthodox of cities—Utrecht. A professor of Utrecht, M. van Heusde, sought to open a new horizon to religious belief; M. Hofstede de Goot, of the University of Groningen, participated in his ideas, and joined him; and in that way was formed the nucleus of a theological society, resident in the latter city, who, rebellious against synodal protestantism, and formally denying all human authority in matters of religion, are seeking to initiate a type of Christianity peculiar to the Netherlands, of which it would be difficult to give a clear idea, for the reason that those who profess it, and propagate it in their writings, are themselves very obscure in their exposition. In all this heterodoxy, observes Esquiroz,—which can, without serious danger, be introduced into the country, because, in the midst of the agitation of religious ideas, the customs, forms, and traditions of the ancient faith remain immutable—there is a grave and delicate point upon which the orthodox are always trying to trip up their adversary, and never succeeding—the divinity of Jesus Christ. Upon this point the thought of the heterodox is involved in a cloud. For them, Jesus Christ is the most perfect type of humanity, the messenger of God, the image of God. But is he

God in person? They put this question aside with every sort of scholastic subtlety. Some, for example, proclaim their belief in his divinity, but not in his deity—an answer so obscure as to be almost equivalent to a negation. For which reasons the doctrine of Dutch heterodoxy may be called a sentimental deism, more or less bound to the poetical side of Christianity. The ardor of religious questions, however, is decreasing every year. The students of the University of Groningen are more interested in literature and science, towards which ends they form societies for readings and study in common, above all of practical science, which predilection is one of the most marked characteristics of the Frieslanders, with whom those of Groningen have many features of resemblance and numerous ties of relationship. The students of Groningen are more quiet and more studious than those of Leyden, who, as far as it is possible to be wild in Holland, have the reputation of being wild.

Besides the glory of the university, which dates from 1614, Groningen has that of having given birth to several men illustrious in the arts and sciences, about whom it is pleasant to hear Messer Ludovico Guicciardini dilate in his vivid and forcible style. He appears to have had a peculiar affection for the place. First of all he places Ridolpho Agricola, " to whom, among other authors, Erasmus in his writings gives immense praise, saying that on that side of the mountains among men of literary gifts there is none greater nor more complete than he, and that there is no honest discipline, wherein he, with any artisan you will, may not contend ; among Greeks and Latins the best of all; in poetry another Virgil, in oratory another Politian; most eloquent, a philosopher, a musician, and writer of many excellent works, with many other rare graces and felicities to him attributed." He goes on to speak of " Vesellius, called Basil, excellent philosopher, of so much doctrine, virtue, and science in every faculty, as appears in an infinite number of his works, written and given to the press, and who is likewise called *the light of the world.*" And he continues that for fear of not being able to worthily praise this Vesellius and this Agricola, who are "the two stars of Groeninghen," he prefers to be silent, "and leave the page white for anyone who shall know better than he how to exalt their names and their country." Finally he cites the name of " another great man, a citizen he also of the same land, called Rinierius Predinius, most worthy author of divers books written with consummate honor and laudation." Besides these may be named the famous orientalist Albert Schultens, the Baron Ruperda, Abraham Frommins, and others.

In the costume and aspect of the people there is, for a stranger, little difference from those of Friesland. Only the helmets of the women are different. At Leuwarde the greater part of them are of silver; at Groningen they are all of gold, and in the exact form of a helmet, covering the whole head; but there are fewer to be seen. Ladies, it is understood, do not wear them any more; the richer peasant women have also left them off, in order to be more like ladies; and now it is only the servant-maids who can boast themselves legitimate descendants of those armed virgins, who, according to the ancient Germanic mythology, presided over battles.

With regard to manners and customs, I had some precious notes from a personage of Groningen, which I think are not to be found in any book of travels. There the customs which relate to the lives of girls and married women are entirely different from ours. Among us (in Italy), a girl who marries comes out of a state of subjection, almost of imprisonment, to enter one of perfect liberty, where she finds herself suddenly surrounded by the consideration, homage, and admiration of those who had formerly neglected her. In Groningen, on the contrary, liberty and gallantry are privileges of the girls, and the married women live surrounded and hemmed in by a hundred precautions and watchful eyes, and are treated with cold respect, almost neglect. The young men devote themselves to girls only, and a great deal of liberty is conceded to them. A young fellow who visits in a family, even if he is not an intimate friend, offers to accompany the daughters, or one daughter, to concert or theatre, at night, in a carriage, alone, and father and mother make no opposition; and if anyone did, he would pass for a fool or an ill-bred person, and would be blamed and laughed at. A young couple may be engaged for years; and during the whole time they are seen together every day, taking long walks, remaining alone together in the house, and in the evening, before separating, standing by the half hour in the door with no one near them. Girls of fifteen years of age, daughters of the first families, traverse the city from one end of it to the other, going to and coming from school, even towards evening, alone, and, should they stop and speak with anyone, nobody pays any attention. On the contrary, if a married woman assumes the smallest liberty of action, there is no end to the comment she excites; but that happens so seldom that it may almost be said never to happen at all. "Our young men," said my informant, "are not at all dangerous. They can be gallant with girls, because the girls are timid, and their timidity encourages them; but with ladies they are too shy. Within my memory there have been but two notorious cases of conjugal infidelity in this city." And he told me about them. "So it is, my dear Sir," he added, putting his hand upon my knee, "that here we make no conquests, except in agriculture, and he who wishes to make them in another field, must first go before a notary and make his attestation that his intentions are to fight the good fight according to law, and with an honest purpose for peace in the end." Arguing, wrongly, from my silence, that this state of things was not to my taste, he added: "Such is our way of life; tedious if you will, but wholesome. You drink the cup of life all at once, we take it slowly and in small mouthfuls. You, perhaps, enjoy more, but we are more constantly content." "God bless you!" said I. "God convert you!" he replied.

But let us come to the market, which was the last spectacle of life that I saw in Holland.

Early in the morning I took a turn about the city to see the peasants come in. Every hour arrived a train which brought a crowd of them; by every country road there came brightly-painted wagons, drawn by five black horses, and bringing majestic married couples; by every canal arrived boats with sails, full of produce; in a few hours the city was full of noise and people. The peasants, male, are all dressed in cloth almost black, with a woollen cravat, gloves, and watch-chain, and carry a large leathern portfolio, a cigar in the mouth, and a countenance of serene contentment. The peasant women are beflowered, bejewelled, beribboned, like the Madonna of the Spanish churches. The business of the market over, they invade the shops and restaurants, not as our peasants do, who look timidly about them with an air of asking leave to enter, but with the look and bearing of persons who know themselves to be welcome. In the restaurants the tables are speedily covered with bottles of claret and Rhine wine; in the shops the clerks hasten to take down their merchandize. The women are received like princesses, and they spend, indeed, in a princely manner. Incidents occur which I have heard described by eyewitnesses. A merchant dealing with one of the ladies of the city, names the price of a silk dress. "Too dear," answers the lady. "I take it," says a peasant woman standing by, and she does so. Another peasant is buying a pianoforte. The dealer shows her one which cost one thousand francs. "Have you none dearer?" says she, "all my friends have pianofortes at a thousand francs." Husband and wife are passing a printseller's window, and see an oil-painting in a gilt frame displayed therein. They stop, and discover in it some vague resemblance to their own house and garden. The wife says "Let us buy it." The husband answers "Let us buy it." They enter the shop, count out there and then three hundred florins, and carry off the picture.

When they have completed their purchases, they visit the museums, enter the cafés and read the journals, or take a turn about the city, casting compassionate glances at all that population of shopkeepers, clerks, professors, officials, proprietors, who in other countries are envied by those who till the ground, but here are regarded by them in the light of poor people. A stranger to the real condition of things might believe, at sight of this spectacle, that he had arrived in a country where some great social revolution had taken place, and that the newly enriched had come into the city to triumph over the despoiled citizens. But the finest sight is in the evening when they go back to their villages and their factories. Then all the country roads are covered with those curious wagons all driven at top speed, trying to outstrip one another, even the women urging on the horses, and the victorious ones cracking their whips in sign of triumph. The air resounds with song and laughter, until at last the festive tumult is lost in the endless green of the fields together with the last red rays of sunset.

FROM GRONINGEN TO ARNHEM.

At Groningen I turned my back upon the North Sea, my face to Germany, my heart to Italy, and began my homeward journey, rapidly crossing the three Dutch provinces of the Drenta, Over-Yssel, and Gueldres, which extend around the gulf of the Zuyder Zee between Friesland and Utrecht; a part of Holland that would be wearisome to anyone who travelled without the curiosity of an agriculturist or a naturalist, but not without its charm to those who have a strong love of nature. Throughout the journey the sky was in harmony with the aspect of the country, all monotonous and grey; and I was almost constantly alone. So I was able to enjoy the melancholy beauty of the spectacle in silence.

Leaving the province of Groningen and entering that of the Drenta, there is a sudden change in the aspect of the country. On every side, as far as the eye can see, extend immense fields covered with underbrush and brambles, in which there is no path, nor house, nor stream, nor hedge, nor any indication of labor or habitation to be seen. A few clumps of small oaks, which are considered as traces of the former existence of ancient forests, are the only objects which rise above the surrounding underbrush; the partridge, the hare, and the wild cock are the only living creatures that meet the eye of the traveller. You think you are at the end of this desert-land, when it begins again; bush succeeds to bush, and solitude to solitude. On the dreary plain are seen here and there small mounds, which some believe to have been raised by the Celts, and others by the Germans, in which excavators have found earthen vessels, saws and hammers, calcined bones, stones for grinding grain, arrow-heads, and rings which are supposed to have served for money. Besides these mounds, there have been found, and still remain, immense masses of red granite, piled up and arranged in a form revealing the intention of a monument, either an altar or a tomb, but without inscription, naked and solitary, like monster aerolites fallen in the midst of the desert. In the country they are called tombs of the Huns; tradition attributes them to the bands of Attila; the people say that they were brought into Holland by an ancient race of giants; the geologists believe that they came from Norway on the back of antediluvian glaciers; and the historian loses himself in vain conjectures. Everything in this strange province is antique and mysterious. The customs of primitive Germany are found here, tillage of the ground is common on the *esschen*, the rustic horn calling the peasants to labor, the houses described by Roman historians, and over all this ancient world the perpetual mystery of an immense silence:

>" . . . . . . ove per poco
> Il cor non si spaura."

As you go onwards you begin to see marshes, great pools of water, zones of muddy ground, intersected by canals of blackish water, ditches deep and long like trenches, heaps of sods of the color of bitumen, a few boats, a few human beings. These are the peat-fields, whose name alone excites in the mind a hundred fantastic images:—the vast and slow conflagration of the earth; floating tracts of land with their inhabitants and cattle upon the waters of the ancient lakes; forests wandering in the gulfs; fields torn from the mainland and beaten by the tempests of the sea; immense clouds of smoke rising from the smouldering peat-grounds of the Drenta, and driven by the north wind over the half of Europe, as far as Paris, Switzerland, the Danube. Peat— live earth, as it is called by the Dutch peasant—is the principal wealth of the Drenta, and one of the most profitable in all Holland. It gives work to thousands of hands; almost all the population of Holland use it for fuel; it serves many uses, with the sods the foundations of houses are strengthened, with the ashes the land is fertilised, metals are polished with the soot, and herrings are dried in the smoke of it. On the waters of the Wahal, the Leek, the Meuse, on the canals of Friesland and Groningen, on the Zuyder Zee, everywhere circulate the boats which carry the great national combustible. Exhausted peat-fields are converted into meadows, vegetable gardens, fertile oases. Assen, the capital city of the Dreuta, is the centre of all this work of transformation. A great canal, into which run all the smaller canals of the peat district, extends almost entirely across the Dreuta from Assen as far as the town of Meppel. Everywhere they are working to bring the land under tillage. The population of the province, which counted a little more than thirty thousand at the end of the last century, is now almost three times that number.

Beyond Meppel you enter the province of Over-Yssel, which for a certain distance presents much the same aspect as that of the Dreuta—underbrush, peat swamps, and solitude; and you arrive in a short time at a village, if village it can be called, the strangest that the human mind can conceive. It consists of a row of rustic cottages, with wooden fronts and thatched roofs, which succeed one another, at a certain distance from each other, for the length of more than eight kilometres, planted each upon a narrow bank of earth which extends as far as the eye can see, and surrounded by a ditch full of water-plants, upon whose edge rise groups of alders, poplars, and willows. The inhabitants of this village, which is divided into two parts, called respectively, Rouveen and Staphorst, are the descendants of two ancient Frisian colonies, who have religiously preserved the costume, manners, and traditions of their forefathers, and live at ease on the produce of their lands and some small manufactures peculiar to the place. In this singular village there are no cafés and no streets, because their ancestors had not the former, and for the latter there is no need, the houses being all planted in one long row. The inhabitants are all Calvinists, sober, austere, and laborious. The men knit their own stockings in the intervals of time when not occupied in the cultivation of the ground; and such is their abhorrence of idleness, that when they meet in council to deliberate upon the affairs of the village, each man brings his knitting, in order not to have his hands unoccupied during the discussion. The commune possesses six thousand hectares of land, divided into nine hundred zones, or strips, about five thousand yards in length and thirty in width. Almost all the inhabitants are proprietors, can read and write, have a horse and eight or ten cows, never leave their colony, marry where they are born, pass their lives upon the same spot of ground, and close their eyes under the same roof where their fathers, grandfathers, and great-grandfathers lived and died.

As you go on beyond Over-Yssel the country changes its aspect. Near Zvolle, the native town of the painter Lerburg, capital of the province, with about twenty thousand inhabitants, there are fine roads, bordered by trees, which refresh the eye after the bare and dreary country you have just traversed. Here, in the little convent of St. Agnes, lived and died, at the age of sixty-four, Thomas à Kempis, the reputed author of the "Imitation of Jesus Christ."

On every side now the brambly waste recedes, giving place to patches of verdure, fields and meadows, and new plantations; houses rise, herds of cattle are seen, and new canals run from the peat swamps to a great one called the Dedemsvaart, the main artery of Over-Yssel, which has transformed the desolate country into a flourishing province, where an industrious population advances like a victorious army, where the poor find work, the laborer becomes a proprietor, the proprietor grows rich, and all have the hope of a prosperous future. From hence, the road, following the course of the Yssel, enters Salland, the Sala of the ancients, where dwelt the Franco-Salii before going south to the conquest of Gaul, where the Salique law originated, at Salcheim and Windcheim, which still exist under the names of Salk and Windesheim, and where agricultural traditions and customs of those antique times are still existent. Finally the road reaches Deventer, the last town in Over-Yssel, the city of James Gronovius, of carpets and ginger-bread, which still preserves, in one of its public halls, the boiler in which counterfeiters were boiled alive, and which rejoices in the neighborhood of the castle of Loo, the favorite residence of the King of Holland. Beyond Deventer begins the province of Gueldres.

Here the spectacle changes. You are skirting the land inhabited by the ancient Saxons, the Veluwe, a sandy region extending between the Rhine, the Yssel, and the Zuyder Zee, where a few villages are scattered here and there over an undulating plain, like a tempestuous sea. Wherever the eye turns it sees nothing but arid hills, the most distant veiled in a bluish mist, the others in part darkened by a wild vegetation, in part white with the shifting sands which the wind spreads over the face of the country. There are no trees and no houses; all is solitary, bare, dreary as a steppe in Tartary; and the frightful silence of these solitudes is only broken by the song of the lark and the murmur of the bee. Yet in some portions of this region the Dutch people, with their patient courage, and at the cost of infinite labor, have succeeded in making the pine, the beech, and the oak grow; they have even formed fine parks and have created complete groves, covering with useful plants, in less than thirty years, more than ten thousand hectares of land, and raising populous and flourishing villages where there was neither wood nor stone nor water, and where the first settlers were obliged to shelter themselves in caves dug out of the ground and covered with turf.

The road passes near the city of Zutphen and soon reaches Arnhem, the capital of Gueldres, a pretty and notable town posted on the right bank of the Rhine, in a region covered with lovely hills which have earned for it the name of the Dutch Switzerland, and inhabited by a people who have the reputation of being the most poetic in Holland, according to the proverb which describes them as "Great in courage, poor in purse, sword in hand." But a traveller from the south of Europe finds here nothing remarkable either in the country or its inhabitants; and the same may be said of Limburg and Southern Brabant, the only two provinces of Holland which I did not think it necessary to visit. So after seeing Arnhem I left for Cologne. The sky was darker and lower than it had been throughout the day, and I, though at heart glad to return to Italy, felt the weight of the depressing atmosphere, and, leaning on the window of the carriage, looked silently at the landscape, more like one who was leaving his native country than one who was departing from a foreign land. I found myself close to the German frontier almost without consciousness of the distance I had passed over, and roused by the voice of another traveller, looked about me and saw a windmill, by which I knew that we were still in Holland. But the land, the vegetation, the form of the houses, the language of my travelling companions, were no longer the same. I turned to that windmill as the last image of Holland, and contemplated it with much the same interest as that with which I had greeted the first, seen one year before on the banks of the Scheldt. As I gazed, something seemed to be moving with it in the circle of its mighty wings. My heart beat more quickly. I looked again, and saw the flags of ships, the tree-bordered canals, the pointed gables of houses, the flower-decked windows, the silver helmets, the livid sea, the downs, the fishermen of Scheveningen, Rembrandt, William of Orange, Erasmus, Barendz, my friends, and all the most beautiful and noble images of that glorious, modest, and austere country; and as if I beheld them in reality, I kept my eyes fixed, with a sentiment of respect and tenderness, upon the windmill, until it appeared a black cross through the mist which covered the landscape; and when even that vision had disappeared, I felt like one who departs upon a journey from which he shall never return, and sees the face of his last friend grow dim and vanish on the shore.

www.ingramcontent.com/pod-product-compliance
Lightning Source LLC
Chambersburg PA
CBHW020122020526
44111CB00049B/569